"The legend of Bluebeard has long captured the interest and imagination of academics and public alike. Now, at last, a definitive first rate historical account of the man behind the legend. Must reading for all those captivated by the Bluebeard story."
>—Kenneth Feinberg, Esq., Victims' Compensation Advocate: 9/11, Virginia Tech, BP, Boston Marathon, GM

"Valerie Ogden's real-life monster, Gilles de Rais, leaps from the pages of her sensational narrative to challenge our notions of the limits of human depravity. Once one of the richest men in 15th century France and a principal comrade-in-arms and protector of Jeanne d'Arc, de Rais is the model upon which the horrific legend of Bluebeard is built. Meticulously researched in breathtaking detail, Ogden's description of the unspeakable carnal desires and blood lust that drove Gilles de Rais into ever more abhorrent acts against the scores of innocent children who were inveigled into his clutches make Jack the Ripper's crimes a Sunday picnic by comparison. Ogden searches for answers to what drove the fiend to act and why the Church granted him absolution for his crimes. Not for the faint hearted."
>—Richard Ben-Veniste, Esq., Mayer Brown, LLP Special Watergate Prosecutor and 9/11 Commission Member

BLUEBEARD

Brave Warrior, Brutal Psychopath

By Valerie Ogden

Foreword by
Michael Kane, former Special Prosecutor,
JonBenet Ramsey Murder Case

History Publishing Company
Palisades, New York

Copyright©2014 by Valerie Ogden
Ogden, Valerie

LCCN:
ISBN: 9781940773070 (QP)
ISBN: 9781940773087 (eBook)

SAN: 850-5942

Ogden, Valerie.

   Bluebeard : brave warrior, brutal psychopath / by Valerie Ogden ;
foreword by Michael Kane, former Special Prosecutor, JonBenet Ramsey
murder case. -- Palisades, New York : History Publishing Company,
[2014]

      p. ; cm.

      ISBN: 978-1-940773-07-0 (pbk.) ; 978-1-940773-08-7 (eBk.)
      Includes bibliographical references and index.
      Summary: Baron Gilles de Rais, Marshall of France, Joan of Arc's
close companion on the battlefield, one of the wealthiest and most
respected men in France, became a notorious serial killer, nicknamed
Bluebeard, who performed bizarre sexual rituals, brutal mutilations and
murders on hundreds of children. How and why did this happen? Was it
the barbarity of war that turned this celebrated hero into a monster?--
Publisher.

      1. Rais, Gilles de, 1404-1440. 2. Rais, Gilles de, 1404-1440--
Psychology. 3. France--History--Charles VII, 1422-1461--Biography.
4. Marshals--France--Biography. 5. Criminals--France--Biography.
6. Joan, of Arc, Saint, 1412-1431. 7. Hundred Years' War, 1339-1453.
8. Bluebeard (Legendary character) I. Title.

DC102.8.R2 O43 2014   2014940661
944./026092--dc23   1410

Published in the United States of America by
History Publishing Company, LLC
Palisades, New York

Printed in the United States on acid-free paper

First Edition

Cover photo: www.istockphoto.com—Cover and interior design.www.aulicinodesign.com

To the end of cannonballs

TABLE OF CONTENTS

FOREWORD

Born to wealthy, benevolent, and highly placed parents at the turn of the fifteenth century, Gilles de Rais had prospects that few children of the era could have hoped for. He loved and admired his father, Guy II, and was doted on by his mother, Marie. But his idyllic family life was cut short at the age of eleven by the tragic, painful death of Guy II, who succumbed to an attack by a wild animal, followed soon thereafter by the loss of his mother. Transformed so quickly from a happy childhood to being an orphan, Gilles endured the loss of his parents in silence and solitude, alone in the vast expanse of his fortress-home, tormented by the belief that their passing was inflicted through the vengeance of God Himself.

Though he inherited the immense wealth of his parents, Gilles was deprived of their moral compass when his maternal grandfather, Jean de Craon—a sixty-year-old best described as a thug—managed to seize custody of the boy despite Guy II's testamentary will directing that he and his year-old brother, Rene, be raised by a cousin. De Craon's interest in assuming responsibility for the children was based not on any affection for his daughter's offspring, but purely on his own self-interest in securing control over enormous stretches of land and other resources. His influence steered young Gilles along a path that Guy II had hoped to avoid.

Valerie Ogden's introductory chapters thus set the backdrop for a fascinating perspective on the life of Gilles de Rais, a medieval French nobleman, warrior, and hero who became the scourge of his day–and generations that followed—as the infamous "Bluebeard." Ms. Ogden blends a wonderful talent for describing scenes and events in a captivating story while faithfully employing scholarly attributions for every detail. The result is a page-turner, a true tale of a man known as much for his bravery and loyalty in battle at the side of Joan of Arc as for his savage sexual and masochistic desires, manifested by the kidnapping, rape, and murder of countless children.

The book is not confined to presenting a well-written story documenting the history behind the reign of terror imposed on Europe by the infamous Bluebeard. Ms. Ogden infuses it with her own hypotheses and invites the reader to explore the enigma that was the life of Gilles de Rais. Was his obsession with sexual exploitation of children born from his own melancholy childhood and being raised by an uncaring, amoral grandfather? Was it the product of depression and hopelessness following the martyrdom of his hero, Joan, and his demotion by the king he so loyally served? Was it what would be diagnosed today as post-traumatic stress disorder after years of witnessing and partaking in unimaginable slaughter? Or had the lawlessness in the wake of the Hundred Years' War simply devalued life to the point that perverted and maniacal pleasures and unspeakable torture of children could be self-tolerated if not rationalized?

Ms. Ogden offers no definitive conclusions, but by raising these questions, adds a dimension that takes the work beyond being a very good story to one that provokes a serious discussion about criminal responsibility and accountability. Her questions are as relevant to some of today's serial killers as they are to Bluebeard.

The conclusion of the book presents a tutorial on the politics and the interplay between civil and ecclesiastical jurisdiction over crime and punishment in medieval Europe. Within that, we find a vivid description of a man apparently wracked with guilt, seeking redemption and forgiveness through confession, and accepting, even inviting, the harshest of retributions for his crimes. Like the people who witnessed the human devastation brought on by his horrible deeds, yet nevertheless prayed for the repose of his soul, the reader is left with a sense of pity for this complex individual.

—Michael Kane, *Esquire*

Introduction

Oliver Davel, about seven years old, was walking along the crowded Rue de Marche with his grandmother. When she looked around, she could not find him. He had disappeared without a trace.

Jean Fouger's delicate child was last seen playing with sticks near the Saint-Donatien parish on a sunless day. He wore a special cloak of homespun wool made by his mother.

Jean Jeudon's boy, a slender twelve-year-old with big, brown eyes, apprenticed to a furrier, went to the castle to deliver a message. He did not return.

A diminutive figure dressed in grey, with a black veil and hood, approached children tending animals in the fields or begging barefoot by the road. She caressed them, flattered them. She put them at ease, promising a better life. Then she whisked them off to the dark corners of the castle.

There were others, many, many others. Long after, when lists were made, the names of youngsters who had vanished included boys and girls from all over the countryside, but at the time, nobody kept track of the missing. Nobody recognized the unfolding catastrophe.

Sometimes people thought they heard horrible cries from inside the castle walls, but no one dared question the lord who ruled from within. No one came forward to talk about the disturbing incidents. No one, least of all the poor, the simple, the wretched, dared point a finger. Menacing bands of men lurked in the shadows. They served the mighty Lord of Machecoul, Nantes, and the surrounding estates. This powerful baron could throw his subjects into his dungeons or kill them outright.

Nevertheless, the drumbeat of concern mounted as the number of children who disappeared reached alarming proportions. Word spread in the markets; rumor passed from neighbor to neighbor in the village communities of illiterate peasants and tradesmen, in the still-wild surrounding areas of gloomy woods, untamed creeks, and swampy plains. As scores of children continued to vanish, the mighty lord became the prime suspect in their abduction. Evidence of his crimes kept surfacing.

* * *

For centuries after this august lord died, the very mention of his legendary nickname, Bluebeard, made those who lived in France tremble. Born Gilles de Rais, he is remembered for his horrific deeds as a fiendish pedophile. He sodomized, then butchered hundreds of children in bizarre sexual rituals and delighted in watching them die as he satisfied his own desires. The crimes of Bluebeard are much more sinister than those of most serial killers as we think of them today, for Gilles de Rais persuaded many associates, especially his homosexual bed partners, to assist in procuring innocents for him, and to participate in his frightful crimes.

Still, Bluebeard possessed extraordinary, even admirable, qualities. His life reflected two disparate aspects of the man that seem difficult to put together. Gilles de Rais was the paragon of the high medieval prince, almost a Renaissance man in his talents and accomplishments. Marshal of France and friend of the king, he fought alongside Joan of Arc at Orleans and was honored by Charles VII for his service to the Crown. A mighty baron and a great entertainer, as well as a renowned intellectual, he staged grandiose theatrical events, commissioned musical compositions, collected art, and assembled an impressive library.

But following his heroic military defense of France, Baron de Rais somehow became a homicidal sexual psychopath, a serial killer. He went through a life-changing crisis that turned him from the path of a noble warrior and set him off on a series of shocking adventures that led to his ruin. A shattering incident must have occurred. There is no clear explanation of what exactly happened; there is only speculation.

CHAPTER ONE

BLUEBEARD'S CASTLE

CHAMPTOCÉ LOOMED ABOVE THE RIGHT BANK OF THE LOIRE RIVER, colossal and impenetrable. Visible for miles, the castle sat on nine hundred acres of land. A thick curtain wall, thirty feet wide, and eleven tall towers with battlements, all of it built of grey stone, formed the outermost part of the compound. An inner stone wall, twenty-one feet wide, encircled the enormous square keep, the central citadel, with its four solid-granite pillars. Measuring close to seventy-five feet in diameter, soaring one hundred fifty feet into the sky, the citadel with its pillars dominated the landscape. It served as the lord's residence and the center of courtly life. It also functioned as the last defensive refuge for the compound.

Situated in the western part of the duchy of Anjou and close to the border of Brittany, the castle's location afforded excellent protection from enemy assault, a requirement for a stronghold during the Middle Ages. The castle's defenses had been designed into its structure. Anyone attempting to climb the ramparts would be shot by archers from two directions simultaneously. Vaulted subterranean tunnels, which could be closed off by trapdoors, connected the fortification's outer walls to all areas of the inner castle through a network of musty secret passageways. These long underground corridors served as supply and escape routes during a siege and allowed defenders to clear out material thrown in by attackers.

Champtocé's five-story gatehouse, with its own complex of towers, bridges, and barriers, rose out of a large moat filled with water. It provided the only entrance into the castle, guarded by the seventy-five battle-ready soldiers quartered there. They directed the raising and lowering of the wooden drawbridge and controlled the portcullis, a heavy, protective gate of thick oak, covered with iron plating. Time spent at this crucial post proved uneventful for the most part, and the men-at-arms passed the time amusing themselves gambling with cards, playing whistles and pipes, and telling each other twaddling jokes.

The vast estate of Champtocé, as big as some medieval towns, easily accommodated its lords and ladies, their retainers, servants, and domestic animals, in addition to a military troop of four hundred. The many outbuildings constructed within the bailey, the open area inside the castle complex, included a Romanesque chapel, stables with verdant pasture nearby, barracks for the armed garrison, and a large kitchen. Plots of herbs, including marjoram, chamomile, basil, sweet fennel, mint, germander, and lavender, grew in profusion in the gardens close to the kitchen. So did all kinds of flowers: roses, heliotropes, violets, poppies, daffodils, iris, and gladiolus. Pine woods, fruit trees, and a fish pond stocked regularly with trout and pike were nearby, and a deep well located in the fully enclosed inner cobblestone courtyard, along with cisterns dug throughout the grounds, supplied drinking water.

The offices of the castle seigneury, which handled the castle's financial and administrative matters, were also in the bailey. Because Champtocé bordered the provinces of Anjou and Brittany, its owners had the right to collect a toll from all boats carrying merchandise between these two territories on the Loire River. The income was hefty. Tradesmen found the charges exorbitant and unjust. Nevertheless, transporting goods on the river was the safest way of ensuring their arrival, as thieves lay in ambush behind hedges and trees dotting the land routes, and even the main roads were rutted and difficult.

While the castle's exterior was stark and daunting, as soon as the servants flung open the elaborately decorated inner doors to the castle, the mood and aesthetic changed. Champtocé's interior was luxurious, positively exuberant. Hundreds of wax tapers illuminated its halls and rooms. Gold and silver cloth, together with tapestries from the prestigious Ile-de-France and Arras studios, adorned the walls; more than just decorative, they provided insulation against dampness and cold. Where the castle walls remained exposed, they were beautifully decorated with elaborate drawings of oak leaves. Thick carpets covered the marble and jade floors, and the best Italian artists of the day had been brought in to enhance the brilliant red-and-blue ceilings with paintings. The arches, vaults, and pillars in the principal state apartments were painted jonquil, indigo, crimson, and aquamarine. Enormous fireplaces with mantled chimneys warmed the great hall along with the private rooms. The library, paneled in Irish oak, contained elegant, leather-bound, illuminated manuscripts, including Augustine's *City of God*, Ovid's *Metamorphoses*, and Suetonius's *De Vita Caesarum*, depicting the cruel lives of the Caesars.

The immense sleeping chambers included splendid hand-carved wooden armchairs cushioned with leather, footstools, and intricately inlaid clothing chests. The lord, his family, and visitors slept in great beds atop a carpeted dais, raised three steps above the rest of the room. The beds had silk canopies, pulled back during daylight hours and closed at night for privacy, as well as protection from drafts. Feather mattresses covered with sheets of silk, heavy wool blankets, and furs provided comfort and warmth. In each room, sweet-scented rose water was available in a gold pitcher embossed with ancient Greek designs.

The small, leaded-glass windowpanes in the sleeping quarters afforded a spellbinding view of the Loire, its banks of gold sand dappled with sunlight through willow trees. In the distance, yellow-billed cuckoos warbled in an azure sky; grape vines carpeted lush hillsides; fertile fields undulated with grain.

Even the plumbing system was sophisticated. A cistern on the top floor of Champtocé supplied running water which fed sinks throughout the castle. Toilets with cold stone seats protruded from an outside wall. Odoriferous waste slid through the hole in the floor to a pit regularly flushed[1] by a servant called a gong farmer.

Champtocé's bulging silhouette towered above a bustling village of huts and half-timbered frame houses crammed cheek by jowl. Smoke curled from chimneys, while carpenters, bakers, butchers, blacksmiths, and potters worked out of the main room of their homes, which doubled as their shops. Fishermen repaired mesh or woven nets alongside the banks of the Loire in all sorts of weather. Short, dusty streets in town curved down to the majestic Loire. When it rained, the mud and stone lanes became streams of smelly garbage, urine, and manure which raced down into the river.

A simple but lovely church was the focal point of village life. Hawkers with their baskets, peddlers with their assorted trinkets, peasants with their small and large carts, their well-worn wagons, their overburdened oxen and sheep, continually moved around this Romanesque tribute to God. Using soap made from goat tallow and beech ash, women cleaned clothes nearby in the wash pool, a tank fed by a spring. They also sold butter, cheese, and eggs by the church steps, idly gossiping together. Throughout the day and into the night villagers entered the church by the grey-green granite stoop, to be greeted by a whiff of incense drifting about the building. Mural paintings in the apse depicted Christ of the Apocalypse surrounded by angels. Late twelfth-century stained-glass windows displayed a serene Virgin and Child in various postures of beatitude.

In medieval France, the rich did not forget the poor, and as in many other villages, a hospice for the impoverished stood near the castle's outer wall. Its large patient hall, where nuns tended to the sick, consisted of three naves with gracefully shaped arches. The village inn also abutted the castle wall. While limited to tiny communal sleeping quarters upstairs and one public room on the ground floor, it was lively and louse-free. Good food and estimable wine could be bought there at an honest price. Chickens as well as geese nibbled around the dung heap and ash pile in the sliver of a backyard, destined to become dinner for boisterous guests when they grew plump. One can imagine the occasional hungry dog darting into the yard and slinking off with one of the birds to devour it in a scarcely used passageway close to the fortress which reeked of old rotting fish guts plus other piles of rubbish.

* * *

The baby born in 1404 at Champtocé Castle seemed extremely fortunate. Four of the mightiest feudal dynasties in Western France came together in the boy's cradle. By his father, Guy II, he was a Laval, one of the richest, most respected families in France. Their extensive tracts of land encompassed a great part of the Northwest. By his mother, Marie, he was a descendant of the foremost Houses of Machecoul and de Craon. The union of Guy II and Marie had not been a love match. Strictly political and financial in nature, their marriage allowed Guy to inherit the de Rais name from an elderly baroness who was the last of that respected line of nobility. More important, after he received her vast fortune, he quadrupled his wealth, Champtocé being but one of the ancient lady's many rich holdings.

The newly wed Guy and Marie, now addressed as the Baron and Baroness de Rais, took up residence at Champtocé when the old aristocrat passed away. They called their first child Gilles, affirming their promise to name him after Saint Gilles if he gave them a boy. Gilles de Rais's baptism in the charming Champtocé village church, with its bells pealing, was a grand event. All the great neighboring landholders attended. Riding handsome horses that danced past onlookers, they came attired in cloaks lined with luxuriant fur, in richly woven, nap-raised Bruge woolens, in voluptuous green, blue, red, and gold silks from Venice. After the ceremony, they visited with the family at the castle. Standing next to the blazing logs in the great fireplace in the grand hall, they offered toasts of congratulations with Hypocras, the favorite drink of the local nobility, a heavy red wine mulled with various spices including cinnamon, mace, and white ginger.

Nevertheless, Gilles de Rais, born in a chamber in the Champtocé tower that was known as "the dark tower," came to believe he was brought forth under the curse of a black planet. When Gilles was eleven, a year after the birth of his brother, Rene, named for Lord Rene of Anjou, their father was out hunting in the woods near the chateau. Guy was charged by a wild boar and gored, and the attack led to his slow, excruciating death. Gilles admired his father, and this accident in 1415 took a very positive influence out of his life. Gilles imagined that the black planet hovered over Champtocé, and that it inflicted more vengeance that same year when his mother also died. Gilles never fully expressed his grief or suffering about these early losses, which he regarded as ominous omens. Like most Europeans in the Middle Ages, he assumed the cosmic dance of the stars and planets influenced his life.

With his parents gone, Gilles had no one to confide in, no one to dispel his fears. Like many young children who lose their parents, he became preoccupied with the death of his loved ones. He suffered from his loss in morbid silence, and the young baron turned into a brooding, solitary child inhabiting a lonely, spacious castle. Years later, de Rais's manservant, Henriet, at his confession before a secular court looking into Gilles's crimes admitted "… he heard the said lord say that there was no man alive who could ever understand what he had done, and it was because of his planet that he did such things."[2]

Fate made Gilles de Rais an orphan, but it also gave him a huge gift, possession of the immense properties of his deceased father and mother, large fortresses and beautiful land, covered variously with vineyards, rolling hills, villages, and tracts of forest and salt marshes. However, he was taught nothing of the moral obligations and personal accountability that properly came with such an inheritance.

In his last will and testament, which he authorized on his deathbed, Guy II designated a cousin as the guardian of his children. Guy knew all too well what type of man his father-in-law, Jean de Craon, was and did not want to entrust his children to him. Nevertheless, after Guy's death, Jean de Craon successfully contested the will and became the guardian of eleven-year-old Gilles and one-year-old Rene.

De Craon wanted control of Gilles's huge fortune. By the feudal laws of primogeniture, and following Norman tradition, the firstborn son inherited the bulk of his parents' estates, to the exclusion of any younger siblings. Nobles believed that if they divided their lands among their sons, stronger neighbors would attempt to take over the smaller estates. Thus all of his parents' great wealth went to Gilles, and de Craon was bent on possessing it.

Two honorable clergy, Gilles's tutors, agreed with Guy's assessment of de Craon. When Gilles's father was alive, they made sure the young Baron de Rais was well schooled in morals, ethics, religion, arithmetic, and the humanities. They abruptly left Champtocé Castle after de Craon placed Gilles and Rene in his own care. These men considered him to be no better than a thug, who did not care about the education or the responsibilities of fledgling noblemen.

This sixty-year-old de Craon relied on banditry to get what he wanted. Although he possessed substantial noble credentials as a powerful vassal of the Dukes of Anjou and Brittany, and was already extremely rich, wealth was what Jean de Craon worshipped. Avaricious, savage, and a miser without scruples, de Craon showed little respect for anything. "If one puts aside a totally exterior respectability, Jean de Craon has the outlook and the facility, if one likes, of a purse snatcher,"[3] insisted George Bataille, a noted French writer and historian. De Craon once even authorized an armed attack on the Queen of Sicily, Yolande d'Aragon, as she enjoyed a ride on her horse through the elm and cedar-covered hillocks in her own Angevine domain. The queen, also the Duchess of Anjou, was relieved of her jewelry beneath a peaceful blue sky. Her escorts had their horses as well as their baggage stolen, and were obliged to walk many miles back toward Yolande's castle before her servants found them.

Displaying little empathy for Gilles's losses, Grandfather de Craon set an atrocious personal example. The greatest lesson de Craon imparted to Gilles as heir to a vast empire was that he remained above the laws of France. Other than that, de Craon essentially left his grandson to run free with little oversight, with one exception. He insisted Gilles receive extensive military training as a knight.

Like many bereaved children, de Rais showed abnormal anger and defiance. Perhaps he felt a need to control his environment, since he lived with an amoral grandfather, and without supervision. The mature Gilles, playing upon the sympathy of the judges during his public confession to an ecclesiastical court in Nantes, admitted he amused himself in any way he saw fit as a child and blamed his offenses on his grandfather's lack of discipline. He told the court he sought his grandfather's attention, and the most dramatic way to be noticed, he thought, was to inflict pain on servants, retainers, and other juveniles. He did all the evil of which he was capable. "I placed all my hope, intent and effort in these illicit and shameful things and…increased these improper acts for the purpose of bringing about"[4] suffering. He laughed as these individuals twisted in pain. De Craon never heeded Gilles's improprieties, never reprimanded him, never showed him any love. (Of all the abuses a child might suffer, a profound sense of abandonment and rejection causes the most harm later on.)

Once in a while, de Craon indulged Gilles, who hated to be bored. To entertain him, Grandfather Jean assembled a mock court for him, made up of twelve and thirteen-year-old boys. The mission of these young courtiers was to serve Gilles and obey his commands. Little was sacred to him, and he so liked to dominate, so liked to punish these boys, that he pushed them beyond the limits of their tolerance for him. The French historian, Joseph Rouille, alluded to his acts being "homosexual in nature."[5] In hindsight, it appears de Rais displayed an antisocial personality disorder early on. While no single childhood problem infallibly signifies future criminality, the impulsive and improper choices he made with his peers, when some did not submit to him, indicated that the rage, fear, and bewilderment he experienced after his parents' deaths had not gone away.

Roger de Briqueville, a cousin from the Normandy region of France, his family financially ruined during the Hundred Years' War, came into the de Craon household as a page when he and de Rais were teenagers. Later, Roger, a puny bantam with flame-red hair, became a fugitive, accused of assisting de Rais in his brutal adult crimes. In an attempt to clear his name, de Briqueville, in letters seeking a pardon from the King of France (*Lettres de grace accordees par Charles VII a Roger de Briqueville, le 24 mai, 1446*),[6] accused de Rais of bullying him even when they were children. De Briqueville alleged that Gilles frequently tied him up with narrow leather straps, bit him ferociously, and sodomized him. De Briqueville said he was petrified of de Rais because of his cruel, vicious nature and his fascination with unhealthy pursuits. A strong boy like de Rais might easily have dominated the weaker de Briqueville. Yet, with a background of neglect, some children tend to become violent and abusive from a very early age. A youngster like de Rais, who enjoyed many abnormal pastimes, must be considered predisposed, but not necessarily predestined, to develop dangerous social and mental problems.

The only exception to de Craon's serious inattention to Gilles was his aforementioned insistence de Rais train to become a skilled feudal knight. He made de Rais spend hours learning the subtleties of sword fighting, jousting, and hand-to-hand combat. While the martial games of young lords of that era were always dangerous, Gilles outdid his adversaries during matches. He enjoyed being the most savage, the most victorious; he reveled in attracting attention and would take any challenge. On one occasion, fighting with swords and daggers, Gilles stuck an opponent with such force he killed the boy on the spot.[7] De Rais had not intended to fell the youth, but he showed little remorse after the squire died.

De Rais's many unhealthy childhood interests probably foretold his eventual penchant for committing serial murders. But along with seeking the roots of his later depraved conduct in the pathological behavior of his early years, the terrible emotional shock de Rais, a hero of the Hundred Years' War, received fighting for his country must also be considered. That trauma made him lose all rational control. As will be discussed, the possibility strongly exists that Gilles de Rais suffered from PTSD, post-traumatic stress disorder, and that the illness triggered his underlying psychopathy.

In a striking contrast to the appalling behavior of his childhood, Gilles de Rais was also an enthusiastic young scholar, taken up with learning. At his father's request, he read and recited Latin and Greek by the time he was seven; encouraged by his tutors, he subsequently immersed himself in the classics. Later on, he showed an interest in science, art, music, theater, literature, and gemology, and developed a fine taste for expensive furniture and fabrics, such as sensual silks and rich brocades. Gilles, an avid reader, always traveled with books. He kept a painter in his entourage, who illuminated his manuscripts with exquisite letterings and miniatures. De Rais even enjoyed coloring the enamels in the gold bindings himself.

The British writer Wyndham Lewis imagined the bookshelves in Gilles's library brimming with extensive manuscripts, written in glossy black ink, illuminated in thick gold and color. In his book, *The Soul of Marshal Gilles de Raiz*, he noted that educated French noblemen of that time often had a variety of manuscripts in their possession, including Latin classics, books of hours, missals, Scriptural commentaries, manuals of devotion, volumes of heraldry, hawking, farriery, and such standard French works as the *Chanson de Roland, the Miracles de Notre-Dame*, and Rutebeuf's *Theophile*.

The nineteenth-century priest, Eugene Bossard, insisted Gilles's redeeming characteristic was his keen curiosity about literature and art. He described de Rais in his rich biography, *Gilles de Rais, Marechal de France, dit Barbe Bleue*, as "one of the most well-informed men of his time," "…one of the best intellects of the century," possessing an extraordinary command of Latin, and speaking it eloquently.[8]

Like initiate knights of his age, de Rais was not only brought up learning the art of waging war but also appreciating the literature available to the elite of the time. He mastered both in his youth. As an adult, he excelled in fighting and proved to be a remarkable intellectual who enjoyed commissioning musical compositions, collecting art, assembling an impressive library, and staging grandiose theatrical events. His passion for erudition, as well as his great respect for beauty and intelligence, made him stand out, looking more like a cultured nobleman of the Renaissance than a chevalier of the Middle Ages.

* * *

Jean de Craon, on the other hand, cared nothing for these finer aspects of medieval life; his command of Latin, for example, was minimal. He thought only about enriching his coffers, and thus he betrothed Gilles at thirteen to a four-year-old Norman orphan. The marriage would have made the house of de Craon-de Rais the most powerful in all of France.[9] But her guardian wanted her for his own seven-year-old son, also a Norman. De Craon went to her financially strapped grandfather, offering to pay his debts if he approved the forthcoming union. The furious guardian called upon the Parliament of Paris, the highest arbiter in France, to settle the dispute. The contract of marriage was declared null and void, since both children needed to be fourteen to marry. The young girl entered a convent soon after and the dispute became moot.

Ten months later, de Craon found a better match for Gilles. She was the niece of Jean V, the Duke of Brittany, and de Rais's feudal overlord. Aware of Gilles's wealth, the duke heartily encouraged the union. A gigantic gathering of Breton nobility took place in the majestic Romanesque Cathedral at Vannes, the ancient capital of Brittany, for the announcement of Gilles's second engagement. The duke wore an ermine-trimmed, purple vest and an ancient Breton mantle for the occasion. It is not clear why this intended marriage never occurred.

Perhaps the nuptials were abandoned because de Craon discovered an even richer heiress, with an enormous dowry. Catherine de Thouars's lands would greatly augment the de Craon-de Rais estates, as her immense properties encompassed the splendid chateau of Tiffauges and other smaller castles, located at the point where Poitou, Angers, and Brittany converged. She was Gilles's fourth cousin, though, and the Roman Catholic Church forbade a union between such close kin.

In the Middle Ages, prohibitions relating to marriage, as well as intercourse with a relative, reached a degree unheard of in any other society. These were most draconian in the tenth, eleventh, and twelfth century. Sexual intercourse between all relatives connected by consanguinity or compaternity (a spiritual affinity between a child's parents and the godparents) to the fourth degree was banned.[10] In fifteenth-century France, these taboos still extended to fourth cousins, adopted relatives, and spiritual relations designated at baptisms.[11]

The restrictions of the Catholic Church did not deter de Craon. The morning after Catherine de Thouars's father died unexpectedly from a high fever, de Craon, along with Gilles and a party of men-at-arms, surrounded her when she was out on her customary ride. They kidnapped her and whisked her away to a chapel, where a monk married the two sixteen-year-olds, a gloating Gilles and a bewildered Catherine.

De Craon had rushed to abduct Catherine because he did not want to give any rivals a chance to claim her hand, and her vast holdings. Eighteen months later, after the Catholic Church received a very nice contribution from de Craon, the Bishop of Angers, following detailed instructions from Rome, joined the fourth cousins properly in holy matrimony with great pomp and circumstance. They were remarried at a nuptial High Mass in the parish church of St. Maurice-de-Chalonnes; musicians led the wedding party there. To make the ceremony eloquent and memorable, de Rais chose and supplied exquisite vestments for the clergy, as well as resplendent wall hangings, carpets, and gold and silver candlesticks; he also suggested the music for the Mass. He wore a splendid jouvence-blue, velvet gown and a rich indigo silken doublet with puffed sleeves. Catherine, at his request, appeared in a red, fully beaded French-lace bodice and taffeta skirt made by hand. (Only the very rich could afford such colors and fabrics.) Elaborate wedding festivities followed the church ceremonies, and large numbers of guests, along with throngs of peasants from the countryside, enjoyed the fanfare of lavish feasts and lively entertainment provided by the very contented Jean de Craon.

A year after Catherine's father passed away, but before she was properly married to Gilles by the church, Catherine's mother had wedded a young, penniless, but able chamberlain of the Dauphin's court. With her new husband, Catherine's mother fought de Craon's seizure of Catherine and her possessions, with dire consequences. De Craon's soldiers abducted Catherine's mother and transported her to Champtocé, where de Craon, aided by de Rais, shoved her into a sack and threatened to drown her in the Loire River if she did not meet their demands. Her husband sent three messengers, including his brother, to de Craon, with orders to cease and desist from his criminal behavior. De Craon scoffed at the demands, and De Rais showed no empathy as his grandfather ordered the emissaries thrown into a deep pit half full of water and left there. The brother died from the ordeal; the other two never fully recovered from their harsh treatment.

Once she was released, Catherine's mother and her husband appealed to the Dauphin, Charles de Ponthieu. He sent a royal commission of inquiry, headed by the president of the Parliament of Poitou, to investigate. De Craon and de Rais ordered their men-at-arms to rough up the delegation before it even reached Champtocé. The commissioners were so intimidated that they galloped back to Poitou without ever talking to de Rais or de Craon. The Dauphin was indignant and imposed a harsh fine on the two, which was never paid.

The inquiry by the Parliament of Poitou, and his mother-in-law's brute treatment, were inconsequential to de Rais, who now shared his grandfather's values: acquisitions were paramount. With the properties gained through his wife, he now possessed lands from the Loire River on the north, the Atlantic Ocean on the west, the further shore of Lake Grand-Lieu on the east (adjoining

Nantes), and the frontiers of Poitou to the south. At eighteen, Baron Gilles de Rais also had a grandiose sense of self-worth.

* * *

Gilles de Rais and his grandfather, Jean de Craon, had felt no remorse carrying off Catherine de Thouars and forcing her to marry Gilles, but when the Duke of Brittany was kidnapped that same year, they were outraged. They came to his rescue without hesitation, not only saving his life but also his principality. De Craon, especially, recognized that if they freed him, the Duke would reward them generously with money and land. While that was straightforward enough for de Rais and de Craon, the circumstances that had brought the situation about were more complicated.

Duke Jean V of Brittany had not fulfilled his promise to the French Dauphin to raise troops to fight against the English in the Hundred Years' War, the series of battles between the French and the English for the French throne, taking place over the course of a century, primarily on French soil. The Duke of Brittany, who was also the Dauphin's brother-in-law, had catered to both sides in the war. Some accounts describe the duke as cunning, heartless, greedy. His people called Jean V the Wise, though, because he represented the interests of his province well, through his intelligence and crafty diplomacy.

Promising his services to the French, he threw his support to the English the very next day. There were reasons for the duke's duplicity; his widowed mother, Jeanne de Navarre, had married Henry IV, King of England. Thus Jean V had very personal ties to that country. Along with many others, Jean V thought the Dauphin weak and vacillating, without the proper aptitude to govern France. The Dauphin was sarcastically referred to as the King of Bourges, because with no regular army, no financial backing, and no allies, after the Duke of Burgundy and English sympathizers took over his residence in Paris, the Dauphin had escaped to

Bourges, a town in southeastern France, to form an embryonic government.

Aware of the duke's double dealings, as well as his insults, the Dauphin backed a plot to trap Jean V, to teach him a lesson about loyalty. He invited the duke to a banquet at a luxurious castle. When the duke arrived, he was chained and thrown into the dungeon, where he nearly starved to death.

As counselors of the province of Brittany, Jean de Craon and his grandson, Gilles de Rais, were called to the parliament at Vannes. The Duchess of Brittany, with her two young children at her side, made a dramatic appeal to the States-General of Brittany to come to the aid of her imprisoned husband. Insulted by the assault on Duke Jean, his vassals took up arms.

In the past, de Craon and the Houses of Laval, Gilles's father's family, had backed a faction called the Penthievres in an incessant and ancient feud with the rival Monforts. Both groups claimed the right to rule Brittany. But now, with their noble Breton peers, de Craon and de Rais swore upon the cross to fight for the duke, a Montfort, to do all they could "physically and monetarily"[12] until they obtained his release. They raised red banners, which symbolized an immediate willingness to fight to the death. Fifty thousand Monfort men marched to battle against the Penthievres who held the duke. At a time when the entire French army had totaled fifty thousand soldiers at Crecy, sixty thousand at Agincourt, and twenty thousand at Poitiers, cataclysmic contests already lost by the French in the Hundred Years' War, this was a very large force.

The Monfort-Penthievres feud must be viewed alongside the broader events affecting France at that time. The battles of Poitiers, Crecy, and Agincourt caused profound social and economic upheaval persisting well into the fifteenth century. Terror and turmoil engulfed the country. The English victories wiped out the greater part of the French aristocracy, destroyed morale and pride, and ruined the economy as well as everyday life. These debacles created a dismal landscape for the thousands of dispossessed. English troops stationed within France faced overwhelming hatred and intense resistance which they countered with brutal reprisals.

In each of those major battles, the English, with one-fourth the numbers of the French, used archers, drawn from the English peasantry, equipped with long bows and steel-tipped arrows to destroy their enemy. The proud French nobility scorned these commoners, thought them unmanly, but the French knights were decimated.

After English archers ran out of arrows during the clash at Poitiers, they joined their infantry in the fierce struggle against the French, using whatever weapons they found. The Dauphin of France withdrew from the savage fight so that his men could regroup. Having witnessed this retreat, another wave of French combatants panicked and fled. At this point, English reserves, hidden in the woods, emerged, circled the remaining French, and attacked their flank and rear. The battle collapsed as the King of France, his immediate entourage, and one of his sons were captured. The English demanded France pay a ransom for their imprisoned monarch equivalent to twice the country's yearly income. The king tried to raise the astronomical amount himself. He received permission to leave his internment in England and traveled to France to do so. Unsuccessful, he honored his promise to return to captivity in the Tower of London, where he died a few months later.

During the battles at Crecy and Agincourt, the overconfident French cavalry worried the skirmish would be over before they had a chance to fight. Largely unsupported by infantry, they attempted to race toward the English across a muddy field, which became more impassible by the second. (It rained before both Crecy and Agincourt, with the muck knee-deep in some places.)

Bogged down in the sodden ground, the knights became easy targets for English archers, whose arrows blackened the sky.

English bowmen also aimed at the knights' war horses, and hundreds of prized destriers and coursers were cut down or wounded. Crazed, bleeding, screaming, whinnying, flailing uncontrollably, these regal animals struggled in vain to pull themselves out of the sludge. They suffered agonizing deaths. The few riderless horses that survived panicked and galloped back through the advancing French line, causing more havoc. In their headlong flight, they trampled and crushed some of the knights already thrown to the ground.

Most of the French nobles shot down remained helplessly trapped in the mud. They lay beneath their chargers, entangled in their own swords, lances, shields, leg armor, spurs. English pikeman and Welsh soldiers equipped with knives walked through the field, massacring them by the thousands. The preferred method of killing the defenseless knights was to lift their visors and shove daggers into their eyes. The upper crust of France, those who frequented the court and owned large tracts of land, was practically annihilated on these fields of slaughter.

At Agincourt, the contest was over within an hour. Like so many prominent French aristocrats, Gilles de Rais's grandfather, Jean de Craon, lost a relative there, his only son and heir. The English army also took a great number of prisoners, but did not have the manpower to guard them. Rather than allow the French the chance to offer the customary ransom in exchange for their release, King Henry V of England ordered their death. Only the most illustrious knights were spared.

Some historians downplay Henry's acts of vengeance, looking upon him as a flawed but courageous man. They believe Henry killed French prisoners by the thousands because he feared the French might rearm themselves from the weapons strewn upon the field and overpower his troops. Other researchers are not as charitable. They see him as a greedy, paranoid psychopath who brought a religious fanaticism to his campaigns and enjoyed watching prisoners burn alive.[13]

After the French debacles, heavy smoke and haze choked the air for days. English heralds wandered over the blood-soaked fields of combat and tallied the number of stiff and mangled corpses, crawling with small black flies. At Crecy there were "eleven great (French) princes slain, twelve hundred knights, and more than thirty thousand other";[14] at Poitiers, four thousand five hundred in total. The estimate for the French annihilation at Agincourt ranged between four thousand to eleven thousand dead.

Combined English fatalities for the three battles did not reach a thousand. One of their wounded was Sir Peers Legh. His faithful mastiff stood over him, protecting him throughout the battle of Agincourt. (Although Sir Legh died a short time later, the mastiff returned home to become the forefather of a pedigree which figures prominently in the modern English mastiff breed.)

In the Monfort-Penthievres engagement, which took place a few years after Agincourt, though the combatants were all countrymen, assaults on the enemy were just as brutal. In the attempt to liberate the Duke of Brittany, Gilles de Rais organized several companies of men-at-arms, which he commanded. While one of the youngest captains in the field, Gilles's courage and ability as a strategist stood out. He seemed to have grasped the complex art of war, for he planned and successfully executed an audacious siege on Lamballe, located near Mont St. Michel in the Gulf of St. Malo. He reveled in the challenge, in the stimulation of battle, in the bloodshed. He also turned his murderous impulses against the enemy.

Bugles blew; drums rolled as the assault commenced. De Rais ordered his nine-foot-long, wrought-iron cannons, some weighing up to a quarter of a ton, to fire stone balls incessantly against the Lamballe castle. Cannon after cannon spewed flames and smoke, their stone balls tearing through parts of the stronghold, their thundering tremors relentless. Fires broke out in the fortification with columns of crackling heat rising toward the sky. Some Penthievres soldiers, set ablaze during the pounding, had their clothes burned off. They ran from the turrets in a futile attempt to escape their pain. Others remained, mortally wounded, with causalities mounting. The surviving defenders, fatigued but unscathed, knew the dark sky with its flying projectiles could rain flashing destruction on them at any moment. They desperately tried to fling Monfort ladders back with forked poles, and dropped an avalanche of rocks along with hot water from the machicolations, openings built into overhangs on top of the castle walls. Archers sent volley after volley of arrows hissing from their crossbows into the concentration of attacking men. Gilles's troops dodged these defensive tactics as best they could. The soldiers kept on charging, though some men had stones crash onto their helmets, wounding or stunning them, and many died from the arrows pouring down. With his insane disregard for danger, Gilles roused the rest of his forces to follow him in a mad, direct assault. Still braving arrows and rocks, they encircled the heavily fortified but crumbling fasthold and steadily scaled the walls of the fortress in three different areas, to divide the enemy's guard.

As the walls were mounted, De Rais ordered a battering ram, called the "tortoise" for how slowly it moved when being wheeled into place, to break down the fasthold gatehouse. Leaving nothing to chance, de Rais also brought in a wooden siege tower. His soldiers climbed up protected ladders inside the tower, to a drawbridge at the top. At Gilles's command the drawbridge was dropped to the castle wall, so that more of his men could swarm in.

While Monfort forces flooded the fortification, their excited cries gave way to shrieks of pain. Some were gruesomely cut to pieces; some were smacked so hard in the mouth their teeth came out the back of their heads as they crashed into Penthievres wielding leaden maces, axes, swords. Both sides, now covered with sweat and blood, bashed out each other's brains, intestines, muscles, eyes, noses, eardrums, kneecaps; it was an orgy of brutality, and dead and maimed men lay everywhere. Despite the fight put up by the defenders, de Rais's unrelenting assaults, his reckless brute force, eventually resulted in a capitulation by the demoralized Penthievres.

Despite Gilles's win, the castles and baronies of the Laval-Rais nobility, as well as some of Jean de Craon's holdings, were razed. Their Monfort allies incurred massive destruction too. Nevertheless, de Rais and his compatriots fought on from there, retaking strongholds such as Jugon, Chateaulin, Brune, and La Roche-Derrien. Many of the inhabitants of these areas were murdered in the Monfort-Penthievres civil war "in a time when a particular hatred is exercised under the guise of a public hatred."[15] Fear and dread spread throughout the region.

In this damaging French feud, the Monfort side gained revenge when their forces, including de Rais, freed the imprisoned duke. With bells clanging throughout the vibrant Breton city, young Baron de Rais accompanied the liberated Duke Jean V into Nantes. Crooked, cobbled streets opened onto broad spaces with overhanging gables, spires reaching toward Heaven, and the masses hailing de Rais for his triumphant deeds. He reared his sleek, prancing paltry many times in acknowledgment. Breathtakingly attired in dazzling armor, a breastplate detailed in bronze eagles, richly embossed gauntlets, and wearing a flamberge sword with a silver pommel, he reveled in the admiration of the jubilant crowd. The duke granted him numerous properties confiscated from the enemy in recognition of his assistance, including fiefs belonging to the Count of Penthievres and his brother. Jean V also gave Gilles and his grandfather a large annuity derived from the rents of another Penthievres possession,[16] but kept the use of the lucrative lands for himself.

Soldiering had won great honors for Gilles's famous ancestors, three venerated fourteenth-century heroes of the Hundred Years' War. With his brief military experience, de Rais found the occupation so exhilarating, the acclaim so enticing, that he decided he too would become a professional warrior, following that noble tradition. The nineteenth-century French priest, Eugene Bossard, in his comprehensive study of Gilles, offered the opinion that after the Monfort-Pentrievres struggle, "He looked upon the art of war as a profound science; de Guesclin, his great-uncle, Olivier de Clisson, his neighbor and relative, Brumor de Laval, his grandfather, furnished him with grand lessons about glory that at the very least he had to equal. His ambition was jogged by the recitation of their feats. To be admired like these patriarchs became one of his passions."[17]

Gilles's exploits in Brittany were the prelude to his brave defense of France as he aspired to as much glory as his ancestors, if not more. Combat also provided the fire he needed in his life; he savored the fury, the killing, the challenge, appetites that expressed themselves most horribly after he left the military, when he turned into a psychopath, and fed those hungers with the murder of children.

After the duke's liberation, Jean de Craon's political associations proved invaluable to Gilles's military ambitions. His connection to Yolande, the Duchess of Anjou, was particularly helpful. Before he robbed her of her jewels, Yolande had invited de Craon to govern her Anjou province. She was also the Dauphin's mother-in-law, and she urged de Craon and de Rais to persuade the freed Duke Jean of Brittany to make amends with the Dauphin, and assist him in his fight against the English. They obliged, urging Duke Jean to meet with the Dauphin, Charles de Ponthieu.

The reconciliation between Charles de Ponthieu and Duke Jean de Monfort took place at the Dauphin's Saumur Castle, standing above the Loire Valley. The Dauphin and Jean V agreed upon the details of Brittany's alliance with France on a sultry mid-summer morning, looking out on a panoramic view of the town and the countryside, prolific with grapevines and orchards. To show their solidarity, they celebrated Mass together three times in the Dauphin's refreshingly cool personal chapel.

De Craon, present at Saumur during the detente between the Dauphin and Duke Jean V, invited the Dauphin to Champtocé, despite the uncertainty of the Dauphin's reign as the future King of France. By the Treaty of Troyes, the Dauphin's father, Charles VI, suffering from schizophrenia, had recognized Henry V of England as his successor. Nevertheless, de Craon hoped the Dauphin would recognize from the grandeur of Champtocé that Gilles could sponsor numerous armed engagements against the English if given a serious military command.

CHAPTER TWO

A COUNTRY OF THIEVES/
A BANQUET FOR KINGS

FRANCE REMAINED PARALYZED DURING THE EARLY PART OF THE
fifteenth century. It faced a series of crises that stretched its
resources and society to their limits. Treachery and cruelty knew no
bounds. Savagery became an acceptable part of life. The Monfort-
Penthievres battle was just one of the local vendettas, and with epi-
demics and burning rage resulting from the Hundred Years' War, it
all combined to weigh down the realm. The nobility cared only
about its own enrichment and displayed no social or national conscience. Expediency outbalanced morality. Loyalty was for sale to
the highest bidder. Duke Jean V of Brittany, the Dauphin's brother-in-law, was not the only lord to change sides during the struggle
with England; de Craon was not the only thievish member of the
gentry. Gilles de Rais lived and fought battles in that tumultuous
time. The events he witnessed or knew about could conceivably
have stoked his smoldering lust for blood. Eventually, his own
demented sexual rituals, his sadistic massacres, his unthinkable acts,
reflected the worst of France's deep pathologies.

The weak but beloved King Charles VI could not prevent his subjects' faithlessness. He had sporadic attacks of insanity, passing in and out of reality for many years. Neglected at times by all but his mistress, he wandered about in rags, reportedly stank like rotten eggs, and lived in his own filth. Sometimes he had hallucinations, believing he was made of glass. At other times he thought thousands of steel points were pricking him. Because of his condition, today diagnosed as schizophrenia, he was helpless to end the Hundred Years' War. Seizing upon Charles VI's frail mental state, Henry V of England landed on French soil determined to snatch the French Crown. His men plundered the countryside for two months, leading up to the great battle of Agincourt.

During Charles's bouts with insanity, his nephew, John of Burgundy, married to the wealthy heiress of the Kingdom of Flanders, served as Regent of France. Along with the vast lands he acquired from his wife, the position of regent made him very strong politically. However, when Charles was more lucid, his younger brother, Louis, Duke of Orleans, attempted to fill the political vacuum left by the demented king. John and Louis each profited financially when in power; for example, their territories were exempt from taxation during their tenures as de facto ruler. Chaos reigned at court and throughout France while these two self-interested nobles vied to govern the country.

A few years before the bitter French defeat at Agincourt, the Duke of Burgundy, called John the Fearless (a nickname he earned after fighting against the Ottoman Empire with great bravery), staged a civil war against the faction led by the Duke of Orleans, who ruled France at that moment. One of Louis's acts had been to exclude the Dukedom of Burgundy from receiving money from the French court. Infuriated, John ordered the brutal assassination of the Duke of Orleans. The attack on the king's brother (also the queen's lover) took place at night as Orleans left the queen's house, the Hotel Montaigu, after the two had made love to lute music. As

Orleans mounted his horse on a dimly lit Parisian street, seventeen assassins hired by Burgundy closed in around him. They toppled him from his mount and amputated his arms, leaving him defenseless. In his book on de Rais, Wyndham Lewis (who co-wrote the first version of Alfred Hitchcock's *The Man Who Knew Too Much*), imagined how the scene played out:

"At the Duke's scream, a window opened in the house of a bourgeois down the street and a woman shrieked 'Murder!' It was soon over. When the gang had vanished, a tall cloaked figure with a hat pulled over its face was seen to issue with a torch from the Duke of Burgundy's town house, higher up the street, and to inspect the body lying sprawled in the kennel. The job had been efficiently done, shipshape and Chicago-fashion; Orleans had been hacked almost in pieces." [1]

John then mercilessly massacred Orleans's followers, called Armagnacs. An ardent English sympathizer, John unleashed this struggle not only out of revenge, but also to take control of Parisian politics and the debilitated king. The Sorbonne dons, on the side of the English, justified Orleans's murder, insisting he wanted to become king himself. Gibbets were strung up all over the French capital. Carpenters were commissioned to make more gallows. When these were full, trees were used. So many bodies were thrown into the Seine that it was said to be impassable in many places. Wolves roamed the suburbs of this devastated city, devouring the numerous carcasses of victims who clashed with the Duke of Burgundy.

Although the Duke of Burgundy talked of helping Charles VI at Agincourt, his troops never engaged in the fight (nor did those of Jean V of Brittany). Instead, when Henry V of England overran northern France after Agincourt, he formed a powerful alliance with John the Fearless. This Duke schemed with Henry V to take the Crown of France from the children of Charles VI and bestow it upon England. The French queen, Isabelle of Bavaria, sided with the Duke of Burgundy and betrayed the French, consenting to have her offspring renounce the French throne. Within twelve months of this agreement between the queen and the Duke of Burgundy, her oldest son was dead. A year later, her second son, then Dauphin of France, perished. Both brothers had been in the Duke of Burgundy's care.

These deaths led to the involvement of the House of Anjou and Yolande of Aragon, Duchess of Anjou (well-known to Gilles de Rais and Jean de Craon), in the struggle for the survival of the Valois royal dynasty in France.

Before these suspicious deaths occurred, Yolande of Aragon had arranged for her daughter to marry Charles, third son of King Charles VI and Queen Isabelle of France. At his birth, he became the Count of Ponthieu, a small province in northern France under the suzerainty of the dukes of Normandy, located near the English Channel. Yolande took her prospective son-in-law to her court in Angers, and raised him with her own family, acting as a substitute mother.

After the deaths of his older brothers, Queen Isabelle ordered that Charles de Ponthieu, then fourteen and married, should be brought back to the French court. Yolande refused. Determined to keep Charles from his treacherous mother and her dangerous Burgundian allies, she replied to Isabelle, "We have not nurtured and cherished this one for you to make him die like his brothers, or go mad like his father, or to become English like you. I keep him for my own. Come and take him if you dare."[2]

Rumors began to circulate that Charles VI's surviving son, Charles de Ponthieu, might be a bastard. Believing her future lay with the English claim to the French throne, and living under the protection of the Duke of Burgundy, Isabelle started to refer to her child as the "so-called Dauphin." Queen Isabelle's extramarital activities were a regular feature of Parisian gossip, and her sexual escapades lent credence to the rumors.

The chitter-chatter did not stop with her dalliances. Foreign-born, she was an unpopular queen, and many considered her reprehensible. She was thought to be unstable, and known to be petrified of thunder; she had a special apparatus built to keep her safe during storms. She also feared crossing bridges, and would only do so after a balustrade had been erected. She was psychosomatic and insisted on taking pilgrimages to cure her menstrual problems. Stories spread that the queen applied a mixture of boars' brains, wolves' blood, and crocodile glands to her face regularly during the day to retain a youthful, alluring image. She suffered from gout, possibly because of her rich diet, and toward the end of her life she became so obese she needed to be pushed around in a wheelchair. [3]

While Isabelle was more interested in maintaining her fading beauty than helping French citizens or her son, whom they saw as the true successor to Charles VI, she was not without her virtues. To her credit, she patronized Christine de Pizan, the first woman in Western literature to make a living from her writing. An avid collector of jewels, Isabelle also commissioned some of the most splendid objects of goldsmiths' art from the late Middle Ages. And while ill-equipped to do so, before she became aligned with the English she dutifully attempted to rule France as the queen consort during her husband's episodes of insanity.

The scandal the queen created over the question of her son's birth unnerved both him and the nation. Charles de Ponthieu was tortured by doubts about his legitimacy, his right to the Crown. Groups allied to the English at the French court played upon de Ponthieu's misgivings until Yolande of Aragon put an end to the insinuations. She met with Charles VI in one of his more lucid moments and prevailed upon him to sign a decree making Charles de Ponthieu lieutenant general of the kingdom. By acknowledging that the young Dauphin was his child, and appointing him to defend his land, Charles VI removed any question that his only remaining son was the rightful heir to the French Crown. The act also removed Queen Isabelle from any claim to be regent.

Contemporaries greatly admired Yolande of Aragon. The notable chronicler, Jean Juvenal de Ursins, one of the main sources of information on the Battle of Agincourt, described her as "the prettiest woman in the kingdom." An observer named Bourdigne, writing about the events surrounding the House of Anjou, reported that "she was said to be the wisest and most beautiful princess in Christendom." Her grandson, who would become King Louis XI of France, recalled that she had "A man's heart in a woman's body."[4] The twentieth-century French historian, Phillippe Erlanger, in *Charles VII et son mystere*, noted that the Duchess of Anjou continues to be unappreciated for her genius, for her positive influence during the reign of Charles VII, and for being the pivotal force in his life for forty-two years.

Despite Yolande's support, Charles de Ponthieu appeared passive, even helpless, after he inherited the throne. He had trouble making decisions, and he continued to obsess over his ability to govern. When the Dauphin did make a decision, the consequences were usually disastrous. Passing through the village of Azay-le-Rideau, whose chateau stood at the edge of the Loire River on the main road from Tours to Chinon, Charles felt insulted by the local militia. He ordered the towers of the mansion burnt down, the captain beheaded, and three hundred members of his guard hanged. After word of Charles's spiteful order spread, this remarkable village was known for a time as Azay-le-Brule, Azay the Burnt.

Charles was also poorly advised by his council, packed with incompetents. Without understanding the ramifications of the act, his close advisors ordered the murder of the Duke of Burgundy, whom they considered a traitor, because of his allegiance to the English. Not only had he arranged for the deaths of the two oldest sons of Charles VI, heirs to the French throne, but he also assassinated the Duke of Orleans, the king's younger brother and leader of the Armagnac faction, which resulted in further bloodshed in the ongoing civil war.

The Duke of Burgundy, upset with the terms imposed on him by his English allies, had asked for a meeting with the Dauphin. The Dauphin's advisors saw this as an opportunity to assassinate the duke and agreed to the rendezvous. They believed this would put an end to the feud between the Dauphin's supporters and those loyal to the Duke of Burgundy. They further assumed that the duke's demise would result in honest negotiations between the now-leaderless Burgundians and the Armagnacs, who after the death of the Duke of Orleans backed the Dauphin and the Count of Armagnac.

Burgundy's assassination was carried out on a bridge at Montereau-sur-Yonne, a town in the Ils-de-France region. Like the Duke of Orleans, he was hacked to death. The Dauphin witnessed the murder but had no idea it would occur; he thought he was going to talk to the duke about the possibility of a rapprochement. Burgundy's supporters assumed the Dauphin was complicit, though, and thus the plan backfired. Hostilities between the Burgundians and the Armagnacs became even more savage. In addition, the duke had an able successor in his son, Philip the Good. Philip immediately strengthened the Burgundian alliance with the English, which led to the Treaty of Troyes, whereby the insane Charles VI was persuaded to designate Henry V of England as the next King of France. [5]

While Charles de Ponthieu's courtiers were politically inept, they still knew how to steal whatever they could from him. The Dauphin had become so poor that when he needed new slippers, a simple cobbler would not accept his note of credit. His council told him that in order to prevent the bankruptcy of the realm, he should continue wearing wet boots instead of slippers, along with clothes that were nearly threadbare at the seams. As Charles desperately pawned his crown jewels in an attempt to shore up the French Treasury, these men arrogantly spent the sums saved by the Dauphin for their own pleasure and folly.

The pliant, pallid Dauphin was simply not a man who commanded respect. He had inherited a feeble body, short, spindly legs, knock-knees, and a long red nose from his parents and ancestors. There is a painting in the Louvre of the Dauphin after he became Charles VII by the celebrated fifteenth-century French portraitist, Jean Fouquet. He depicts Charles as an unhappy weakling "with pinched and meager features,"[6] "a bestial face, with the eyes of a small-town usurer and the sly psalm-singing mouth that butter wouldn't melt in…a debauched priest who has a bad cold and has been drinking sour wine."[7]

The Dauphin's unsightly appearance, along with his disturbing behavior, did not inspire his subjects. With lackluster support, wicked advisors, and a frail mind, his domains shrank until they encompassed only central and southeastern France.

* * *

Despite Charles de Ponthieu's overwhelming tribulations, he remained the Dauphin of France, and Gilles de Rais wanted de Ponthieu to offer him a military assignment fighting the English. Accordingly, de Craon prepared for Charles's visit to Champtocé in the fall of 1425. Bright pennons of rich green and carmine-red sendal, a fine, light, thin silk, flew from every turret, and colorful banners of the same material extended across the castle's façade. Heavy carpets adorned the courtyard. All the rooms in the grand castle were scrubbed. New silk curtains and bedspreads, along with hangings of fine damask, as well as lustrous wool, adorned the chambers to be used as the royal suite. The imperial emblem, a three-petaled iris flower (the fleur-de-lys), sewn on the linen and also applied to the Dauphin's chair, added to the grandeur of the occasion. Tents assembled in the courtyard accommodated the horsemen who accompanied the future monarch; fields staked outside the castle grounds contained their steeds.[8]

Peasants working for de Craon-de Rais gathered mammoth amounts of provisions for the elaborate feasts to be presented to the Dauphin. The vaulted kitchen, built separately as an outbuilding to reduce the risk of fire, bustled with hunks of meat roasting on spits over a blazing open hearth. Soups and stews simmered in large iron cauldrons; the aroma of baking bread rose from the ovens.

Food prepared in the kitchen was brought into the great main hall of Champtocé through an extended passageway. The hall, a huge multifunctional room used for holidays, festivities, banquets, and receptions acted as the social center of the de Craon-de Rais household. It measured over thirty-two feet high and wide, and sixty-two feet long.

The chamber featured a timber-beamed ceiling, and had three bay windows with transoms nestled into one of the long sides of the wall. Exquisite Parisian tapestries, created before the Hundred Years' War, hid the moisture that dripped down the stone walls. A display of valuable gold vessels glittered ostentatiously in Gothic sideboards with elaborately carved panels near the dais at the far end of the hall, opposite the entrance. The dais, or platform, was raised on two steps. Lords de Craon and de Rais sat at the high stone table there. Long, narrow, rectangular wooden tables, forty-two inches wide, eighty-four inches long, were set up at right angles to the high table; benches without backs provided seating.

A skillfully carved oak mantel portrayed lions combating bears; black marble also adorned the massive fireplace behind the dais. The fire kept de Rais, de Craon, and their guests warm and took away some of the chill that permeated the hall most of the year. The aroma of burning wood filled the massive room.

Adjacent to the great hall was a small, interior Gothic chapel, where only the immediate de Rais-de Craon family could worship. Everyone else used the Romanesque chapel in the bailey. The walls and pillars there painted in vibrant hues of red, blue, green, and gold, presented scenes from the Bible. The gilded altar, decorated with sculptures of saints, rested under the large stained-glass east window.

Daily meals at Champtocé consisted of dinner in the morning, around ten o'clock, and supper at sundown. But for great banquets, like those honoring the Dauphin, all the invitees, arrayed in capes, furs, and costly fabrics brought from the Orient, thronged into the great hall at half-past ten. The women were clothed in floor-length, tight-fitting taffeta and satin, with trims complementing the rich colors of their rustling gowns, maroon and saffron, lemon and poppy, cobalt and apple green. Sumptuous jeweled pendants of rubies and emeralds hung from their bare necks. The men wore exquisite brocade or velvet doublets, tailored tunics with elongated sleeves, fitted closely to the upper body, and resembling a skirt from the waist down. The hem of the doublet fell just below the knee. The noblemen's hose, two very long stockings tied separately to their underwear to keep them up, were in colors that either matched or contrasted with their doublets. Both sexes proudly wore custom-made leather shoes with very pointed toes, called poulaines, the fashion of the day, the higher the rank of the wearer, the longer the pointed toes.

The twenty-one-year-old baron, Gilles de Rais, obsessed with appearance, showed up in a dazzling malachite-green brocaded doublet with a heavily embroidered gold-filigree design. Outfitted in petal-pink stockings, he wore the most outrageously long poulaines. Gold and silver chains adorned his neck. Rings of rubies, emeralds, and sapphires flashed from each finger. (Diamonds were reserved for kings.)

Musicians as well as minstrels in madder-brown gathered to entertain the assemblage before, during, and after the feasts. Located in the gallery above the entrance to the great hall, trumpeters dressed in roan announced the beginning of the banquet with prodigious fanfare.

The Dauphin took his seat at the high table, now covered with a white silk cloth. The ewerer, a household servant who supplied water for hand washing, sipped the water to make sure it was fresh before he poured it over the Dauphin's fingers. He used an aqamanilia, a small metal vessel cast in the form of a lion, for the ritual. He provided perfumed water along with clean towels for the rest of the honored guests. A priest then blessed the food.

The panter, responsible for serving Champtocé's breads and trenchers, carried in the salt cellar. It contained prized salt from Gilles's Marais Breton in his Pays de Retz, just south of the Loire River on the Atlantic coast. (Gilles's last name is rendered in a variety of spellings: Rays, Rais, Raiz, Retz. The latter is mostly used to describe the diverse region he owned.) This marshy area, almost magical with its fig and mimosa trees, palmettos, pampas grass, and yucca, flourished in the mild air of a subtropical microclimate. Its coarse, grey sea salt, then as precious as gold, and today considered the healthiest in the world, was valued for its delicate flavor and the salt's aroma, redolent of the clean sea. Hand harvested every summer from the pristine clay bottoms of the ocean's salt marshes, the sun and wind evaporated the sea water, leaving light crystals to be skimmed with wooden rakes from the surface of the salt pans. Thus the panter proudly placed this fleur de sel, the "flower of salt," before the most honored visitor, the Dauphin.

Now the panter brought decorated breads, which made up the first course, to the tables; these were made from the best flour ground at Champtocé's mill. The upper crusts, normally given to lords de Rais and de Craon, went to the Dauphin. Trenchers, large slices of stale bread, acted as plates; they absorbed gravies and sauces during the repast. French nobility remembered the impoverished, and after a meal the de Craon-de Rais household always donated these plates to the poor, who waited patiently at the castle gate to receive them and bolt them down.

Napkins were supplied, but not forks. Some food was eaten

with silver spoons, the rest with fingers. Everyone including the Dauphin carried a knife in a sheath at the waist, pulling it out to cut up the meat the carver placed on the trencher. A whetstone was available for guests to sharpen their knives right outside the great hall entrance before they dined.

Etiquette dictated that the Dauphin and the rest of the nobility at the tables use the little finger to add sea salt to a dish if they found it bland. The ewerer offered all the guests water between courses to clean their fingers. Banquets at Champtocé combined excellent cooking with formality, sociability, and amusement.

Drums and trumpets announced each new dish as it arrived. A stream of servants carried in mounds of food. Adding to the festivities, jesters in checkered, saw-toothed tunics and close-fitting three-cornered caps with dangling bells popped out from silver platters and jauntily bowed to the Dauphin, as did tumblers dressed in moss green.

Charles de Ponthieu received one surprise after another at this great, lively banquet. He savored the red-herring tart lightly seasoned with saffron, as well as the soft, strangely sweet, lamper eel scented with limes and raisins. He enjoyed finely ground, chewy beef pastries. He also relished eating the young hare subtly flavored with ginger, braised down to a rich, tender essence. Afterward, upon de Rais's urging, he gravitated to the somewhat acidic-tasting pie baked with four and twenty blackbirds.

Champtocé chefs took great pride in making the herons, swans, cranes, buzzards, storks, seagulls, and quail crispy and soft for the Dauphin. These birds, next to appear at the great hall tables, simmered for days in mutton stock, after being cured with a dose of eau de vie, a kind of brandy, together with flagons of wine.

Then came the presentation of the peacock, reassembled with its feathers intact. It had been cooked slowly in duck fat and then honey-glazed with traces of the hot, slightly bitter spice called *maniguette*, or grains of paradise. The Dauphin marveled at both the taste and the form of this culinary feat. Delighted that his pièce de résistance received accolades from the Dauphin, chuckling and chortling, Jean de Craon congratulated his chiefs and himself.

De Rais and de Craon devoured the heavy, lip smacking meat course which followed. It consisted of a pungent wild boar's head and a cow's tongue; fatty pigs' haunches smothered in cloves and oranges, plus a dense chicken broth; stag soaked in goat's milk buried in warm, sweet cardamom; and the guests' favorite, slow-roasted, succulent mutton sprinkled with tarragon, the herb used to ward off dragons. All tossed their leftovers to the dogs.

Young Baroness Catherine de Rais sat at the far left end of the dais. Upset by the lack of attention she received from de Rais, who found her tedious, and preferred peculiar sexual encounters and beating up his servants to being with her, Catherine bravely smiled throughout the banquet. Wearing a sapphire choker and dressed in richly embroidered cerulean damask trimmed with hare, she made polite conversation. She encouraged the ladies at the table to try the crunchy salads, topped with mace, caraway, poppy, rosemary, and hyssop; the greens also contained cooked vegetables, together with the crests, livers, and brains of poultry.

Catherine bored her immediate dinner partners by gleefully listing the ingredients that went into the molded pastries. She proudly explained how the chefs stuffed the dishes with meat, eggs, fruits, or nuts on top of dipping them in sweet and spicy sauces. Catherine was at least well liked by the staff, and the cooks wanted to provide some personal merriment for the neglected baroness. She pointed out to the guests that each of the desserts, accompanied by edible marzipan sculptures of kings, queens, and castles, was decorated with food paints made from the flowers and vegetables grown in Champtocé's gardens.[9] The pastry chefs adorned the queens' robes with a blue similar to the color worn by Catherine at the banquet.

If de Craon loved anything as much as money, it was wine. He kept an ample supply of dry wines as well as the local favorite, Hypocras. He made sure no invitee needed a libation and enjoyed watching his guests lose their inhibitions. He savored the sound of their noble cheer. De Craon also encouraged his visitors to share the beer, plus the fermented mulberry juice served in goblets and a type of bowl called a mager. They eagerly obliged.

The banquet lasted until dark. As the feast ended, servants lit handheld torches to augment the illumination from the wall sconces and candlesticks. Thereafter jugglers sang love songs, played music on lutes as well as harps, and continued to amuse the Dauphin and the assemblage well into the night.

There was a common saying among fifteenth-century French nobility: *Venari, ludere, lavari, bibare; Hoc est vivere!* To hunt, to play, to wash, to drink; this is to live! But hunts, the favored pastime among grand seigneurs, were not scheduled for the Dauphin. Besides a phobia about strangers, and another about bridges, which he shared with his mother, Charles de Ponthieu had a fear of horses. Instead, de Craon and de Rais entertained him with a gluttonous meal every day he stayed at Champtocé.

Thus, an enormous number of cooks were ceaselessly pressed into using their imagination and talent to concoct whimsical and delightful dishes for the Dauphin, while a multitude of scullions cleaned up after the creative chefs. The ritual of the table service initiated at the court of Burgundy was glorified at Champtocé, where the craft of medieval feasting was at its finest.

The twenty-two-year-old future monarch, who barely had money to pay his butcher and none to pay his cobbler, found his luxurious reception at Champtocé overwhelming. When he prepared to leave the castle, he asked Gilles de Rais for loans to keep the Royal Exchequer afloat, funds desperately needed to prop up his dwindling dominions and his nearly empty treasury, at one point down to four ecus. Gilles readily agreed to help. The Dauphin then invited Gilles to reside at his court, and de Rais accepted. However, the Dauphin did not offer Gilles a military appointment.

* * *

The Dauphin's court at Chinon "was a snarl of intrigue complicated by an occasional murder."[10] Charles de Ponthieu's entourage, composed of different cliques, changed constantly as the web of factions routinely tried to remove their rivals. Three predominant groups—the Angevins, beholden to Yolande of Aragon; the Bretons, under Count Arthur de Richemont; and the Gascons, dominated by the Count of Foix—all looked to influence the Dauphin, each party hating its opponents. Local feuds between these three noble houses affected the status of its members at court.

Concerned with his own survival, the Dauphin understood that the men vying to win his favor, whose reputation depended on their standing at Court, could be trusted only as long as they were rewarded. Charles de Ponthieu attempted as best he could to play them off against each other, and considered none of them indispensable, while they all knew there were plenty of courtiers waiting in the wings if they made a false step.[11]

Yolande of Aragon, Charles's mother-in-law, played a prominent role in surrounding the young Valois Dauphin with advisors she knew. She even selected Charles's doctor, who came from the House of Anjou. So that Charles would not be poisoned or stabbed, she brought in watchful servants, too, with the grandmaster of the Dauphin's household being her former retainer. Yolande's influence extended to mistresses of influential men at court and highborn women who shared their beds with powerful men. She bribed them to speak highly of the Dauphin to their paramours.

Gilles de Rais's move to Chinon delighted Yolande. Unaware of any of his outrageous proclivities, she assumed he would offer financial as well as moral support to Charles de Ponthieu. Because of his brave exploits during the Penthievres-Monfort feud, she believed him to be a young man of substance, who might help restore some decency to the decadent court. She was mistaken, and intrigue continued to flourish at Chinon.

Before de Rais's arrival, courtesans loyal to Yolande of Aragon and the Count of Brittany murdered two of Charles de Ponthieu's early favorites, who were despised by the Breton and Angevin factions; they had also formulated the unwise plot to kill the Duke of Burgundy on the Montereau Bridge. The official explanation for the murders was that the Devil possessed them. Witchcraft "was added, de rigeur, to the alleged crimes" of victims of partisan politics. It became part of "the ritual of political assassination to sever a hand, considering it guided by sorcery and the invocation of demons."[12] The Duke of Burgundy's hand had been sliced off during his assassination using this pretext.

One of Yolande close compatriots, Jean Louvet, had also been instrumental in killing the Duke of Burgundy, yet remained a prominent figure at court because of both his alliance with Yolande and his financial acumen. He had ably served in the Angevin *Chambres des Comptes*, the finance chamber, where he made wise decisions about cash reserves, assets, and debts. He understood the importance of a balanced budget. At Yolande's request, Louvet counseled the Dauphin about monetary matters.

Louvet often offered the Dauphin expensive gifts, to stay in his good graces. One time, he lent Charles 4,016 ecus of gold, so that merchants would supply him with gold cloth, silks, furs, silver plate, and jewels, for his personal use, and for New Year's Day gifts.[13] While the Dauphin enjoyed such luxuries, and did his best to maintain the appearance of an extravagant court life, as the times required, these handsome items were extreme departures from his usual, necessary frugality. Louvet knew Ponthieu would never be able to repay the loan.

But the House of Anjou was not impervious, and Jean Louvet, its mainstay, had many enemies. His name was linked to Queen

Isabelle of France, since he was one of her many lovers. Jean V of Brittany disliked him because he supported the Penthievres' claim to rule his duchy. But worst of all, Louvet was associated with the imprudent assassination of the Duke of Burgundy. The Bretons along with the Gascon faction finally made formal allegations against Louvet, citing financial improprieties. Charles never showed gratitude or loyalty to any of his generous benefactors or saviors, and Louvet was no exception. Without asking Louvet if the verbal attacks by his competitors were justified, and excluding his mother-in-law from his decision, the Dauphin dismissed Louvet as his advisor on charges of embezzling, expelling him from Court. [14] At least Louvet left Chinon with his life and all his limbs.

Despite the constant intrigue, De Rais would find that time passed slowly for Charles's entourage of backbiting, mostly impoverished parasites, except when they engaged in their deadly amusements. Bored, continually looking for gaiety and diversion, they filled up their empty days by hunting, playing court tennis, and many table games, such as chess, draughts, and backgammon. They trifled with the card games of *triomphe*, *piquet*, and *trente-et un*, trying to outdo each other's accomplishments. Sometimes the group went on pastoral excursions dressed as shepherds and shepherdesses. They routinely attended religious services. Church rituals afforded only mild fulfillment but gave them the opportunity to display inherited jewels along with sumptuous clothes.

The royals held themselves up as the truest of the nobility. They felt no obligation to assist their countrymen. Instead, they believed the hoi polloi should provide them with a better existence; the common folk needed to pay additional taxes to help out the court. There was nothing inspiring about their self-indulgence and self-absorption.

In the face of what they believed to be their inevitable demise, the royals became financially reckless too, especially after Louvet's expulsion from court. Charles's lords and ladies decided to live life on the grandest of scales, as long as the Dauphin's coffers permitted and the English did not drive them out of France. This was an age devoted to extravagance and unhealthy rules of conduct. The Chinon court was no exception. Most of the nobles at Chinon wore shoes with points so long that chains had to be fastened to the points so that they did not trip. The women paraded around in flowing trains and sweeping dresses, with great headdresses shaped like hearts and butterflies, or in tall steeple caps, so large and high that doorways had to be raised to accommodate them. The men sported extravagant furred, brocaded, and damask doublets. As they awaited their possible banishment from France, black, especially black velvet trimmed with martin, telltale grey, and russet, became the most popular court colors.

* * *

Always looking to be amused, the assembly at Chinon thrilled to the arrival of the dashing twenty-two-year-old Gilles de Rais. He approached Chinon sumptuously attired at the head of a cavalcade of attendants and liveried men-at-arms. He captivated the court even before he dismounted from his high-stepping cordovan paltry with its colorful harness and merry bridle-bells. Not only would his enormous loans to the treasury help bankroll the hedonistic appetites of the lords and ladies, but he also offered great diversion. The women were especially impressed with his money, his extensive, glorious trappings, and his reputation as a fearless soldier. They swarmed around him constantly.

The Baron de Rais showed an indifference to the ladies. He stayed aloof, not because of loyalty to his wife left back at Champtocé, as he had always found her to be a boring nuisance, nor because of his homosexuality. He kept that a secret and had no liaisons, either, with any of the court dandies "moving through rooms hung with tapestries off which smaller rooms opened" as they talked "in low voices, catching the eye of a victim or potential patron."[15] For almost a year, he remained distant from court intrigue and its constant gossip, which he found insufferable. He felt constrained by the social norms of the court.

Instead, de Rais concentrated on impressing the Dauphin, still hoping Charles de Ponthieu would offer him a military assignment fighting the English. He longed for the Dauphin to look upon him favorably, recognize his indifference to the lords and ladies, his readiness to be of the utmost financial assistance to the Crown, and his outstanding reputation as a steadfast soldier. De Rais did not exhibit any of his abnormal childhood traits; he suppressed his savage impulses.

Georges de la Tremouille, Gilles's cousin on the Craon side, desperately wanted to further de Rais's military career as well. Twenty-two years older than Gilles, fat and extremely tall, he was one of the real powers behind the throne. De la Tremouille had served at the Burgundian court, allied with England, for several years. He subsequently switched his allegiance, joining the Dauphin's court in the role of an advisor. Soon after his arrival, de la Tremouille kidnapped and drowned Charles's favorite counselor, Pierre de Glac, then married the man's rich widow, who was an accessory to the crime. After taking the deceased's place on the Dauphin's council, de la Tremouille so impressed the Dauphin that he named de la Tremouille his grand chamberlain. He became the Dauphin's preferred courtier. Charles, as observed in Mary Gordon's book on Joan of Arc, "… had a habit of attaching himself to stronger, older men, most notably the Duke de la Tremouille."[16]

Georges de la Tremouille placed personal advancement above public interest. Jealous and suspicious, he repressed any idea or proposal that did not benefit him, even if that meant betraying the French cause. As for de Rais, Georges had no inkling Gilles might be imbalanced. Gilles's behavior was no different than that of many others at Chinon; he was a more exemplary figure than most, Tremouille observed, for Gilles was politically naïve. He would capitalize on Gilles's innocence. He could use and direct Gilles to help him keep an eye on events on the battlefield and at court. De la Tremouille knew de Rais had the wherewithal to pay a collection of spies, and furthermore, no one suspected de Rais of subterfuge, since his sole desire appeared to be obtaining a military assignment. Thus it was in his interest to cement de Rais's reputation as an important soldier. But first he demanded that Gilles sign a secret pact to serve him at all costs. De Rais believed de la Tremouille would help him get his military commission and eagerly agreed.

Another significant player at court, instrumental in furthering de Rais's career, was Count Arthur de Richemont, the brother of Duke Jean of Brittany. After Yolande of Aragon's successful maneuver to have Jean break from his alliance with the English, she asked his brother to become the Dauphin's constable, assuming the military responsibilities for the Kingdom of Bourges. The count, esteemed as a great warrior, had survived the Battle of Agincourt. Captured and imprisoned in England, his family had paid a substantial ransom for his release. Richemont accepted the appointment and became the head of the Breton faction at court. Honorable, loyal, and energetic, yet austere and upright, he stood out at Chinon for his character, but also for the disfiguring facial scars he received at Agincourt. (Because of his deformity, Charles de Ponthieu always appeared uncomfortable when he talked to him.)

Gilles de Rais's fighting abilities and seriousness impressed de Richemont. At the count's suggestion and with de la Tremouille's approval, the Dauphin finally rewarded de Rais for his perseverance. Charles de Ponthieu presented the now twenty-three-year-old Gilles with a significant armed command. It encompassed the border country between Maine and Anjou, an area harassed by Anglo-Burgundian troops, French soldiers fighting on the side of the English.

Shortly after Gilles's departure for the front, de la Tremouille chased Count de Richemont from court in disgrace, on a trumped up charge of conspiracy. De la Tremouille felt threatened by Richemont. He disliked de Richemont's honesty, as well as his ability to influence the Dauphin.

Ironically, de Richemont had introduced de la Tremouille to the Dauphin. Thinking him an inconsequential adventurer and seeing him as a means of getting rid of the worst of Charles's sycophants, de Richemont had ordered Tremouille to murder the aforementioned advisor, de Glac, detested by Yolande and most of the court. Tremouille was a far more dangerous character, though, and he now had the Dauphin's ear.

De la Tremouille made sure Count de Richemont did not receive the pension he was due when the Dauphin banished him and even tried to have Richemont assassinated. Thereafter, de la Tremouille, with his pudgy hands and his pale complexion, became the strongest presence on Charles de Ponthieu's council.

CHAPTER THREE

BLUEBEARD BRAVE

THE ENGLISH, ALONG WITH THEIR ANGLO-BURGUNDIAN ALLIES, continued to conquer all but central and southeastern France, territory still considered the Dauphin's. De Rais and his military compatriots tried to keep it that way. By the late 1420s, the rest of the country had been picked clean by war. Destruction and carnage prevailed and shaped the landscape. Savagery rent the kingdom asunder. The terrified populace found their lives ruined, as they were tortured and terrorized by the English. The stench of death poisoned the air.

Using a chevauchée, or horse charge, groups of mounted English soldiers brutalized France. This cavalry of a few hundred men totally disrupted rural society, creating economic havoc. They rode through the countryside wasting enemy territory. Farmlands and crops were senselessly obliterated; peasants murdered; animals slaughtered; bridges smashed; villages scorched. Smoke blackened entire regions. In some places, the English impaled inhabitants on stakes and castrated the males as they dangled there. They smashed in the heads of toddlers, roasted people alive, and forced their families to eat their flesh.

Called Goddamns (Godons) by the French, the English also pillaged unfortified towns and manors. Desperate bourgeois dropped heavy objects on the soldiers from the upper stories of their homes. Some English were killed, some injured, but not enough to make a difference. The Goddamns continued to rape, flog, maim, and murder citizens. They threw residents off the roofs of their homes, dumping their mangled bodies into open sewers and ditches when they could not extort valuables.

One English company made a living capturing castles, then selling them back to their original owners. Another group of Goddamns controlled forty strongholds, plundering at will from Orleans to Vezelay, southeast of Paris. Chevauchée became very profitable for the English. They acquired vast amounts of booty, including a great number of valuable horses. These raids had political significance as well, in that they called into question the Valois capacity to defend their land and protect their people.

Normandy, one of the first provinces occupied by the Goddamns, suffered the most. Resentment grew among peasants, laborers, monks, merchants, country gentlemen, and aristocrats, including the father of Roger de Bricqueville, the young cousin of de Rais brought into the household as a page by de Craon when the boys were teens. A guerilla movement arose against the English, among all segments of the population. Trained dogs hunted down these Norman resistance fighters. Anyone caught, male or female, was buried alive in heaps of manure or executed. The Goddamns piled the dead on top of each other, leaving their carcasses to rot in public squares.

In this Hundred Years' War, the wasted lands, overall poverty, and constant fear of death dispersed thousands from their homes throughout France, and reduced them to living scarecrows. Misery and despair were etched in their pinched faces; many were sick, tormented by rickets.[1] Even thieves became apprehensive of the emaciated, ragtag souls wandering over the land in search of food.[2]

Vast clouds of circling black crows signaled their every move. These noisy flocks with their piercing caws feasted well when they spotted the dead. So did wolves.

Hedges took over in many towns; houses were overgrown with weeds. Main thoroughfares sprouted high grasses. The only inhabitants of immense areas of France were wild boar, as vicious as the one that killed Gilles de Rais's father in the forests of Champtocé. Five residents lived in Limoges. One half the population of Lyon fled beyond France's borders into the Holy Roman Empire. Delegates from the University of Paris proclaimed that if an end to the war was not forthcoming, the French would have to leave France.[3]

As the Goddamns advanced into the Dauphin's lands, de Rais took part in brutal fights in the Anjou province, ruled by the Dauphin's mother-in-law. Here he received the stimulation and thrills he constantly craved, for the battles were savage. Along with other young warriors, Gilles brazenly assaulted the strongholds secured by the English. These knights had the support of the head of the Angevin resistance, a knowledgeable, spirited powerhouse named Amboise de Lore, who brought his remarkable troop of men with him. These were skillful scouts and skirmishers. These brothers-at-arms, with de Lore's assistance, brazenly retook the renowned fortresses of Rainefort, Lude, and Malicorne.

Two lanes lined with grand cypresses led up to Rainefort Castle; a sultry June sun shone directly on the small leaves and rounded cones of the fine trees, which whispered quietly in a summer breeze. Crickets made warm chirping sounds rubbing their front wings together underneath the trees. Suddenly, de Rais's forces appeared on the pathways, luring the Goddamns out of the Rainefort fortification. To the English, they seemed to be a very small troop that could easily be destroyed. But as soon as the encounter began, the rest of de Rais's men emerged. Braying with fury, they hacked, tore, sliced, and skewered their enemy with fearsome bladed halberds and piked spontoons. These weapons, designed to kill in close combat, and used by the English as well, brought the combatants so near to each other that they could look into the eyes of their opponents, smell each other's rancid breath. Injured French and English soldiers, gibbering in terror and pain, crawled away from the battle, dragging themselves through the blood-soaked earth and over the dead bodies of the fallen.

A week before, Gilles had sent in sappers to undermine the structure at Rainefort. These men dug tunnels underneath three corners of the castle walls, reinforcing them with wood brought in surreptitiously from the surrounding countryside. As the battle for Rainefort progressed, the worn-out sappers surfaced. They set the wood on fire, which caused the tunnels to collapse, severely damaging the heavy corner walls.

Overwhelmed by the numerous French, who continued to gain yard after yard of ground, the Goddamns stampeded back to the crumbling battlements. There they observed the devastation which had already occurred, their fallen comrades' bloating bodies, the disintegrating stronghold affording scant protection.

Lax as well as overconfident because of their many victories throughout France, the English at Rainefort had made no provision for a siege, idly waiting for additional supplies. Now the terror-stricken soldiers faced a desperate predicament. Even if the castle walls were stabilized, they knew the French attackers could still starve them to death over a period of weeks, due to the limited amount of food on hand. Worst of all, Rainefort only had one well with suitable drinking water. The Goddamns had no choice. Standing on the parapets of the towers, they yelled down to the French. If the French halted their attack, the Goddamns would vacate the castle the next day, in the event that their reinforcements, soldiers and rations, did not arrive by then, as they were anticipating. The English even handed over some of their men as hostages to back up their pledge. Additional troops did not appear and the French, including de Rais, let the English leave Rainefort, as promised, taking their injured with them.

Next Gilles de Rais achieved an astonishing personal victory at Lude. He first directed the battle from a ridge near the castle just after sunrise, as the sky filled with strong red hues, colors portending the turbulence to follow. He raised his sword in the air, the signal for the battle to begin. The silence of the early carnelian morning was shattered as his iron culverins battered the stronghold without relief. In addition to this relentless assault from the cannons, two massive catapults, stationed one thousand feet away, sent stones, burning wood, and the corpses of livestock over the walls into the fortification. They hit the defenders with devastating accuracy, often smashing heads, scattering body parts, and setting sections of the castle on fire. Gilles had carefully planned his attack; diverse bombardments came from all directions, sending severed limbs flying, and stunning the tense survivors, many splattered with their colleagues' blood. Some of the dead, looking as though they were about to participate in a retreat, had fallen on top of each other with their eyes and mouths open.

After an hour of observing the destruction he had wrought, the enemy suffering, the turreted grey towers and walls disappearing in vast banks of smoke, an exhilarated de Rais dismounted from his chestnut destrier. He gave the horse, extremely agitated by the intense cannon fire, to his squire, who led it away.

De Rais's bombardment now afforded ground troops the opportunity to invade the fortification. Along with his men, he began a charge on foot through the choking clouds of smoke. With fists pumped in the air, their fierce battle roars reverberating throughout the castle above them, they bolted toward the stronghold, ready to fight, easily securing scaling ladders to the weakened six-towered fortification. With shields and new helmets, paid for by de Rais and forged to withstand the rocks and boiling water thrown down upon them, his troop met with scant opposition as they clambered up the walls.

Gilles entered the castle first. He immediately encountered the

English commander, Blackburn, a crusty colossus. Lunging, smiting, stabbing, the two battled in furious hand-to-hand combat. Winded, gasping for breath, Blackburn, the mighty giant, loudly roared and vowed to fight to the death. Gilles obliged. His men-at-arms reported that de Rais raised his weapon above his head and brought it down with great force; with one thwack, Gilles split Blackburn in half. Following de Rais's example, his troop began to lop off the heads and appendages of the dazed enemy without mercy; they battered, tore, ripped, and slaughtered their foe. The frightened English left standing gave up their arms after seeing their leader and comrades butchered. Quivering wrecks, they were grief-stricken, shocked by what occurred. Some wet themselves in their nervousness.

News of the surrender of Rainforte and Lude reached the Goddamns holding Malicorne. Believing an impending siege to be imminent, the English placed vast quantities of dry Burgundy grass, a fodder crop, in a large circle twelve hundred yards from the stronghold, spreading oil over it to make it burn easily. When they saw five hundred French marching toward the fortification, the English defenders set the grass on fire with a flaming arrow, to burn and kill as many of the invaders as they could. French foot soldiers, aware of this tactic, stopped short of the grass.

De Rais ordered one hundred of his archers to shoot an incessant and lethal barrage of projectiles from their longbows into Malicorne. Missiles flying over them, the rest of his troop pounded the castle with cannonballs that cracked the walls, bastions, and towers. The English cringed under this assault from the sky, which delivered a loud, violent death to many stationed there.

In addition, as soon as the heat from the Burgundy grass had died down and the heavy choking dust settled, French foot soldiers were free to surround the castle. They began an attack with support from strong artillery. De Rais and his comrades led the assault. Torrents of arrows, darts, and javelins rained down from the battlements onto the French rushing the parapets. The English madly pitched spiked hammers called gudendags at the attackers. As a last resort, the frantic Goddamns hurled sand at the enemy, hoping it would get into their armor and make the soldiers itch.

Outnumbering the four hundred men stationed in the English garrison, French forces now crawled over the castle walls. Vicious brawls ensued. Using the sharp side of their heavy shields along with their swords, the French, bent on revenge for the atrocities committed in their country by the Goddamns, struck out ruthlessly. They screamed out insults as they hit, maimed, and killed many of the exhausted Goddamns. They clubbed out their eyes, ears, testicles, brains. The English fought back with swords as well as bill-hooks, hatchets, mallets, stones, and any other weapon they could find. A still-warm arm trailing blood, a severed foot, half a body, a decapitated head would scud through the air. English resistance dwindled as the toll of their dead and wounded grew with the insensate savagery of the continuing French offensive. The haggard captain in charge of the garrison, covered in sweat and grime, surrendered to prevent further casualties. With his voice dry, he stammered out a capitulation. His surviving troop remained silent and morose, filled with shame at their total rout, and in the face of the excruciating pain of the injured.

In keeping with medieval tradition, all the Goddamns were released after they paid a hefty fee. At that time, handing over a nice ransom to the conquering army was common during war. The losers gained their freedom and could fight their enemy again in later battles. The winning party took over the territory, purchasing additional arms plus supplies with their adversary's money.

French mercenaries fighting for the English at Malicorne were also taken prisoner. Gilles's companions, possibly hoping to extract money, wanted to spare these men, but de Rais insisted they be put to death. He remained uncompromising. Perhaps preoccupied with fighting, he failed to understand his comrades' wishes, or he might have truly considered such individuals traitors, and wanted to make an example of them. Whatever the reason, the executions proceeded, and Gilles showed no pity. As he watched these mercenaries hang, he said with an icy nod of his head, "…one can die for France, but not abandon it." ("…l'on pouvait mourir pour la France, mais non pas l'abandonner.")[4]

Gilles de Rais's reputation for military know-how, bravery, and ferocity on the battlefield took shape after these few French triumphs. His victories became beacons in a dark time, as the English kept on extending their reach, holding most of France. And combat continued to satisfy his savage psychological needs.

* * *

Such absurdity; such incredible claims; such presumption! Hostility mounted in the huge hall on the first floor of the grand castle at Chinon. A fire roared up the great chimney as three hundred lords, knights, and ladies of the court, decked out in their finest gold and silver cloth, gathered by the light of fifty torches one early March evening. Charles de Ponthieu was daffy, perhaps insane like his father. He had consented to talk to someone that anyone could see was no more than an unwashed lowlife, a girl no less, who came from a small village in the province of Champagne. It was preposterous that the Dauphin would even consider receiving this illiterate seventeen-year-old peasant promising to liberate France from the English invaders and make him king.

For the Dauphin, it was a time to grasp at straws. The kingdom of France lay in ruin. Charles de Ponthieu feared he might be exiled, as the English kept advancing. Despite the few successes of Gilles de Rais and his comrades in the Angevin and Maine territory, the English claimed most of his war-torn country. The Dauphin's mother-in-law along with his wife appeared sympathetic to his meeting with the young, uneducated maiden. They understood the Dauphin's dire situation. Gilles de Rais, also present, remained curious about the girl rather than antagonistic.

The French attributed the current horrors of the Hundred Years' War to the Dauphin's inability to beat back the Goddamns. The war as well as heavy taxation made the Dauphin's government extremely unpopular. His mother's notorious history and accusations of bastardry, along with his father's insanity and designation of Henry V as his successor, subjected Charles de Ponthieu to the derision of his subjects. Still, despite these calamities, deep and universal sentiment persisted that the King of France held a venerated position. There was only one monarch appointed by God, by tradition. Perhaps that is why rumors began to spread about a virgin savior of France who was coming to the Dauphin's aid.

Indeed, a young peasant girl, Joan of Arc, from the tiny village of Domremy along the Meuse River, heard the voices of Saints Catherine, Margaret, and Michael. Always speaking to her from over her right shoulder and accompanied by a great light, they urged her to rescue France. The town official of Vaucouleurs, the walled city near Joan's home, had been persuaded she might do so. He paid for her trip to Chinon. He wrote to Charles that she accurately predicted a devastating outcome for the French at the Battle of the Herrings, when French forces unsuccessfully attacked a much smaller English convoy delivering salted herrings to their soldiers stationed at Orleans.

As soon as she arrived at the grand hall in Chinon, Joan of Arc immediately went to Charles, who was hiding behind some members of his court. She fell to her knees and told Charles that God had sent her to give succor to him, the lawful King of France, and to the kingdom. The apprehensive Dauphin, with his skeptical court, was far from certain that this young maiden, dressed in her humble red peasant clothes, was genuine.

However, Gilles de Rais was immediately spellbound by Joan of Arc. After seeing her, he concluded her mission to crown the

Dauphin king was God's intent. De Rais persuaded his Laval relatives, as well as one of the Dauphin's most highly regarded cousins, to believe in her. The Bastard of Orleans, Jean Dunois, the illegitimate son of the Duke of Orleans and the handsome leader of that besieged town, accepted her willingly, too.

Lawyers and doctors of theology at Poitiers questioned Joan of Arc intensely. She was also physically examined to make sure she was a virgin; otherwise, she would have been considered a witch. As everyone in the fifteenth century knew, one only became a witch by having intercourse with the Devil.

Still unsure of her ordained role, the Dauphin commanded that a suit of steel be fashioned for Joan at Tours, famous for its armorers. Made of polished, unbrowned steel, it gave Joan of Arc a striking, ethereal appearance. She seemed to be an apparition engulfed in white, glimmering armor. Her prized white linen banner, fringed in silk, depicting God holding the world, also came from Tours.[5]

Charles initially offered Joan a command of fifteen men, but before he even received the positive written report from the examiners, he made her commander in chief of his French forces. She impatiently set off to liberate the cathedral town of Orleans from the English.

Joan of Arc requested that the Dauphin allow Gilles de Rais to be her protector on the battlefield. She must have observed something in his character, in his bearing, that drew her to him. Wyndam Lewis, in *The Soul of Marshal Gilles Du Raiz*, suggested that the Dauphin's primary advisor, de la Tremouille, approved of and suggested the appointment for sinister reasons. He thought observation, rather than "benevolent" safekeeping, was de la Tremouille's motive. But Gilles de Rais remained loyal to Joan throughout their time together; there was never a hint of his twisted behavior when he fought with her.

When she saw that her army could not cross into Orleans by a bridge held by the English, Joan entrusted Gilles to take the troops back to Blois. Without hesitation, de Rais led Joan's men on the sixty-mile round trip so that they could safely enter Orleans on the other side of the Loire River. As it happened, George de la Tremouille had purposely sent Joan up the wrong side of the Loire, and Gilles's successful execution of Joan's order made his cousin furious. Wyndham Lewis wryly continued his commentary: "If his fat kinsman ever looked to Gilles de Raiz for what is called in modern politics a double-cross, he was to be grievously disappointed." 6

* * *

It was the royal decree that captains and all other ranks of soldier follow Joan's leadership as commander in chief. But as she looked around the cobbled stone labyrinth of Blois, where her troops gathered for the attack on Orleans, Joan was shocked by her army's behavior. All she could see was barbarous drinking, pernicious gambling, depraved ribaldry, and wicked whoring.

Her captains were the heavy-drinking, irreverent, war-worn leaders of bands loyal to the Dauphin. De Rais's bawdy companions in the Maine and Anjou battles were representative. Unflinching, hot-headed, and savage, they became the fear, the marvel of France; they battled and robbed, and left the morals of the troops to priests.

None of this would have been surprising to somebody less innocent. Joan's soldiers were like many armies of the time, a licentious lot of sinners. "A hundred years of war and crime had yielded this human harvest." 7 Boisterous and abusive, these hardened men filled the wine shops of Blois. They staggered around the tiny streets, urinating on posts exquisitely carved with acrobats and jugglers adorning some of the corbelled two-story houses. Outside the doors of the beautiful St. Nicholas Church, inebriated, rowdy throngs yelled insults and assaulted each other as they gathered around fierce, sometimes explosive betting games. Ladies of the night and infantrymen seemed to fornicate everywhere; they grappled in front of half-timbered homes, on street corners, at the back of the Benedictine Abbey, in the Beauvoir Tower, the ancient square integrated into the town's fortifications. Rampant bestiality also ran unchecked along the banks of the Loire, purportedly matching the times of Genghis Khan, when his soldiers took on sheep for carnal pleasure.

Joan of Arc called her captains together. She ordered the sinfulness to stop immediately. The orgies and the vulgarity must end; the prostitutes must leave camp. She commanded the captains to attend mass and say their prayers along with their men, for they were to be a part of an army lead by Heaven. She told them the English were winning the war because the French were so unrighteous. (The Goddamns, actually, were not very different. Accustomed to rape, pillage, and murder in France, they continued the same behavior when they returned to English soil.)

Incredibly enough, the violent French chiefs agreed to go to confession. The soldiers at first were astonished by Joan's ultimatum, since swearing and debauchery had been learned at an early age. However, they were spellbound as Joan, a figure in white armor, rode among them. In reverence to her, they discontinued their crude behavior and put their faith in Joan and her voices. They bit their lips to keep from swearing and marched after her banner with the image of Christ. Her mendicant friar led the troops, singing hymns and anthems. Raucous exuberance gave way to sober piety.

* * *

Orleans held great significance for the English as well as the French. It remained the gateway to the center of Charles's power. The French needed the town as a bulkhead, forestalling any English offensive southward. The English saw Orleans as a pivotal base from which they could easily conquer the rest of the Dauphin's territory.

An English army of four thousand, later to be joined by fifteen hundred of their Burgundian allies, surrounded the city. Orleans, unlike many towns conquered by the Goddamns, was heavily fortified, protected by 5,400 citizens able to bear arms. They divided into thirty-four companies that manned each of the thirty-four towers on the walls of the city. Orleans was so well provisioned that its townsfolk burnt the surrounding suburbs to a distance of 219 yards before the English assault. This strategy made every move of the English more difficult, as they were easily observed, and denied them any immediate source of food. But the Goddamns remained confident of victory, certain they would receive adequate Burgundian reinforcements.

The siege began nicely for the English. Early on, the Goddamns seized five stone towers, called bastilles. Some of them contained outer embankments or boulevards. All were situated to the west of Orleans in the direction of Blois, only a few hundred yards apart. By capturing these bastilles, the English believed they could control every entrance into Orleans in that direction. The Goddamns also intended to take the last gate, the Burgundy Gate, situated on the eastern side of the town, and then starve the populace until Orleans capitulated.

For seven months the English barraged Orleans, but it resisted effectively. The town, well equipped with gunpowder artillery, was capably managed in its defense against the besiegers by Dunois, the Bastard of Orleans. Yet as the months passed, it became difficult to bring in adequate supplies through the Burgundy Gate.

While Dunois directed specific operations within the city, he had no authority to implement a long-range strategy for Orleans, or employ troops outside the town. The Dauphin was in charge of the overall defense of Orleans. After he received some money for the relief of Orleans from the States General of the central and southern provinces, which remained loyal to him, he proceeded with a plan to liberate the town. The Dauphin had directed his favorite noblemen assigned to his army to assemble a good-sized force. Four thousand knights willingly set off for Orleans. On their way, they intercepted a supply convoy to the north of the town carrying dried herring to the English garrisoned there intended for the English soldiers, who were Catholic at that time, as a substitute for meat during Lent, the forty days of strict penitence before Easter. Being a much larger and a more-skilled military unit, the French anticipated victory. They attacked the 1,500 Goddamns, but the English dramatically held off the French, finally destroying them as Joan of Arc had predicted. Once again, the defeat of the elite cavalry by the English humiliated the French still faithful to the Dauphin. The engagement became known as the Day of the Herrings, a derisive reference to the fish left scattered about the battlefield.

The battle had an immediate impact on morale. It reinforced a sense of futility felt by the citizens of Orleans, as well as most of those serving in the French army. Support for Orleans became nonexistent, as did the city's chances for survival. When provisions dried up, French aristocrats within Orleans abandoned the town. The remaining, famished residents slowly sank into despair.

But the balance suddenly shifted. A chance cannon shot tore away half of the fiery English commander's face. He died a week later, a more cautious leader replacing him. The Burgundians defected after the Goddamns refused Orleans's request to be put under their protection if and when the town surrendered. (The Goddamns were known to hack off heads or torture inhabitants of towns that had resisted their attacks. Orleans residents expected to be treated more leniently by the Burgundians, even though they were English allies.) The English also became bogged down as additional troops and equipment, both needed to breach the huge walls, did not arrive. The Burgundy Gate remained passable; supplies continued to trickle into Orleans.

Joan of Arc, her banner flying in the wind, entered the town by the Burgundy Gate with some of her knights on the evening of April 29, 1429. She was warmly greeted by all the remaining citizens. Her courage was infectious. While she waited for her troops, marching from Blois under Gilles de Rais's command, Joan spent her days on the town's ramparts appearing before enemy positions. She yelled threats to the English, warning them that their army would be driven out of France by force unless they departed forthwith. The Goddamns replied, calling her a whore, a sorceress. They hollered that she should return to her cattle or they would burn her.

Joan's first engagement with the English at Orleans occurred near the fortified Church of St. Loup, outside the city walls. What began as a skirmish evolved into a small battle between a troop of French and English soldiers. Joan was taking a nap as it began. When she received reports of the ongoing fight, she hastily mounted her horse, speeding through the Burgundy Gate. A large town militia scrambled after her to add its support.

Joan raised her banner while soldiers followed her, shouting, "Hurrah for the Maid." The combined French force rushed at the Goddamns positioned in a ditch before St. Loup. The English, overpowered by numbers, hastily retreated toward the St. Loup church. Two hundred men were cut down, and forty more were taken prisoner after they sought refuge in the church. They had outraced their French pursuers and hurriedly put on robes; when the French arrived, they claimed to be priests. Joan ordered that they be spared, as she did not want to violate Church sanctity.[8]

St. Loup was Joan's first battle. She wept at the sight of so many bleeding corpses, the mutilated bodies of men who had died without confession.

The contest for the Fort of St. Jean le Blanc and the St. Augustine Monastery soon ensued. Racing to St. Jean le Blanc, the French found it deserted. As a tactical ruse, the Goddamns had left some abandoned equipment at the fort, after they saw the size of the approaching French army. The English then covertly withdrew to the bigger, sturdier St. Augustine, gaining time to fortify its ruins.

The combined English troops of 450 initially repulsed the French assault with arrows, crossbow bolts, and cannonballs. They had also planted many calltrop, spiked balls intended to cripple horses. The French panicked and abandoned Joan, leaving her alone at the boulevard, the outer embankment. Gilles de Rais immediately ordered his men to rejoin her; he protected her himself, his sword and destrier becoming her shield. When Joan defiantly planted her standard, her other soldiers returned.[9]

Their courage now restored, the French piled into the life-or-death struggle from all directions. They kept up their onslaught throughout the afternoon. The English quailed when they saw what they believed to be a final charge from Hell. It was not an assault from the French military, but from Joan, that hair-raising enchantress in white, who galloped straight at them. Her horse ran so fast it left its shadow in the dust, and the English imagined that fire flew from its hooves. The French successfully broke the Goddamns at the Augustines.

Chroniclers of the time mention twenty-four-year-old Gilles de Rais twice at the Battle of Orleans; they commend him for bringing needed reinforcements to Joan at the Augustines, and after pulling her to safety when she was seriously injured during the intense fight for the Tourelles, he went on to fiercely attack the enemy.

The impossible occurred for the French at the Tourelles, that stone tower on the far end of Orleans. The Tourelles, well commanded by the English knight, Glasdale, was thought to be impenetrable. Its garrison numbered five hundred men-at-arms and archers. Nevertheless, the French began a direct, frontal offense on the fortified fasthold. First, they attempted to undermine its bridge arches, part of the structure's foundation. At the same time, the town militia filled in the ditch approaching the Tourelles.

French forces then gained ground, and Joan accompanied the army as it moved forward. She sprang off her black charger, placing the first scaling ladder against the wall. As she had uncannily foretold, she was badly wounded attempting to mount one of the ladders. In the midst of the fight, a bolt from an English crossbow struck her with such force between her shoulder and throat that it pierced her armor, projecting six inches behind her neck. She fell backwards. Gilles de Rais and other captains who witnessed the incident rushed to her. They carried her to safety, to dress her deep gash. Joan pulled out the arrow herself, crying with pain. A compress of fat and olive oil relieved her distress.

The Goddamns, superstitious like all medieval Catholics, considered a woman leading an army of men to be a conjurer of Satan. Overjoyed she was injured, they began to jump around and sing, "The witch is dead! The witch is dead!" When they heard the English jeers and saw Joan felled, the French lost spirit. The Goddamns stationed in the bulwark of the Tourelles easily repulsed the halfhearted efforts of the French struggling up the walls. Commander Dunois prepared to break off the engagement as the tide of battle shifted in the direction of the English.

Joan recovered. Her saints appeared to her, and she overcame her weakness. She spurred on the French once again, late in the afternoon. At the sight of this revered girl, her standard blowing free, her troops rallied; drums and bugles sounded the assault as their fierce charge was renewed.

When the attack began on the Tourelles, the Orleans townsfolk sent out their own surprise to the Goddamns. They cut loose a barge loaded with flammable material including wood, horse bones, shoes, sulfur, and other unpleasant, smelly items, which they ignited at the end of an island near the Tourelles. Slowly, stealthily, the burning barge drifted under the wooden drawbridge joining the outer embankment with the Tourelles.

The English, busily fighting to keep the French off the draw-bridge, did not notice the barge until smoke began to rise beneath them. As they attempted to cross back over the bridge to retreat into the Tourelles, they finally smelled the pitch and heard the crackle of flames.[10] Damaged by the weight of the men, as well as by the heat of the fire, the blazing structure fell apart. Five cannon shots from the city carried the remnants away. Three hundred Goddamns, including their leader, Glasdale, ended up in the swollen Loire River; all drowned because of their heavy armor. The two hundred English who made their way back to the Tourelles or who battled inside the tower were surrounded. They did not resist. Those not butchered by the French became prisoners.

The next day the English who held the remaining towers assembled in battle formation outside the town. French forces quickly gathered, advanced, and faced the Goddamns. They were eager for another fight, but Joan forbade any combat since it was Sunday, the day of worship. The two armies eyed each other for an hour. Abruptly, the English turned away from the French and marched off. The siege of Orleans was over.

Overwhelmed with joy, Joan led her astonished soldiers and the elated citizens of Orleans in a solemn procession around the city walls. Kneeling, they all gave thanks to God for His deliverance of the town. Bells rang throughout the city, trumpets sounded, people cried "Noel," and Orleans reveled all night. In less than a week, Joan of Arc, seventeen years old, carried off one of the decisive battles of the world and remapped French destiny.

CHAPTER 4

THE INSPIRATION AND MARTYR OF FRANCE

THE MAID OF ORLEANS, AS JOAN OF ARC WAS NOW CALLED, became the inspiration of France. She rode on to many victories against the English. The Baron de Rais paid for new troops who helped Joan rid the Loire Valley of the Goddamns. He insisted that his Laval cousins mortgage some of their choice properties to assist Joan, as the Dauphin did not have the financial resources to do so. With Gilles and her other revered captains at her side, she took Jargeau (Charles singled out de Rais and rewarded him for his actions in recovering this village, east of Orleans), Meun, Beaugency, and Patay in one week. The English captured and killed in Patay alone amounted to four thousand. Perhaps if Joan had then gone on to Paris, she would have conquered it as well, given the adoration and assistance she received wherever she went. However, her voices directed her to take Charles to his coronation instead.

Joan's spectacular advances on the territories held by the English, which soon included Auxerre, Troyes, and Chalons, successfully cleared the way for the Dauphin to enter Reims. Bells rang and vast crowds wildly cheered as Charles de Ponthieu, now popular on the strength of Joan's victories, was crowned King Charles VII of France in an elaborate ceremony lasting over five hours.

De Rais's part in Joan's successful campaign through the Loire Valley enhanced his own career, and Charles next ordered him to accompany a religious cavalcade transporting the holy oil kept at the Abbey of Saint Remy for the official coronation. A drop from the sacred ampoule, guarded within the abbey, had been used to anoint every French king since Clovis was enthroned in 496. De Rais was one of four knights handpicked by Charles, and along with other nobles, fully armed and mounted, in splendid harness, and carrying silk banners with their family emblems, led the procession of churchmen in scarlet and purple robes to the Cathedral of Reims.

The Grand Prior of Saint Remy, sitting on the back of a white horse, beneath a jeweled canopy, bore the vial, or holy chrism, in its case suspended from his neck by a gold chain.[1] When Gilles and the other knights approached the richly patterned west front of the cathedral, the smiling sculptured angel on the left of the farthest doorway, known as the *Sourire de Reims*, appeared to be particularly happy. They rode their palfreys into the exquisite cathedral, packed with people, through the great main door, a beautiful rose window above it, to the choir, where they dismounted. The prior presented the precious anointing oil to the Archbishop of Reims in his grand costume, his miter on his head, his cross in his hand. The monarch awaiting the oil was in tears. Holding her standard, Joan of Arc wept too as she wrapped herself around Charles's knees; the crown was finally his. Overwhelmed, de Rais shared in Joan's great joy. His heroine, the savior of France, had successfully accomplished the mission her voices commanded.

One of Charles's first acts as king was to make the Baron Gilles de Rais a Marshal of France, the highest military rank in the army.

He was not the only marshal, but he would command the Crown's troops and carry a baton as a symbol of distinction.[2] In recognition of Gilles de Rais's loyalty, inspiring service, and heroic deeds, the king also permitted him to display a border of the royal symbol, the fleur-de-lys, on his own coat of arms. Gilles was not yet twenty-five years old when these great honors were bestowed upon him. He had won these considerations by his bold defense of France and his relentless support of Joan of Arc. No one questioned his mental stability. He had become a legendary warrior, a partner of the Maid. He had a lifetime of distinguished service to look forward to.

After the coronation, Gilles declined Charles's invitation to return to his court. Instead, de Rais joined Joan's army at Senlis, some thirty-seven miles north and slightly east of Paris. The Maid's voices did not tell her she would have any more victories, but she marched on to Paris with her troops anyway, longing to finish her work and send the Goddamns back to their island. She immediately captured the Saint-Honore Gate on the outskirts of the city. During a day of hard fighting, her men, led by de Rais, gained ground around the tall ramparts by the gate (today in the center of town, near the Theatre Francais square and the Rue de Rivoli; Joan's gilded equestrian statue presently guards that street). The French forces continued their struggle with the assistance of the many Parisians hostile to the Goddamns.

But the Duke of Burgundy, Philip the Good, who supported the English, was up to no good. He sent word to the newly anointed king that if he halted the Maid's attacks now, the duke, in charge of Paris, would later turn the city over to Charles. Georges de la Tremouille, the French chancellor, advised the king to follow a policy of negotiation and appeasement with the English in regard to Paris, and urged him to sign a truce.

Twentieth-century historians have concluded that de la Tremouille purposely gave Charles bad counsel. Wyndam Lewis railed, "Fat La Tremouille...A cynic, sleepless and insatiable in intrigue, inscrutable, ruthless without scruple, having no ideal but the benefit of Georges de la Tremouille, had been bred up at the Court of Burgundy, and was suspected all his life of having a foot in both camps."[3] Vita Sackville-West, noted for her work on Joan of Arc, went even further. She characterized Tremouille as an English sympathizer and corrupt statesman, his collaboration with the enemy extensive and ongoing. George Bataille felt "beyond a doubt" de la Tremouille was responsible for the king's decision to abandon the siege of Paris.

In order to save his own fortress from English occupation, for example, de la Tremouille plotted with the Goddamns to impede Charles's journey to Reims for his coronation.[4] He insisted the route to Reims remained too dangerous; intimidated, Charles dillydallied. But after the Maid's victories in the Loire Valley and elsewhere, public support overcame de la Tremouille's attempts to prevent Charles's installation as king.

Another court favorite, Regnault de Chartres, the Archbishop of Reims at the time of Charles's accession to the throne, was in league with de la Tremouille and the Goddamns as well. Though a churchman of high rank, the archbishop displayed little vision regarding the Catholic faith. He thought of his religion as a set of doctrines, and having neither charity nor piety in his heart, like de la Tremouille, he pursued his own personal aggrandizement. These two, de Chartres and de la Tremouille, did not hesitate to obstruct Joan's Paris offensive.[5]

Heeding de la Tremouille's and the archbishop's counsel, Charles ordered his commander in chief to desist from further fighting. Joan ignored the king and continued to attack his foes. Waving her banner, she tirelessly encouraged her troops, and could be heard above the clamor urging the Parisian garrison to surrender. At Vespers, just as it appeared Paris would fall, her armor became a shining mark for English arrows, and the Maid was wounded by a crossbow bolt in her thigh. (For decades, a plaque on the Café de la Regence in the Place du Palais-Royal marked the spot where she was injured.) Gilles de Rais led her to safety, and believing she might die, Joan requested that her devoted companion, who fought with her all the way from Blois to Reims and then Paris, stay with her through the night. This would be their last military action together, and the last time they saw each other.

Gilles's cousin, de la Tremouille, insisted Charles VII call de Rais back from Paris forthwith. Because Gilles had demonstrated his military prowess, de la Tremouille now saw him as another threat; Gilles could undermine his disreputable stratagems. Joan's valorous and faithful Gilles, "*valeureux et fidele*," as she described him, a far cry from how he had been characterized in his youth, obeyed the command.

Joan recovered sufficiently from her wounds, yet she did not capture Paris. De la Tremouille and the Archbishop of Reims had sold out the French cause in that city well before her attack, for an attractive sum of money the Duke of Burgundy dangled in front of them. Weeping, her hopes dashed, Joan left Paris. First, though, she laid her armor upon the altar in the Cathedral of Saint Denis, whose name was the war cry of France, and offered it to him. She felt her equipment was useless, as the king had now disbanded his army for the winter, possibly for economic reasons. Thirteen hundred ecus of silver and gold, sent from the town of Bourges to assist in the struggle against the English in Paris, had mysteriously disappeared during de la Tremouille's custodianship, before it could be used to pay the troops fighting there.

When the truce with Burgundy expired the next spring, Joan anxiously renewed her mission to rid Paris and France of the Goddamns. She remained such an inspiration to the French that the citizens of Melun, twenty-five miles southeast of Paris, rose up when they heard she would be attempting to liberate their city.

After ten years of siege by the English that had them eating rats to survive, they walloped the English garrison and ejected them. The town's new allegiance to France permitted Joan passage of the Seine River.

As she approached Melun, Joan's voices warned her she would be captured in the near future. They told her this was God's plan, but He would be with her. She begged Saint Catherine and Saint Margaret to tell her when this would occur, and later confessed that had she known, she would not have engaged in battle that day.

Subsequently, a delegation from Compiegne met with the Maid, pleading with her to rid their town of the English. They explained they had a meager supply of food within the town, and while they had access to the countryside, the crops had been destroyed by skirmishes; a siege by the Goddamns would be short and successful. She accepted the challenge willingly, even though many of her captains and soldiers had drifted away, due to her limited resources. The Archbishop of Reims also popped up, urging capitulation.

The enemy had set up three camps across the Oise River from Compiegne. One was manned by the Burgundians, two miles above the town; another, guarded by the English, was three-quarters of a mile downriver; and the third was directly opposite Compiegne, located at the end of a bridge over the Oise. Joan and the governor of the town, Guillaume de Flavy, decided the latter camp could easily be destroyed by a swift charge across the bridge by Joan and her soldiers. They would be reinforced by de Flavy's archers and culverins placed along the walls and banks of Compiegne. Joan would be able to break up the camp and ride back across the bridge before the enemy at the other locations became aware of what had occurred.

The attack went as planned. However, some Burgundians witnessed the skirmish and quickly sent word to the other camps, whose troops galloped to the rescue of their comrades. Joan and her soldiers could have retreated over the bridge when they saw the larger forces bearing down on them. Instead, they met the onslaught of men and drove off these advancing troops. Fierce fighting continued with additional English soldiers and Burgundians, who greatly outnumbered the French. Five hundred of the enemy cut Joan's men off from behind.

Now Joan and her troop retreated in desperation toward the bridge, attempting to cross it and enter the town to regroup. Soldiers from both sides tried to cram onto the bridge and slash their way across it, and from the walls of Compiegne, the governor, de Flavy, watched bloody rampage approach his town. He ordered the drawbridge raised and the gate shut. He later claimed he was afraid the English would gain access to the city, but suspicion remains that de Flavy, a relative of the Archbishop of Reims and a deputy to de la Tremouille, purposely betrayed Joan.

On the Compiegne side of the river the land was low and wet; causeways led to sodden meadows along the river bank outside the walls of the town. Joan and her band successfully crossed the bridge, but were compelled to leave the causeways and were forced into the meadows. They bravely resisted but were overpowered by the enemy, bent on capturing the "witch." In late afternoon, Burgundians seized Joan by her cape and dragged her off her horse, while the residents of Compiegne looked on, shuddering.

French citizens, French nobles, French peasants all mourned in their hearts; they could not believe their heroine was taken from them. But when he heard the news about Joan, the Duke of Burgundy ordered a *Te Deum*, a hymn thanking God for a special blessing, to be sung in all the churches of Paris. The University of Paris, loyal to Burgundy and the English, attempted to get Joan into its hands. Two days after she became a prisoner, the faculty at the theological college, subject only to ecclesiastical law, mandated that the Burgundians turn her over. As English surrogates, they could try her as a witch and heretic.

She was initially held at two Anglo-Burgundian strongholds, Beaulieu and then Beaurevoir. Joan, hoping to escape her fate, jumped out of a tower window at Beaurevoir, a drop of sixty or seventy feet. She survived the incredible fall, dazed but only slightly injured. As soon as she was well enough to travel, she was transferred into English custody. By December 1430, the Goddamns jailed her at the Castle in Rouen, the capital of the Normandy province they controlled, where they intended to bring her to trial.

Weary of the duplicity he found there, Gilles left the court soon after being summoned to join Charles during the Paris offensive. Chroniclers do not mention him again until he surfaced at Louviers, sixteen miles from Rouen, when Joan was captive. Attended by two armed companies of men, de Rais, now twenty-six, planned a daring rescue of the Maid that involved retaking Rouen and the castle where she was imprisoned. The Angevin firebrand and soldier of fortune, La Hire, and the Duke of Alencon, whom Joan called *le Beau Duc*, the handsome duke, participated in this bold scheme. For six months these three fighters, combining their forces, made forays against the Goddamns, who put up great resistance.

Frustrated by his inability to break the English, de Rais devised a new plan to save Joan. He believed that the English lookouts at Rouen Castle would leave their posts to seek shelter on cold winter nights. When they did, he would set ladders against the high stone walls. With fifteen of his captains, he would mount the walls, killing any sentinels they encountered. A company of men would be covertly stationed right outside the castle, to be called upon for reinforcements. After scaling the walls, Gilles counted on finding Joan in one of the frigid towers, and overpowering her drunken English jailors, who had been described by a notary in Rouen as "miserable men, mere tramps, who sang and rioted and buffeted her about, taunting her with her fate."[6] After plucking Joan from her dungeon, de Rais and his group would fight off any other attackers and bring the Maid to safety by climbing down the ladders his troop protected from below.[7]

The English learned of the plan and threatened to toss Joan into the Seine rather than give her up. The raid de Rais envisioned never materialized, nor did Gilles successfully repulse the English at Rouen until well after Joan of Arc had been burned at the stake. Even so, his willingness to risk his own life to save her illustrated the marshal's courage, his humility, his loyalty to this simple, saintly peasant girl. Ever protecting and commanding by her side, de Rais's life had been changed by Joan. But the black planet bringing misfortune hovered above him once again, waiting to tear his life apart.

* * *

Charles VII said nothing, did nothing to save Joan of Arc. A great French churchman, the Archbishop of Embrun, wrote the King. "For the recovery of this girl and for the ransom of her life, I bid you spare neither means nor money, unless you would incur the indelible shame of disgraceful ingratitude."[8]

The king remained silent. If his military could not free Joan, he held some high-ranking English prisoners. By the medieval conventions of war he could have easily exchanged them for Joan, or he could have offered a ransom for her. But Charles VII had his crown, his cities on the Loire; he was no longer in personal danger. Weak and self-indulgent, he showed no more indebtedness to the Maid than he did to anyone else who had helped him or would help him preserve his realm. Mary Gordon in her book *Joan of Arc* observed: "Because he had no personal loyalty to her, because he was interested in her only in what she could represent, when her representations failed to be of use to him, she ceased to exist as important or, perhaps, even real.[9]

The recently crowned monarch agreed with de la Tremouille and Regnault de Chartres, who recommended that he abandon

Joan of Arc, their enemy. They advised him she was not needed anymore, reinforcing Charles's own thoughts. De Chartres hardly disguised his antagonism toward Joan. After her capture at Compiegne, he told its inhabitants she "raised herself in pride." [10] He described her as a willful individual who did not listen to advice.

The English could not suppress their glee at Joan's apprehension. She was too dangerous to be kept alive. She had thwarted their attempts to take France. She also spread panic within the English army. Many soldiers, who were very religious, believed her to be the handmaiden of the Devil and were frightened of her, which was a terrible embarrassment for the English.

Since the Goddamns wanted Joan dead, they intended to have the Catholic Church try her as a heretic, a blasphemer, and a witch, with the assistance of the University of Paris. Her conviction would mean Charles had acquired his crown through sorcery; that would make young Henry VI of England the rightful King of France. The ten-year-old was so crowned that December, in Notre Dame Cathedral, Paris.

The Goddamns selected Pierre Cauchon, the Bishop of Beauvais, to bring Joan to trial. The Maid had been captured in his diocese, thus Cauchon was entitled to take possession of her and preside at her trial. The bishop, for his part, assumed that if he successfully convicted the Maid, he would be promoted to Archbishop of Rouen, a prestigious appointment. He needed the town's approval to gain that post, so he was trying very hard to convince the public of Joan's guilt, and kept up a constant dialogue with the people to persuade them. An ardent English sympathizer, he claimed he prosecuted Joan for the good of her soul. He wanted the citizens of Rouen to believe that her salvation was his only motivation; he wanted his prosecution of Joan to appear so conscientious, his conduct so irreproachable, no one would doubt his integrity.

Cauchon not only directed the preliminary hearings, but also the trial, with no secular examination proposed. Some of the priests Cauchon summoned to assist him did not like the prospect of ecclesiastical action against Joan of Arc, the heroine of France. Furious at any reproof, the bishop denounced those who opposed him, threatening to kill them. One conscientious objector acted as though he were a drunkard in order to be disqualified to serve as a judge. Another, Nicolas de Houppeville, who was thrown in jail by Cauchon, later testified: "I have never thought that the Bishop of Beauvais engaged in this trial for the good of the faith and through zeal for justice, with the desire to redeem Joan. He simply obeyed the hate he had conceived for her because of her devotion to the party of the King of France, and merely followed his own inclinations. I saw this when he rendered an account to the regent of his negotiations for the purchase of Joan, being unable to contain himself with joy."[11]

Cauchon finally selected a tribunal to consider Joan's offenses against the Church. It was made up of men loyal to the English cause. Throughout Joan of Arc's six-month trial, her sixty judges mainly consisted of French theologians and doctors from the University of Paris. Another twenty to thirty specialists, sympathetic to the English, appeared from time to time. Vita Sackville-West, in her book praising Joan of Arc, argued that "Jeanne was not tried by the Church at all, but only by a small and hostile section of it. Even the most impartially minded arbitrator must find himself unable to deny the force of this assertion....Whatever the authority of the Bishop of Beauvais within his own diocese, there is no getting away from the fact that, in the name of justice, the tribunal ought to have included at least a proportion of unprejudiced divines, even allowing that we might be going too far in expecting to find a proportion drawn from the party specifically favourable to Jeanne."[12]

Though accused in an ecclesiastical court, the Maid was illegally incarcerated at a secular prison within the Castle of Rouen, and guarded by inebriated English soldiers. Kept in an iron cage, chained by the neck, hands, and feet, at first she was not granted any religious privileges because of the grave charges against her, which involved heresy and dressing as a man. However, she continued to wear men's attire in her cell to maintain her modesty.

The nineteen-year-old Joan, who could neither read nor write, had no advocate, but responded well to the many technical questions posed by scornful judges. The topic of her submission to the Church was not even mentioned until the fourth week of the trial, even though Joan's indictment referred to her as a heretic. Instead, the learned men from Paris were more concerned with why she wore men's clothes and how she communicated with her voices; both of these accusations involved idolatry. Cauchon hoped to trick Joan into saying she touched and smelled her voices, the voices of Saints Catherine, Margaret, and Michael. If she did, she would have committed the sin of idolatry, and her trial would be over. For this reason, the judges concentrated on learning more from Joan about her voices. Joan repeatedly responded in the first weeks of her trial that God had sent voices so that she could help liberate France from its oppressors. She made no reference to touching her saints. In response to the accusation of "idolatrous transvestism," Joan simply stated that she wore male outfits to safeguard her virginity, not to set herself up as an idol.

The trial against Joan of Arc was modeled on an exhaustive Inquisitional inquiry, the accusations all religious. Joan was continually threatened with torture if she did not give up her evil ways. A change of venue occurred during one court session toward the end of her trial, so that she would feel pressure to confess. On May 8, two years to the day from when she departed Orleans after successfully returning it to the French, she was interrogated in the Grosse Tour of the Rouen Castle. On her way to meet with the judges, she observed the castle's torture chamber where executioners stood beside their frightful instruments. Joan told her inquisitors they could put her on the rack, but she would give them her same story afterward. She received additional warnings from her judges; they were losing patience, and if she did not recant and submit to the Church, death by fire awaited her. The judges prodded her. She struggled with the decision of whether to betray her voices or be burned at the stake, which she greatly feared. Mary Gordon remarked in her book, Joan of Arc, that the preservation of her virginity was pivotal to her; her body's destruction by fire meant an unclean end.[13]

Meanwhile, Cauchon continued with his attempt to sway the Rouen public, to make his case against Joan. He repeatedly told the inhabitants he truly sought her redemption. "With all his heart" he "desperately" wanted her to reject the Devil.

The Maid of Orleans, taken to the cemetery of St. Ouen, was formally excommunicated there. Under duress, head shaved, and dressed as a woman, she finally consented to sign a retraction of her voices and visions. By doing so, she believed she would avoid being burned at the stake. She also thought she would be set free. Before she signed the retraction, though, she protested an examiner's insulting characterization of Charles VII, the king who betrayed her, as a man who lacked true Christian piety.

"By my faith, messire," she responded, "with all due reverence I dare say to you, and to swear at the risk of my life, that he is the most noble Christian of all Christians, and best loves the faith and the Church. He is by no means what you say!"[14] The examiner ordered one of his underlings to "tell her to be quiet."

Joan of Arc's judges took the renunciation of her voices and her sworn allegiance to the Catholic Church to represent her submission to that holy authority. Even so, they sentenced her to a permanent incarceration. While dismayed that she would never hear the joyful sounds of spring in her father's garden, Joan consoled herself by thinking she would at least be taken to a Church prison with female attendants. Instead she was returned to the sour stench of her cell at Rouen Castle. Cauchon sent emissaries to Joan, to tell her she was fortunate the Church had shown her such mercy. Then these men insisted she keep on wearing women's garb, warning her that any lapse on her part would result in dire consequences.

While Cauchon's functionaries threatened Joan about any further conduct that went against the Church, the bishop persuaded the English and the Burgundians, furious with Joan's repudiation because it meant she escaped execution, that his plan to kill her was progressing smoothly. He told them to be patient. The court he had packed with English admirers had won over the people of Rouen. He maintained that simple folk believed Joan's return from the road to perdition was entirely due to the judges' insistence she renounce her satanic voices and evil behavior. Cauchon pointed out to the Goddamns that Joan's retraction of her sins and her allegiance to the Church also put her in a far more precarious position. There was no reprieve in Christendom for a relapsed heretic who might take up her old ways, such as obeying the commands of the devilish voices she purportedly heard, or dressing as a man. The inhabitants of Rouen would understand that Joan had to be dealt with harshly if she disobeyed the Church when she had promised to renounce Satan.

A few days after Cauchon's messengers had warned Joan about the consequences of wearing men's clothing, her jailors took away her women's attire, on Cauchon's instructions. She had no choice but to put on the male garments left in her cell, which reeked of greasy brew, urine, and filth.

A tribune of thirty-seven revisited a summary of Joan's offenses and proceeded to deliberate her fate in the serene chapel of the archbishop's Rouen palace. They decided Joan should indeed be treated as a relapsed heretic, unanimously voting to put her to death. These men of learning found that Joan had proved herself to be a dangerous, unorthodox renegade, a witch whose voices represented evil. Her pride, mentioned by Regnault de Chartres at Compiegne and noted with disdain by her French interrogators at her trial, was her downfall. They reasoned that ordinary people could not communicate with saints as easily as Joan swore she did. Her judges saw that the Church would be unnecessary if such an occurrence was not an aberration prompted by the Devil. The general public needed the Catholic clergy as intermediaries with God, for Satan was never too busy to try to tempt Christians away from their fidelity to the Lord Almighty.

Holy Catholic doctrine forbade taking a life. Thus the ecclesiastical assessors handed Joan over to the civil powers, requesting that they deal with her "tenderly," an euphemism for death by fire.

Clad in a long white robe, wearing the square paper cap of the condemned, Joan left her prison the next day in the executioner's cart. Surrounded by an armed guard, she was brought to the old Rouen Market, an open square teeming with people. A temporary structure had been erected with a post and chains. Two English soldiers seized Joan, hurrying her to a stake where they bound her tightly around the waist. She asked God's pardon for her judges, for the English, for Charles VII of France. She called out the names of her saints, Michael, Margaret, Catherine. She prayed to Jesus and begged for a cross to be held up so she could see it. The executioner lit the flaming torch. Then the Maid of Miracles, deserted by the king she crowned, the city she rescued, and the captains she led to victory, burned to death. Hers was a slow and excruciating death, as those who killed her were ordered to distance her from the flames.

Many French who witnessed Joan's demise sobbed openly. So did some English soldiers. As she perished, one exclaimed, "Ill fares the English land. We have killed a holy woman."[15] As with every death by fire, an unforgettable stench permeated the marketplace for days.

* * *

The countryside hummed with the news of Joan's death. Gilles, stationed sixteen miles away in Louviers, knew exactly what had occurred. Furious and determined to avenge her killing, he, along with the Duke d'Alencon, La Hire, and their companies of men, attacked Rouen in June, 1431, with some success, but were unable to oust the English.

Numb after the finality of Joan's death sank in, the new Marshal of France tried to repress his painful loss. He showed no immediate emotional distress, continuing in the role he knew best, that of a soldier. He honored his oath of loyalty to his cousin and the king, mostly performing the duties Georges de la Tremouille considered advantageous to his own interests. With the French regaining their land, de la Tremouille's loyalty to the Goddamns diminished. He ordered Gilles, now twenty-eight, to take part in a few important engagements, which the French won, especially the Battle of Lagny. This victory assured Charles VII control over the lower Marne region near Paris. Marshal de Rais's significant accomplishments at Lagny, where he and other captains forced the English to lift the siege of that town, and the Tourelles, earned him renown acclaim. He distinguished himself during both battles, and the memory of his heroism persisted after his death.

Two years after Lagny, Charles VII had to order this Marshal of France to come to the aid of the Duke of Bourbon. The reprimand by the King provided the first inkling of the mental transformation de Rais was undergoing. The Monarch demanded de Rais dispatch a large number of troops to Burgundy to assist Bourbon, who was engaged in a ferocious struggle there. The marshal always kept two hundred cavalry and an establishment of men at his disposal. His armor-clad, well-appointed company was battle ready. He could have easily drawn from his servants, his tenants at Champtocé, Tiffauges, and Machecoul, for additional support.

Currently short of funds and with scant enthusiasm for fighting, Gilles asked his cousin, de la Tremouille, to loan him twelve thousand gold crowns so that he could raise an army. The corpulent and now former counselor to the Crown had fallen from grace and had been driven from court, his life spared after an assassination attempt had failed because the killer's sword could not penetrate his huge mounds of flesh. But while he was Charles's favorite, de la Tremouille had accumulated or stolen enough wealth to give Gilles the money he asked for. In exchange, de la Tremouille took out a mortgage on de Rais's breathtaking castle, Champtocé.

Once Gilles received the funds from his cousin, he ignored the battle in Burgundy and sent his younger brother, Rene de la Suze, to fight in his place. Instead, he presided over a most lavish theatrical production at Orleans, which glorified Joan of Arc. De la Tremouille's advance partially paid for the show. De Rais had reached an unexpected turning point in his life.

Even in the last days of feudalism, such behavior amounted to insubordination, especially from a Marshal of France. His conduct could have been construed as treasonous; he could have been labeled a deserter. The exasperated king summoned de Rais to a meeting. True to his own timid character, Charles never asked Gilles why he did not follow orders, especially since he held such an important military position. The king simply informed him that he would never hold another administrative post. Charles VII decreed Gilles de Rais dishonorably retired from military service, yet allowed him to keep his rank and baton. In effect, the Marshal of France was stripped of all but his trappings.

De Rais was not shamed. He did not care. Joan's death had crushed him. His despair over her loss was overwhelming, becoming greater all the time. It brought on or exacerbated his mental deterioration. Gilles had been fiercely attached to Joan of Arc; his close contact with the Maid on the battlefield, her devotion to God, her distinct mission, her passionate resolve, had been a monumental inducement for de Rais to live honorably. This Marshal of France, whose integrity, civility, and mental stability had been questioned before he met Joan, totally believed in her. An ennobled Gilles rode the path to greatness with the Maid, and he subsumed himself to her for the good of God and France. She was not only the inspiration of her country but also the spur and symbol of a newborn idealism for de Rais.

Gilles had witnessed her miracles: Joan prayed for the wind to shift during the occupation of Orleans, and Gilles watched, stunned, as it slowly changed direction. He saw Joan remove the arrow from her shoulder during the battle for the Tourelles, which resulted in a wound so deep most knights would have quit the battle. Instead, after she recuperated, she forged ahead and brought her troops to victory there. He observed Joan as she prayed to God to lift the siege at Orleans. Within less than a week, the English retreated from that town. Her remarkable prophecies came to fruition, particularly her predictions that the English commander at the Tourelles, Glasdale, would die without bleeding, and more importantly, that Charles would become the legitimate King of France. Joan had swept Gilles away.

Her violent end, which he was helpless to prevent, made no sense to her loyal and valorous Gilles. He could not understand how a saint could have been treated so horribly by man or God. De Rais's "discipline, honor and devotion," observed by Wyndham Lewis and commented upon by Joan herself, perished with his martyred comrade in the flames at Rouen. A radical change now became very apparent in his behavior: patriotism and honor meant nothing to him; he wanted little to do with public service. Furthermore, de la Tremouille, banished from court, lacked the power to order this devastated commander around.

The world closed in around him.

Like many veterans of our day who have experienced trauma during combat and returned home, Gilles had problems navigating within his own circle. His defensive mechanisms started to fall apart. Retreating to his magnificent castles, he felt no need to lead a disciplined life. Any semblance of normalcy disappeared. He now engaged in a debauched existence, living indolently with his homosexual companions. Since he had no work to do, inactivity generated strange, ugly thoughts. He spent his days and nights carousing and intoxicated, possibly as a distraction to get him through the pain of Joan's death. Passing out from drink or exhaustion, he had raging nightmares that would startle him awake, in many instances in a hot or cold sweat. He would be shaking and not know where he was. A sound in his memory made his neck tense. He gulped down more Hypocras.

Grandfather Jean de Craon passed away the year after the Catholic Church burned Joan to ashes. Near the end of his life, this wily old man had second thoughts about his own unruly conduct. He tried to make amends to those he harmed by leaving property and money to his peasants, compensating those he had robbed. He even conferred endowments on two hospitals.[16]

De Craon had condoned Gilles's cruel behavior in the past, but as he lay dying, he became alarmed by de Rais's excessive brutality, his abnormal sexual vices, as well as his extravagances. Supposing Gilles had been corrupted by the Devil's touch, with no idea that Gilles now suffered from serious mental-health problems, he left his sword, together with his breastplate of armor, the symbol of manhood and strength, to his younger grandson, Rene de la Suze, rather than to the Marshal of France.

This snub did not bother de Rais; he had given up being a hero. Free from the tentacles of his grandfather, he remained one of the wealthiest nobles in France. He could act as he saw fit, which he did by shunning all laws of decency and squandering his vast inheritance.

* * *

Historians offer different opinions regarding the impact of Joan of Arc's demise on de Rais and his conduct thereafter. Mary

Gordon referred to Joan's "mysterious connection" to Gilles in Joan of Arc, but simply felt his contact with her did not stop him from becoming a murderer. A. L. Vincent, a British writer and diplomat stationed in France in the nineteenth century, also believed Joan had a supernatural influence on Gilles, "incapable of rationalistic solutions." Vincent, in his history *Gilles de Rais: The Original Bluebeard*, attributed de Rais's transformation to the removal of Joan's incentives for him to act decently, which brought out "the satyr and murderer" who "lay in waiting to fill the gap." He assumed de Rais's cruel conduct in his childhood, which he considered abnormal, gained momentum after Joan's demise.

The roots of Gilles's adult mental disease or diseases were probably planted in his childhood, when he displayed pathological interests. His neglect, and the loss of his parents, presumably resulted in his unusual behavior when he was young, as he later claimed at his trial. Tyrannical, hotheaded, and brutish before his association with Joan, Gilles exhibited many monstrous characteristics early on. Yet he kept his underlying psychopathy—at that time a disorder of character rather than of the mind—in check when he served with Joan. It was only after the Maid died that he reached a stage beyond rescue, becoming a serial killer.

George Bataille presented an extraordinary analysis. His theory did not revolve around Joan's death. Rather, he attributed Gilles's murderous vices to "an ensemble of traditional cruelties and drinking bouts," inherited from savage Germanic ancestors, the Berserkers who terrorized Europe during the early part of the Middle Ages.[17] But Jacques Heers, an esteemed professor at the modern-day Sorbonne (in the past referred to interchangeably as the University of Paris), disagreed. In his history, *Gilles de Rais*, he simply stated that de Rais fell in with bad company after returning to Champtocé following his military service, and did not display homicidal tendencies before that time.

War in any era does not turn soldiers into saints; witnessing atrocities is dehumanizing. De Rais's sad story still has echoes in our time, but with some significant differences. In de Rais's fifteenth century, no one knew about post-traumatic stress disorder; no one could fathom how someone might suffer from bipolar disease or major depression, or that a serial killer might be crippled by one or all of these conditions. Gilles de Rais's subsequent actions appear inexplicable, impossible to truly understand unless such mental illnesses or others, now recognizable, are considered. No handy explanation can be offered, but with today's psychological advances and with mounting case histories about disordered minds readily available and described in books, newspapers, movies, television, and the internet, evidence suggests de Rais experienced something that made him snap.

Post: after the event. Traumatic: emotional shock following a stressful event. Distressing: intensely disturbing. Stress: pressure or tension. Disorder: a lack of order, confusion. PTSD has received enormous attention in recent years. Its symptoms, noted by psychiatrists and veterans, may completely destroy a life. Post-traumatic stress disorder, officially recognized as a "stress-related, combat-induced disorder" in 1980 by the Veterans Administration of the United States, can develop after exposure to any event which results in psychological or physical trauma. Severe or intense trauma can lead to a long-term neurosis. Many suffering from this affliction, not aware of what is really bothering them, simply believe they are going crazy. Shock experienced during wartime is one factor; the sudden, unexpected death of a loved one can also cause PTSD. The combination of both of these events is another hypothesis.

The possibility strongly exists that Gilles suffered from PTSD. When de Rais was just a child, his parents had died unexpectedly. Then his inspiration, Joan, was gone. He felt at fault because he could not stave off these deaths and believed a dark, malicious planet directed his life. Soon after Joan's demise, de Rais displayed most of the symptoms associated with post-traumatic stress disorder: feeling emotionally numb; losing interest in activities that were enjoyable in the past; having angry outbursts; being irritable; having frightening thoughts and nightmares; exhibiting strong guilt and depression; finding it difficult to relax or sleep; wanting to kill oneself or others; suffering from panic attacks.

PTSD is just one of the many psychological illnesses that could have affected de Rais. Bipolar disorder is another possibility. When Gilles left the military, he displayed wild mood fluctuations, too. His lifestyle was replete with warning signs. Gilles would be depressed at times, crying uncontrollably, being irritable, having difficulty making decisions, lacking energy; then he would seem to become manic, preoccupied with everything grandiose, with his concern for wealth and fame, with his spending sprees, with his hypersexual behavior, with his increased energy. Disorders such as PSTD and bipolar disease can blend and become parts of the same mental problem. They occasionally kindle a latent psychopathy which presumably occurred with de Rais, for shortly after he left the military he turned into a cold-blooded serial killer.

The tragedy of this haunted hero is that he attained the pinnacle of success when he fought with Joan of Arc to liberate France. His failures, his transgressions, came in rapid succession thereafter.

CHAPTER FIVE

THEATRICAL MAGNILOQUENCE/ STAGGERING RUIN

THEATER WAS WIDELY POPULAR IN THE FIFTEENTH CENTURY, AND it played a central role in the life of the community. Every large town in Europe had a permanent company of actors who performed medieval productions on the steps of cathedrals, in squares, and in the streets, to the delight of large crowds who loved the pageantry. A carnival atmosphere took over as acrobats, fortune-tellers, merchants, and visitors mingled to watch the plays that gave this diverse audience a connection with each other. The biblical plays, history plays, and saint's plays all supported the people's understanding of themselves as the children of God by providing a history of the world and their place in that history.

At the same time, the public was treated to morality plays steeped in Christian ethics that showed the consequences of good and bad behavior. They also adored the buffoonery of farces and fool's plays, called soties, which offered communal release by creating satirical thrusts at social abuses. The dramatic monologue, very popular as well, was the simplest form of entertainment, entailing a single actor's performance. Examples were the *sermon joyeux*, festival parodies of Sunday church sermons.

Then there were mystery plays, serious plays dealing with religious subjects. The most important type of French mystery play eulogized the life of Jesus, Mary, or the saints. In Paris, the staging of these plays was the sole right of the Confrerie de la Passion. Elsewhere, municipalities usually subsidized these lengthy and costly pieces.

In addition, every great noble or baron offered grandiose stage performances during Church holidays or for his own enjoyment. De Rais was no exception. While he had assisted with the music, the vestments of the clergy, as well as Church trappings for his own wedding, his serious theatrical interests began only after his military service ended, when he lacked direction. He needed to keep busy to avoid constantly being reminded of the loss of Joan of Arc; certain noises, certain smells, triggered his intense distress, his obsession with her death. On a whim he decided to stage productions at Champtocé. As each performance became more elaborate, more sophisticated, the former marshal eagerly embraced this pastime. Like so many nobles of that era, de Rais considered himself to be a patron of the arts and welcomed the numerous poets, writers, and actors who drifted to his castle to become part of his household. They fleshed out the pieces de Rais proudly conceived. These included simple pantomimes and farces; in addition, he concocted soties, a blending of morality plays with farces, which were very popular. The dialogue was packed with puns, and generally portrayed a conversation among idiots ("sots"). Gilles personally supervised all the scripts. He also oversaw the design of the costumes, decorations, and theatrical properties; he commissioned local artists to build his sets. The baron even adjusted the illumination on his stage by directing his servants to walk around and snip the wicks of the candles mounted there.

His growing theatrical company benefitted nicely from his philanthropy. He treated his well-funded troupe of players to lavish meals; they enjoyed plentiful drink, too. As Gilles's endeavors expanded into ten dramatic shows, de Rais also invited the public into his castle to watch his presentations, and always without charge. Champtocé villagers eagerly attended these diversions, telling de Rais how much they enjoyed his entertainment. Delighted, his lordship outfitted them in expensive robes so that they would not stand out jarringly among the nobility.[1] They received free food, complimentary libations.

At the same time that the incensed King of France summoned Gilles to his court, declaring him dishonorably discharged from military service, Gilles introduced his theatrical concoctions to a broader audience than Champtocé's inhabitants, brazenly ignoring the Crown's reprimand. He did not care about the king's disapproval. His love of battle had now been replaced by an infatuation with the theater. He thought his talent so great he rushed off to display his genius by doing a theatrical tour of the major towns in Brittany and elsewhere, which, he was sure, would be beyond all expectation. Word spread, and his magnificent presentations, with splendiferous entrances and exits into and out of cities such as Angers, Bourges, Montlucon, and Nantes, drew wide attention. Nothing compared to de Rais's events staged by his large troupe of actors, supplemented by performers paying dues to various guilds in the towns he frequented. His productions created such interest that all work stopped, all buying and selling halted, something he insured by threatening the public with fines if they did not attend.[2]

At Nantes, for example, a herald, along with four men-at-arms, galloped through the dove-grey streets announcing Baron de Rais's show: "We, noble and powerful baron, Gilles de Rais, Marshal of France, Lord of Champtocé, Tiffauges, Machecoul, St. Etienne de Mer-Morte, Pornic, and other places, do by these presents make known that by permission of the high and powerful seigneur, Jean de Malestroit, by the Grace of God and the Holy Father, Bishop of

Nantes, there will be given on the twenty-first day of the present month, two o'clock in the afternoon, at the Place of Notre Dame, a representation of a Mystery concerning the Life of Our Lord and of Madame the Holy Virgin His Mother."[3]

On the day of the performance, Gilles and his entourage left his residence in Nantes at the Hotel de la Suze accompanied by an honor guard, their Damascene-steel halberds and scabbards glistening in the sun. These soldiers kept the jam-packed, boisterous mob back from the powerful Lord of Brittany. An assistant walked next to Gilles carrying an upturned helmet stuffed with coins. The mighty Baron de Rais tossed these trifling pieces to the multitudes, who trampled each other trying to catch them. He took pleasure in watching the crowds grovel for such pittances.

The Dukes of Anjou and Brittany, even his cousin, Guy de Laval, tried to emulate the Baron de Rais's fabrications, which had become the chitter-chatter of France. They lacked his talent, money, and flair. Duke Rene of Anjou, second son of Yolande of Aragon, nevertheless gave what he considered to be sophisticated plays and parties in his province. Like de Rais, he expended a great deal of money on his performances of the *Mystery of the Resurrection*, dealing with Christ's ascension from the tomb. For his lavish culinary feats, trying to surpass de Rais's grandeur, he imported peacocks, red partridges, and carnations from Provence, a region in the southern part of France where he was count. In addition, he used nutmeg from the Banda Islands of equatorial Indonesia in some of his dishes. None of these novelties had been introduced into Anjou before.[4] A benefactor of the arts like de Rais, patron to the painter Nicolas Froment, he enjoyed bringing new intellectual expressions and objects to his realm.

But Gilles de Rais's productions were the greatest shows in fifteenth-century France, the closest thing in his time to media sensations. A procession of close to one thousand approached each town where Baron de Rais would stage a theatrical event. His herald, dressed in scarlet, holding a shield adorned with the de Rais coat of arms, his two hundred helmeted soldiers, mounted on magnificent cinnamon-colored rounceys with shiny rumps, led the way. Then de Rais's traveling chapel came into view in hierarchical order. All their outfits were magisterial, especially his thirty canons, his chaplains, who appeared in long, trailing, crimson cassocks with cloaks of black fox. Each rode a pure white palfrey. Gilles's choir of breathtaking young boys wearing provocatively short buff tunics and flesh-colored stockings next appeared, on foot.[5] They preceded one hundred valets, along with servants identically liveried in chartreuse and acorn brown.

Retainers in terra-cotta red herded packhorses bearing lavishly carved Gothic coffers whose contents would be used in the performances. These chests contained jeweled vestments of heavy silk brocade and damask, liturgical vessels, plus accessories made by the best French goldsmiths and silversmiths. More ornate wooden boxes carrying albs, amicus, supplicus, altar linen, frontals, hanging tapestries, and choice carpets materialized.[6]

Now the portable organs arrived, each on the shoulders of six strong men. Built exclusively for Gilles de Rais, the organs were assembled at the beginning and dismantled at the end of de Rais's presentations. Music, which Gilles prized, became an intrinsic part of his performances. Minstrels as well as jugglers and actors accompanied the stage properties. This group saluted, smiled at the gaping crowd that gathered. About thirty giggling ladies of the night who followed armies and grand corteges at that time slithered after the musicians, immodestly wiggling their hips, seductively caressing their shabby, worm-eaten fur capes. (Joan of Arc chased these prostitutes out of Blois, when her troops assembled before the siege of Orleans.) Carts transporting precious gold, silver, wines, and arms rolled along behind these women.

At the end of this cavalcade, the grand baron, Gilles de Rais, surrounded by astrologers and magicians, introduced himself to the mass of ogling spectators. He sat astride his glorious, well-fed horse, Cassenoix (Nutcracker). Prinked in his vibrant purple silks, rich saffron brocades, and luxurious sables, consumed by his grandiose sense of self-worth, he acted like an overindulged Roman emperor.

There are no authentic portraits of the Baron de Rais. (The one by the French painter Eloi-Firmin Feron that hangs in Versailles with the other Marshals of France is an imaginary representation.) But it is believed Gilles acquired the infamous name Barbe Blue, Bluebeard, because of his horse, Cassenoix (Nutcracker). Its brilliant black coat, as glossy as satin, changed color according to the light, sometimes giving off a blue reflection. The French call an Arabian horse *une Barbe*.

The *Siege of Orleans* was the acme of Baron de Rais's peerless theatrical creations. He presumed no one would be able to match the grandiloquence of his presentation. Excitement grew within Orleans as word spread that the very rich young Marshal of France, the elegant Gilles de Rais, one of their heroes, intended to present a monumental spectacle about the city's struggle against the Goddamns at his own expense in their town. Orleans had evolved into an inspiring Gothic city, with its strong walls and gabled houses. And its residents, many of whom fought and lived throughout the extended English attack, were a proud lot. These self-reliant locals watched in awe as workmen began to erect a stage higher than a house, half a street long, and sturdy enough to support masses of men and horses as part of de Rais's depictions of battle scenes. They gazed openmouthed at the innumerable barrels of Hypocras, as well as the fine wines, grown on both banks of the Loire in the region, being stored as refreshments for the actors and the spectators underneath the huge platform.

With de Rais's arrival, Orleans became a festive city. The streets, the alleyways, even the Quay Fort-des-Tourelles with its simple commemorative cross to Joan of Arc, exploded in revelry.

Celebrations of that magnitude had not been witnessed since the Maid and her victorious troops liberated the town. De Rais's entourage occupied every principal inn, places with such colorful names as The Sword, The Shield of St. George, The Blackmoor's Head, The Great Salmon, and The Wild Man. Gilles de Rais and his retinue stayed at The Golden Cross. His twenty-year-old brother, Rene de La Suze, specially invited by Gilles to this theatrical commemoration of the Maid, together with his servants, resided at The Little Salmon. Because of de Rais's wasteful spending, which directly affected his inheritance, Lord de la Suze would never warm to his older sibling again after the Orleans spectacle.

His extravagance saw no bounds. Baron de Rais entertained day and night, holding incessant, sumptuous banquets for those of notoriety who came to Orleans from all over France. Nonstop feasts for the populace occurred as well, when the weather was good, and tables could be spread out in the streets. Anyone who found a place gobbled food and sopped up wine at Gilles's expense, causing temporary food shortages from time to time. Gigantic, rollicking, Bacchanalian hordes, reeking of drink, hoping for handouts, waited for de Rais and followed him from the theater to The Golden Cross where he lodged. The Baron's household imitated their master. They supped, they guzzled to extremes, as they gave out favors to friends befitting their position.

Performances of the Siege of Orleans, farces, and other forms of entertainment continued for thirteen months. These were also free to the throngs that poured into Orleans by the thousands. If folk could not afford to take off from work, the beneficent Marshal paid them for their lost wages.

The great Lord of Brittany, thirty-one-year-old Baron de Rais, triumphantly ensconced upon a high throne at the theater, directed his invited guests, lords, bishops, and officers of the Crown, to assume their designated places around him. Regulars grabbed any available seat or stood throughout the show. The entire audience concentrated on de Rais's drama which recounted the daring retaking of Orleans.

The *Siege of Orleans* did not hypnotize, as it was not great theater. Written by an unknown author, who faithfully followed the sequential events of the siege, this verse drama was packed with vain, labored expressions of nationalism. An uninspiring piece, short in literary stature, "like so many themes dealing with patriotism," Wyndham Lewis observed. A humorist as well as historian, Lewis continued, "and for the most part as humdrum as any other chauvinist exercise. It is difficult to write good verse to the glory of man, and the hack of Orleans notably fails to provide moments of beauty and realism one finds everywhere in religious drama."[7]

The *Siege* lacked rolling rhythms in its dramatic passages; it was neither eloquent nor rousing, the language neither rich nor fluid. Its 201 scenes of varying length contained 2,529 lines of mostly boring, rhymed octosyllabic verse as represented by the following passage:

Et n'en a on defailli goute.	And without a doubt.
De la Pucelle, ensomme toute.	The Maid went all about.
On ne luy doit riens refuser;	One could not refuse;
Et que son plaisir escoute	What pleased her to spout
Que Bel Vois luy	In That Beautiful Voice
fait propposer.	she overtured.
Des places qui sont a avoir.	The places we were to conquer.
Au lone la riviere de Loire,	All along the river Loire,
Bon seroit premier les avoir,	Good was her first desire,
Que y nous sont trop en	For we were far from
frontiere,	interventions,
Et en nestoyer le repere,	From clearing out locations,
Ains que proceder plus avant;	So to proceed on with impunity
Et ne vous doubtez de	And not doubt we will have
Victoire	Victory

Que elle vous est	Because she has great
prominent.[8]	Perspicuity.

Nevertheless, the defects detailed above were minor in the totality of the presentation. The work was innovative, actually daring, as the *Siege* had a secular plot, unlike all other medieval dramas, which were based on the lives of saints or on the life of Christ. Moreover, the piece portrayed personages still alive. The simple speeches attributed to Joan were the most moving in the work, and de Rais could have easily remembered them verbatim. Gilles, who commissioned the *Siege*, collaborated with the author, suggesting the outline of the work and the tone of the speeches.

The tableaux placed the piece apart from all medieval entertainment. It contained ornate, glittering stage properties, such as sublime velvets, silks, and ermine, glittering swords and armor, gorgeous wall hangings, choice carpets and splendid furniture. There were no curtains, yet the immense stage was never without players, with scenes going on simultaneously in different planes. The battle sets in particular outrivaled any presentation of that period. With 140 roles, the dressing, mounting, herding of men and horses onto the stage was astonishing. While Gilles used his own actors, he augmented the crowd scenes with 350 local citizens. All paraded around in a new costume at each performance, the old ones being discarded. This superfluity was unique in medieval Europe, since all classes wore the same clothing for weeks on end. (As a result, skin infections were commonplace.)[9]

The piece took a whole day; the action continued without intermissions. It began in England on the eve of the Orleans campaign. The show ended with the return of Joan of Arc to the town after her victory at the village of Patay, another English stronghold on the Loire. De Rais's use of trumpets playing a specific signal call advanced the plot and made the piece more interesting. No less than forty-seven pauses in the script indicated that trumpets should sound. Chimes, bells, and clarions marked the beginning of a battle. Multiple small organs, with keyboards of up to two octaves, announced Heaven's visit to earth; the precise nature of Joan's mission to make the Dauphin King of France was revealed in the story line.

The star of the *Siege* was Gilles de Rais. A tall, handsome actor exuding courtly charm portrayed the former Marshal of France. He had the major role, reciting hundreds of lines. The performer, alone in many scenes with the heroine, Joan of Arc, displayed great devotion and reverence and also protected her from her adversaries. He addressed her as "My Lady." At the beginning, King Charles authoritatively commanded Joan:

> "And to lead your men,
>   Take the Marshal de Rais."

The *Siege* glorified the Maid and de Rais. It also presented the red-nosed Charles as a decisive leader, a characterization many of his subjects disputed.

George Bataille chastised Gilles for his Orleans spectacle: "The need to shine makes his head swim; he cannot resist the possibility of dazzling spectators; he has to astound others through incomparable splendor." [10] A modern psychologist would point out that Bataille's analysis proved de Rais probably suffered from a bipolar affliction as well as PTSD, flaunting the excesses for which he became well-known, seeking intemperate excitement and exaggerated happiness.

Perhaps the *Siege* assuaged Gilles's guilt over Joan's death, his theatrical piece being his grand public eulogy to her. De Rais might have also commissioned the *Siege* to reinstate the memory of Joan and his own days of glory, for after the Maid, Gilles's role in the liberation of France was one of the greatest. Conceivably, he wanted to celebrate that nobler and happy time, a time when his heroism became legendary, when he subjugated himself to the spirituality and passion of Joan of Arc and fought for the salvation of France. He longed for popularity and legitimacy once again. The presentation of the *Siege* and his extravagances at Orleans were his attempts to regain his self-image, his status as a man of great importance. He basked in the adulation as well as the flattery he received. The shadow that walked beside him was the great warrior in his heyday. All confused that brave soldier with the now-broken de Rais. They thought this worthy figure was just expending the money he had, and were most impressed. No one understood he lacked the coping skills to deal with his distress, with the trauma he suffered after Joan's end, and that with his injudicious stagings, he demonstrated a loss of restraint.

De Rais's roots of childhood abnormalities and perversions, controlled when he served with the Maid, now burst forth. He no longer experienced the elation that the savagery of the battlefield had brought him, which he craved. As his mind careened, his lingering taste for blood led him to prey upon vulnerable little targets, children, whom he first raped, then tortured, and then killed. He first began his victimizations at his Champtocé Castle. These occurrences were followed by murders which took place in Orleans as he staged his stupendous theatrical pieces.

Baron de Rais's exorbitant sensationalism precipitated desperate, unplanned borrowing. The bill for the festivities was astronomical. When his credit ran out in Orleans, Gilles, in a depressed and irritable state, together with his immense company, moved on to Montlucon, a town located in the south central uplands of France. It was difficult for him to stop thinking about Joan as he traveled there. His mind was not occupied with images of the little strangers he had killed; instead one nightmare persisted. As storm clouds boiled in the sky, he and Joan rode through the tumult of flying missiles. She carried a small battle-ax in one hand as she led an assault under furious artillery fire. Gilles was struck down at her side, wounded. He could not help her. He fitfully glanced at the wild tragedy about to engulf her...He awoke and was crying.

He thought of suicide but did not have enough energy to carry out his plan. Then his spirits lifted, he drank heavily, and his undertakings continued to be grand. A two-month stay in the foothills of old volcanic mountains, where morning fog dreamily meandered through the hilltops, where constant performances as well as uninterrupted refreshment continued to be offered, also required a gargantuan sum of money. Gilles could only pay a little over half the amount demanded by creditors for his sojourn. He needed to leave two servants behind as collateral at his lodging to placate a furious innkeeper.

De Rais's conduct, so heroic in the Anjou and Maine, at Orleans, Lagny, and the Loire Valley, was now full of the warning signs associated with mental illness. He was on a downward spiral, with his disastrous spending, with his cold-blooded murders. He returned to his castles. However, he would soon be forced to give up lands, estates, personal property to pay for his ostentatious follies. His killing spree would continue during his financial debacles and his forthcoming forays into black magic.

* * *

Jewelry, clothes, swords, pictures, priceless manuscripts, including Ovid's *Metamorphosis*, wagons, harnesses, his beloved horse, Nutcracker, whose coat seemed blue, treasures from his chapel, including a pair of gold chandeliers, silk curtains, a silver reliquary of St. Honore's head, fine vestments...the Baron de Rais sold off any marketable object at a ridiculously low sum when his cash and credit ran out at Orleans, even his most lucrative salt marshes located in the Marais Breton. An avalanche of debt descended upon him. The former Marshal of France was quickly catapulted into bankruptcy.

A millionaire many times over, Gilles did not worship gold, but he felt it was there to be used. He had amassed debts before Orleans. During his early days as a soldier, many of de Rais's smaller estates had been mortgaged to raise armies. Nevertheless, the majority of his properties remained intact, even though he spent enormous sums of money after he left his grandfather's guardianship, which occurred when he married Catherine de Thouars. With most of the de Rais's possessions in landed estates, the revenue they yielded eventually failed to keep up with his expenses. It was simply a matter of time before his properties had to be broken up and sold at vastly discounted prices to pay off his arrears.

Gilles distant cousin, Roger de Bricqueville, came to the de Craon-de Rais household as a penniless teenager. De Bricqueville's family had lost its wealth when Roger's father, the Sire de Laune, opposed the English in the Normandy province. The Goddamns then took over his estates because of his defiance, with the family fleeing to Brittany. De Bricqueville, with his blazing, hungry eyes, felt no affection, loyalty or gratitude to de Rais, who provided for him after his father's unwilling forfeiture. Instead, Roger worked feverishly to pillage Gilles's treasury. He wanted to amass another fortune of his own to make up for the inheritance he had never received.

Determined to profit at de Rais's expense, he hovered over Gilles like a vulture. Happy to fleece Gilles whenever he could, he took advantage of de Rais's mental disorder, his alcoholism, constantly encouraging him to spend freely. He also received a cut from both sides when de Rais sold his riches. Abbot Bossard categorized de Bricqueville as a "tyrant who only thought about ruining" de Rais,[11] intending to leave Gilles destitute. Wyndham Lewis, always stirring the pot of polite sensibility, wrote: "The sudden transference to ostentatious luxury and that strain of piracy running in so many Norman veins may sufficiently explain Roger de Bricqueville's ensuing exploitation of his patron, his cynical indulgence of Gilles's every vicious and extravagant whim..."[12] Lewis alluded to de Rais's psychopathic murders in this quote, as well as his inordinate expenditures. De Bricqueville, as will be noted later, spurred Gilles on to commit his deranged killings.

While Grandfather de Craon managed his properties to an ecu, a trait common to the emerging French bourgeois, de Rais could not be bothered with the daily administration of his estates. Furthermore, he had no clue how to manage his lands. Thus he abandoned his responsibilities and gave over the handling of his entire fortune to his cousin, Roger de Bricqueville, which compounded his impending financial disaster. A deed of procuration, or power of attorney, was signed and sealed before an official of the Provosty of Orleans, permitting de Bricqueville to undertake these duties, with authority to sell his master's castles, lands, and possessions as he saw fit.

The deed also authorized de Bricqueville to contract a marriage for Marie, the only child of Gilles and Catherine de Thouars; he could set her dowry at any sum. Gilles had no interest in his shy, young daughter, born in 1429, or if she were left without any resources. He found both Marie and her mother irritating and paid scant attention to either of them. As a result, they became estranged from him. After his military service ended, and it became apparent he suffered from some mental disability, Maire and Catherine lived a reclusive existence far away at the Pouzauges Castle, which Catherine had brought to the marriage. De Rais had made it clear to his wife that he saw his close associates, now primarily homosexual bed partners, as far more captivating than her. Cunning to the core, de Bricqueville, Gilles's intimate companion and primary counselor, never suggested to de Rais that he should treat his only child more charitably. A small dowry for her meant the parrot-nosed Bricqueville could purloin more riches.

The rest of the baron's entourage also benefited from Gilles's unbridled spending. They helped themselves to de Rais's money trough whenever they could. They relied on his gifts when he had assets. He dispensed liberally to all on his staff, even to his stable boys and grooms. He handed them blank forms which he signed in advance; his followers gleefully filled them out while gold drained from his coffers. He had become so unstable, so crazed, he could not understand the consequences of such acts.

As his headlong spending continued, the king received an anguished plea for help from the de Rais-Laval family. They wanted to put a stop to Gilles's financial debacles. His relatives sent Charles VII a report detailing his fortune and folly. Witnesses testified in the document to his reckless spending, to his total lack of judgment, to his insanity. They cited de Rais's theatrical disaster at Orleans as an example. They further pointed to the greed and dishonesty of his staff. They detailed Gilles's maintenance of an opulent household where he kept an entourage of two hundred men, knights, captains, squires, pages, even a personal herald who accompanied him at all times. De Rais equipped them brilliantly, provided them with stunning palfreys, and overpaid them. They in turn all hired personal attendants requiring exquisite dress and well-appointed steeds. His way of life had become extravagant and delusional, his narcissism overwhelming.

Anyone who showed up at Gilles's castles was welcome. Artists, poets, troubadours, jugglers, scholars, swindlers, numbskulls, and knaves flocked to his gates. The baron gave presents to them when they arrived, money to one and all when they left. De Rais permitted as many as eighty guests at a time to frequent his noisy halls. His cooks were paid on the grandest of scales. Every day an ox was roasted whole in Gilles's huge kitchen. In addition, other heavily spiced meats, along with large quantities of fine wines and Hypocras were consumed. The drunk, tottering horde guzzled and gulped down enough barrels of wine during an evening to stun a hundred horses.

The deacons and canons of Gilles's chapel were singled out in the report to Charles VII because of their lavish dress, their luxurious lifestyle. The canons adorned themselves in trailing, vivid-red robes trimmed with expensive Danish mink. His deacons paraded around in wide-sleeved satin dalmatics. De Rais defrayed their expenses, paid them huge wages. They did little work. He did not care. He believed they added respectability and grandeur to his castles.

Besides his deacons and canons, he employed a considerable number of other ecclesiastics, including an archdeacon, a dean, a vicar, a treasurer, cantors, a schoolmaster, clerks, and a host of choirboys. He gave a few crowns per month to some of his chapel; others received hundreds of crowns. This was serious money at that time, with considerable purchasing power. (The standard weight for the gold crown throughout Europe by 1435 was 3.54 grams.)

De Rais rewarded one member of the choir, Rossignol of La Rochelle, who warbled like a nightingale, with a substantial prebend (an ecclesiastical stipend) for the rest of his life. He also received one of de Rais's small properties. His parents netted two hundred crowns every month. Because of the baron's largesse, the family saved enough money to buy horses, cows, sheep, and poultry, maintaining a very nice lifestyle. De Rais presented another choirboy from Poitiers with the land of La Riviere, close to Machecoul, worth three hundred crowns in an annuity. Gilles adored the boy's chestnut curls and his singing ability. These boys snatched up their money while Gilles cast pearls before swine.

His relatives referred to Gilles's expenditures as "mad expenditures." Their report to the king also listed Gilles's religious accoutrements, among them vermilion altar cloths, green silk curtains, copes of orange-red velvet, hammered chalices encrusted with jewels, baldachins with fabric patterned in gold, detailed with hawks and falcons. The document further stated that his chapel contained a quantity of sumptuous gold and silk cloth vestments, candlesticks, censers, crosses, plates which had cost three times their value, along with several pairs of organs, each one requiring six men to carry. A note in the disclosure to Charles VII further referred to Gilles's outlandish religious displays as simple exhibitionism; the de Rais family thought Gilles devoid of true Christian feeling. Abbot Bossard, in his extensive nineteenth-century work on de Rais, advised his readers that Gilles had indeed forgotten about God. The glory revolved around Gilles, who paid with his gold.[13]

In addition, the relatives took issue with an expensive ecclesiastical foundation the marshal established in Machecoul. Gilles named it The Holy Innocents. He envisioned it being beautifully decorated and lavishly equipped, similar to the renowned chapter in the Lyons Cathedral. De Rais sent a letter to Rome to win the approval of Pope Eugene IV for this endeavor. Eugene, a frugal Augustine friar, had been forewarned by Gilles's wife, Catherine, and his brother, Rene, about the marshal's ostentatious, besotted, and generally unhealthy behavior. The thrifty Pope, who patronized and encouraged the artists Donatello, Fra Angelico, Ghiberti, and Pisanello, denied the baron's request. Catherine and Rene pointed out to the Crown that Gilles went ahead anyway, disrespectfully setting up his extraordinary foundation. It consisted of an entire metropolitan clergy of twenty-five who were dependent upon de Rais for financial support. Wherever he went, Gilles brought along the members of this chapel. Most had servants of their own, and horses, no soft-eyed, old grey mares among them. The de Rais family characterized this retinue of around fifty, which Gilles funded, as lacking piety and discipline. Gilles needed to liquidate a large part of his and the family inheritance to maintain The Holy Innocents.

The king responded. The sound of a trumpet announced the nailing up of the Crown's royal edict. The official decree proclaimed the nobleman Gilles de Rais a prodigal. The edict, posted in the towns of Orleans, Tours, Angers, Champtocé, and Pouzages, besides other places frequented by the former Marshal of France, forbade Charles VII's subjects from entering into contracts with Gilles de Rais. He ordered de Rais to refrain from transferring additional property. Gilles's captains, including the brother of Gilles de Sille, a close associate of de Rais and in his pay, could not surrender the de Rais castles even if they had already been sold. Gilles de Sille, who surfaces later in de Rais's story, lived off de Rais in a most elegant manner. There is no record whether his sibling, the captain, did too.

The king also directed the Parliament of Poitou to appoint a controller to take charge of Gilles's remaining fortune. But Wyndham Lewis, again in his droll manner, remarked: "As for the lawyers of the Parlement of Poitou, who were supposed to be finding a controller for Gilles' finances, they prudently sat mum and let the redoubtable Marshal have his fling."[14] In other words, they were not foolish enough to risk his ire, which could perhaps lead to their deaths.

These lawyers had heard about Gilles's vicious assault on his former tutor, Michel de Fontenay, whom de Rais's father had hired. Out of concern for de Rais, de Fortenay made sure the king's edict of interdiction had been posted in Champtocé, close to the University of Angers. Furious, Gilles went to Angers where this leading citizen and churchman lived. He abducted de Fortenay, for he wanted to punish his tutor, believing the man had betrayed him. De Rais grabbed him from his home with the aid of some of his men-at-arms. They rode to Champtocé with de Fontenay tightly bound by leather straps. Then the fuming de Rais threw him into his prison; later he transferred him to the Machecoul dungeon. Gilles knew de Fortenay was an Angevin priest and a notable, and that there could be consequences for his actions. He was too livid at that point to be concerned. The Bishop of Angers along with de Fortenay's university colleagues protested, stating de Rais did not have the authority to behave so abusively against an ecclesiastic. De Rais then felt obliged to release de Fontenay. The senseless act against this man, responsible for his education, further demonstrated the deterioration of de Rais's state of mind.

Despite the edict, the marshal signed away his larger tracts, as he and his staff needed money. Neighboring landowners, noblemen, merchants, and creditors bought his estates. The Bishop of Nantes, Jean de Malestroit, to emerge prominently in Gilles's future, the Bishop of Angers, who married de Rais and protested de Fortney's kidnapping, his cousin, the oversized George de la Tremouille, as well as the Duke of Brittany were glad to help the marshal out of his financial difficulties by taking over his possessions. All ignored the royal edict.

Breton custom dictated that Jean V de Monfort could not purchase his vassals' lands. But the duke, who had salivated over Gilles's treasured estates for some time, agonized over a way to absorb them. He ultimately decided to seek the approval of the Crown for negotiations with de Rais. He sent his son, attended by a huge escort, to Charles VII because the duke was sure his child, the king's nephew, would obtain his permission to deal with de Rais. Charles VII refused the duke's request after considerable prodding from his advisors. Because of this rejection, Duke Jean, with his pinched nostrils trembling, forbade the king's interdiction against Gilles to be displayed in his duchy. To further spite Charles VII, the duke took away the appointment of Gilles's cousin to the office of Lieutenant General of Brittany. The cousin had served the king's edict on Jean V. Then the duke conferred this same title of Lieutenant General on Gilles de Rais. By giving Gilles this position, the duke not only acted maliciously against the Crown, but he also sought to muddle his real intention of taking over de Rais's properties.

To further obfuscate his scheme, Jean V sent amicable letters to Duke Rene of Anjou, son of Yolande of Aragon and supporter of Charles VII. Jean swore by a sacred oath, "over our Lord's dead body during the singing at Mass,"[15] that he would not procure Gilles's castles of Champtocé and Ingrandes located on the border of the Duke of Anjou's territory. Right after this pledge, Jean V met with de Rais so that he could buy these fortresses.

At the rendezvous between the Duke of Brittany and de Rais, Jean offered Gilles a final proposal regarding the purchase of Champtocé and Ingrandes. Duke Jean reminded Gilles of a three-year mortgage agreement he had made involving the de Rais domains in Brittany. Unless Gilles wanted to rid himself of these lands, including the Machecoul stronghold, he needed to fork over the thirty thousand gold crowns he owed Jean V within a few weeks. If de Rais wished to accept the duke's previous proposition to acquire Champtocé and Ingrandes for one hundred thousand gold crowns, Jean V promised Gilles he could buy back the entire de Rais barony in Brittany in the future. He would also receive the option to repurchase Champtocé and Ingrandes.

De Rais agonized over the puny offer, but he needed the money badly so he reluctantly consented. The duke's eyes sparkled as he bought the magnificent fortifications at rock-bottom prices.

Gilles's relatives were desperate to prevent these transactions. Under the auspices of the Crown, de Rais's brother, Rene de la Suze, and a Laval relative, accompanied by a large armed guard, took over Champtocé, Ingrandes, and then Machecoul. They thought de Rais would dispose of the latter castle as well, transferring it to the Duke of Brittany. Lord Rene de la Suze, whose title originated from the name of a seignory owned by his grandfather, Jean de Craon, was aware that Gilles's mind was failing along with his finances. This younger brother of de Rais, born the same year as Joan of Arc, attempted to keep the family inheritance intact when he petitioned the king to let him take temporary control of de Rais's castles. Gilles did not hold Rene actions against him, and he remained the only family member with whom Gilles had any contact after the king issued his royal order. It is conceivable Gilles did not disassociate himself from his brother because he knew Rene served as a lieutenant to the Constable of France, Arthur de Richemont. Gilles greatly admired de Richemont; they rode to battle together after de Richemont joined Joan of Arc's army. (When de Richemont returned to the court following de la Tremouille's ouster, he consolidated Joan's victories, enabling France to rid itself of the English.)

Lengthy negotiations ensued between Gilles and his family. When Gilles eventually gave his brother seven thousand gold crowns along with another beautiful property, his family reluctantly agreed to his sale of Champtocé and Ingrandes to the Duke of Brittany, and permitted de Rais to take back the three supreme strongholds in contention. Machecoul, as stipulated, would remain with Gilles. Because none of the parties involved wanted to incur the wrath of the king for defying his edict, after the duke's treasurer received the deeds to Ingrandes and Champtocé, a power struggle was staged between the Baron de Rais's brother and the duke's brother at those castles. Duke Jean V bribed the guards to behave as though they had been overpowered by his forces.

Nonetheless, the king's ire immediately fell upon de Rais for defying him. In a voice unusually resonant, but hoarse with anger, he banned his former Marshal of France from court.

* * *

Astrology influenced everyday life in the Middle Ages for all classes. Kings and noblemen had their own personal astrologers, but even peasants worried about the positions of celestial spheres and constellations. All scanned the heavens for signs, portents of what would happen next. After his parents' death, Gilles believed a black planet directed him, even though he had been born a Libra. Those guided by Gilles's zodiacal sign, the symbol of weighted scales, are characterized by their fair-mindedness. Libras, nevertheless, also possess reckless tendencies. "Their love for beauty and pleasure can cost them dearly in their occasional extravagances." [16] None of de Rais's astrologers forecast that this personality trait of Libras would lead to Gilles's ruin. Only Roger de Bricqueville, the Norman cousin responsible for the marshal's finances, could predict Gilles's tragic bankruptcy. Rather than a black planet governing de Rais's ill fortune, de Bricqueville, recognizing that Gilles could not stop his reckless spending, facilitated de Rais's financial demise, which accelerated his psychopathic breakdown.

De Bricqueville understood "the traits, so well displayed by this man of excessive brilliance, who was tormented without cessation; open to all beautiful things (specified above as a description of Libras); capable of being a hero, if he possessed moderation in his desires, he (de Rais) transformed into a villain who had neither the courage nor wisdom to put a brake on any of his passions." Thus Abbot Bossard characterized this complex, troubled soul in his exhaustive study of Gilles de Rais.

(His commentary remains more poignant in the original French: *"Ces traits nous peignent bien le character de cet homme, qu'une ambition demesuree de briller tourment sans cesse; ouvert naturellement a toutes les bells choses; capable de devenir un heros, s'il avait eu de la moderation dans les desirs; et que se transforma si vite en scelerat, pour n'avoir pas eu la sagesse ni le courage de mettre un frein a ses passions."*)[17]

Bossard's analysis of de Rais continues: "If he lived within the boundaries of his birth and fortune, one could sympathize with his attempts to achieve grandeur, but his envy to surpass other men and be the equal of princes and kings promptly thrust him beyond the realm of reason."[18] Again, his description exposed Gilles's abnormalities, most particularly his consistent irresponsibility, impulsivity, and narcissism.

While Rene de la Suze also recognized that Gilles's entire staff was corrupt and stealing from him, he never fully grasped Roger de Bricqueville's extensive power over his sibling. Perhaps Rene would have removed de Bricqueille from the de Rais castles if he knew of his undeniable and ruthless intention to ruin Gilles financially and encourage his total mental collapse.

Some twenty years after his brother's debacles, Rene de la Suze offered a very detailed account of the costly undertakings at Orleans and elsewhere in *Memoire des heritiers*, or *Memory of the heirs*. Drawn up and presented to the King of France and the Duke of Brittany, it was written to justify de la Suze's claims to the ownership of Champtocé. De la Suze wanted to show that Gilles was insane, and thus all his contracts to sell his possessions were null and void. Though a present-day diagnosis of a bipolar illness coupled with PTSD was not possible, de la Suze still addressed Gilles's impulsive wastefulness and the unbridled, manic temperament that disrupted his life and that of his family. It set forth the manner in which Gilles squandered his entire fortune, all his many castles, seigneuries, and lands so assiduously acquired by his ancestors. While it did not touch upon Gilles's serial murders, *Memory* illustrated how de Rais's inheritance was dissipated:

> "He had immense wealth...a fortune far greater than the brothers of the Duke of Brittany...Seduced by the false fawning and damnable covertness of his servants," "pushed by the advice and the exhortations of those surrounding him who only wished to enhance their own fortune," the Baron de Rais was " governed and supported morally in such a fraudulent manner by his false and malicious entourage...who took over the government and administration of his lands and seigneuries; and thus used them for their own pleasure, only thinking of themselves...."

Memory also decried Gilles's demonstrations of religiosity as vainglorious, profligate, and derisive.[19] A similar description of his lack of true religious beliefs had already been submitted to the king.

The conclusion of Memory specified the amount of money raised to pay for Gilles's debacles. The sale of his properties, the rents derived from them, amounted to 180,000 to 200,000 gold crowns, a sizeable sum even today. Starting in 1435, Gilles, then thirty-one, went through that fortune in three years, a stark raving mad accomplishment, and a heartrending fact.

CHAPTER SIX

THE DARK SLOPE

GREEN-TINTED FLAMES, DRIFTING FUMES, WONDROUS SMOKE coughed up from tall bottles like athanors, glass and earthenware vessels deformed in shape, carrying all sorts of unearthly names: violes, crosletz, curcubites, aludels.[1] All over fifteenth-century Europe, alchemists boiled their metals and made their calculations, hoping to produce the Philosopher's Stone, a substance that would transmute base metal into gold; also known as the Elixir of Life, it provided the secret to eternal youth as well.

Alchemists supposed that all substances were made up of one primitive matter which had mercury as its base and which could be separated from the four elements of earth, air, fire, and water. They believed the Philosopher's Stone was created if the residue was properly treated with derivatives of sulfur and arsenic.

Producing gold seems like an unattainable goal, but alchemists applied logic and intellectual discipline to their experimentation. They took pleasure in their labor, and enjoyed working with various substances and diverse tools, as well as maintaining and inspecting their red-hot ovens. They looked forward to erudite dialogue with colleagues.[2] These freethinkers wanted to obtain gold, but they also hoped to attain wisdom by systematically examining the mysteries of life. Black magic, magic practiced in league with the Devil using charms and spells, was not a part of alchemy. But astrology, so important in everyday life at that time, became closely related, because medievals believed that each of the heavenly bodies represented and controlled a particular metal. The positions of these heavenly bodies had an effect on the success or failure in the alchemist's work.

The former Marshal of France, Gilles de Rais, showed little interest in the intellectual exercise involved in the study of alchemy. Instead, de Rais hoped the elusive process of creating gold would remake his fortune. He had learned of the practice in his early military days from an acquaintance, an Angevin knight. The soldier had been accused of heresy, and arrested by order of the Inquisition. The soldier surreptitiously lent de Rais, who visited him in his damp cell, a manual on the art of alchemy, which detailed how to freeze mercury and turn it into quicksilver. It is not known exactly how de Rais knew the knight, but meeting with him would have been easy; access to the prison in the Duke of Anjou's castle would be permitted to a great lord such as Gilles.

At his eventual trial in Nantes, de Rais admitted to the judges "that he had received…a certain book on the art of alchemy."[3] He said he read it out loud a few times in a room at Angers before several listeners. He never specified the audience or the location of the room, but insisted he returned the manual to the knight soon after he borrowed it.

Desperate to recoup his fortune, Gilles actually studied the manuscript in great detail, subsequently giving it to his close associates to read, because the book primarily dealt with the cult of the Devil, and procedures for summoning demons. If his alchemic experiments failed, Gilles assumed he had no other choice than to use black magic to ask Satan for gold, and this manual laid out the specific methods needed to summon him. A circle had to be sketched, with arcane symbols and characters. Charms, spells, animal offerings along with tapers, burning coals, incense, myrrh, and aloes were indispensable. Specific incantations needed to be uttered; they involved swearing upon the Father, Son, and Holy Ghost, the Virgin Mary, and all the saints. Catholic religiosity, so pervasive in the Middle Ages, was practiced even by those invoking the power of evil.

With half his estates lost, with his family appealing to the king to end his excesses, with his treasurer still paying for the Orleans disaster, Gilles was in critical financial straits. He disregarded sanctions banning attempts to make gold, imposed by the late, insane king, Charles VI, and retreated to his favorite castle, the ghostly, grey-stoned Tiffuages, convinced that alchemy would restore his wealth. The austere, mysterious fortification, built on the site of an old castrum, a Gallo-Roman fortress, sat fifty miles from Nantes. There, in the valley of the Crum River, where the lofty outline of the keep grew out of granite rocks, and some eighteen towers encircled a vast esplanade, de Rais established a laboratory for alchemic experiments in one of the distant wings of his impregnable castle. It contained the most current medieval apparatus and paraphernalia.

Unaware of de Rais's intent to produce gold, serfs yoked to the land at Tiffauges spent their arduous days in the dung-colored fields, in the mills, in the granaries, and in the vile-smelling tanneries owned by Gilles. Their ramshackle huts were blackened with soot, the furnishings consisting mainly of lice-ridden straw sleeping pallets. Rats incessantly gnawed upon the thatched roofs. During the summer, these peasants tried to relieve the monotony by adorning their ramshackle homes with bright yellow and purple flowers from the very poisonous henbane plant, shunned by the nobility.

Gilles lived an existence far removed from these workers, especially in the warm months. Every mellow morning, Gilles refreshed himself at the grand castle in a tub filled with tepid water, scented with lavender and cinquefoil. Throughout the year, as he bathed in solitary luxury, he paid particular attention to his hands. He spent an unhealthy amount of time pampering them; he kept many brushes for them. Always dreaming of gold, the Marshal of France then stood by the vast fireplace in his chamber. Sometimes he "dressed himself in a long peach-coloured robe, green slippers and chrysoberyls."[4] Absentmindedly, he munched upon some Brignole plums placed on his favorite white porcelain platter, decorated with gold and green leaves, and drank Hypocras from his bejeweled silver chalice. Some days, particularly when there were bursts of rain, he hated looking out on what he perceived to be a melancholic landscape. As he fell into his black depression, totally exhausted on those occasions, after having uncontrollable thoughts about Joan of Arc, he directed that the castle's mullioned windows be covered. Finally, after recovering from his deep despondency, he would order fiery torches, together with girandoles, lit throughout the high-vaulted rooms. Only then did the great Lord de Rais descend from his stone chamber. He strolled down the winding staircases and narrow corridors into his laboratory, so that he could carefully inspect his steaming furnaces, his bubbly vessels of distillation, his retorts, his alembics.

To operate this laboratory effectively, the marshal sent his trusted friend, Gilles de Sille, another distant relative, whose cousin became Grandfather de Craon's second wife, to the north of France to seek out individuals who understood the science involved in producing gold. Word spread. Men and women cognizant of this art from all over France, as well as Germany, Italy, and England, knew of a very rich nobleman's interest in obtaining alchemic results, no matter how they were achieved.

Magicians and charlatans, rather than true alchemists, scrambled to find their way to his lordship. Master alchemists from

Paris, the hermetists's center, found the route too dangerous, since the English blocked the main roads. They preferred to work secretly with their colleagues under the vaults of the Notre Dame Cathedral. Their fear of traveling to Tiffauges was reinforced when they heard that an acquaintance drowned as he crossed a river to get there, after being engulfed in a thick, freezing fog. When he eventually confessed before an ecclesiastical tribunal, Gilles would testify to this occurrence, and to the fact: "...he sent the said Gilles de Silles into a region farther north, to find these alchemists"[5] so as to persuade them to come to Tiffauges.

Another alchemist perished in a cold drizzle as soon as he reached de Rais's territories. Again, Gilles acknowledged this occurrence at his trial. He went on to attribute these "unlucky deaths...to divine clemency, and the intercession of the Church, from which his heart and his belief have never strayed. It had mercifully arrived and prevented him from succumbing to so many tests and perils..."[6] This passionate avowal seemed completely genuine, since those who lived in Europe during the Middle Ages believed God and the Devil were always present and competed for one's allegiance. Gilles thought of himself as a devout Christian, even though he more than dabbled in many forbidden practices, including alchemy, black magic and, worst of all, murder. Like most serial killers, he dehumanized his victims. And similar to other French nobility of that time, he believed indigent children, his main prey, were only a step above dumb animals. (It is worth noting, however, that unlike our current picture of psychopathic serial killers, Gilles never hurt or tortured animals, sometimes showing them great affection, as in the case of his horse, Nutcracker.) Thus, despite his butchery, he could justify his conviction that he remained a good Catholic. Besides, he only looked to Satan temporarily, to restore his fortune. Contrary to his family's perception, he also believed his extravagant religious displays enhanced his standing with God.

Jean Petit, a Parisian goldsmith, along with a simple English blacksmith, were two of the first to find their way to the castle. De Rais was thrilled to have them join his entourage. Gilles then hired many slick adventurers from Italy, where alchemy was practiced openly. Impatient to obtain the philosopher's gold, de Rais insisted that these men conduct continuous experiments. However, each and every one of the laborious endeavors remained inconclusive.

Gilles became frenzied as the failures continued. Wrapped in orange brocade, adorned with emerald rings, he read and reread the manuscripts of Nicholas Flamel, the fourteenth-century Parisian purported to have fabricated gold. He devoured the practitioner's impenetrable numerical offerings. Yet the texts remained incomprehensible to him.[7] His cupbearer brought him more and more Hypocras in a giant goblet. His anticipation grew. With hands shaking, de Rais paced his laboratory, as thick grey plumes of smoke puffed up, disappearing below the vast ceiling. He peered at the contraptions, the gourds, the lodestones, the tripods. He roamed the desolate hallways, desperately looking for an insight into Flamel's alchemic riddles.

A goldsmith from Angers showed up on an unseasonably sticky spring afternoon. Short, unshaven, with thin, grey, oily hair curling at its tips, he said he was familiar with alchemy but demanded to work alone, in complete silence. He ordered de Rais's servants to bring the heavy trunks containing his equipment into the laboratory. Instead of thanking the men for their assistance, the goldsmith yelled at them to leave the room. Hours went by, but the alchemist did not appear. Gilles's valets finally investigated. They found the lush passed out, lying prostrate on top a multitude of empty bottles. Gilles immediately kicked out the inebriate. Grimacing most unpleasantly, the drunk still left with a silver mark, the installment payment he had already received.

Gilles became an even greater insomniac as the alchemic disappointments escalated. He went long days and nights without sleep[8] to avoid nightmares. While he drank immoderate amounts of Hypocras, he ate very little. His eyes, now pale, darted nervously from one object to another in the laboratory. He impatiently watched over his alchemists, who worked incessantly, striving for tangible results. All of their attempts to concoct gold cost de Rais dearly. He still hoped for a miracle, but the fiasco dragged on.

While his experiments continued, de Rais needed to deal with other matters, and reminders of the Maid kept occurring. A woman claiming to be Joan of Arc duped him, along with many of his comrades-at-arms and scores of simple folk, including the real Maid's two brothers. The municipality of Orleans even offered festivals in her honor. She resembled the Maid in stature, but seemed less ardent. She attributed this lack of verve to her long incarceration. The false Joan rode a horse and gave orders to soldiers, which they obeyed. She insisted she had escaped from the flames set by her English captors. All of the Maid's admirers prayed the story was true. Gilles especially hoped this was the case, for he worshiped Joan, whose death contributed to or was the main cause of his creeping mental decline, his probable PTSD, his psychopathy.

Charles VII unmasked this imposter's string of lies when he met with her. He identified her as a half sister who could not tell him about a confidence he and the true Joan of Arc shared.[9] (The secret involved the confirmation by the Maid of Charles's legitimate claim to the French throne.) Thereafter, this Joan, who took on the title of Lady des Armoires, admitted she was married with two children. She again acted out her charade in Paris, but the parliament and the university immediately exposed her and made her confess to her deceit. Neither of those illustrious institutions, still supporting the English, wanted another French heroine to surface. After a tearful acknowledgement, she and her family hastily departed for Rome, where she said she intended to ask the

Pope to pardon her sins. She might have also chosen that city because a large French colony lived there at that time, or she might have intended to bamboozle the Italian residents with more of her fabrications.

Before the king discovered she was a fraud, Marshal de Rais engaged this imposter to retake Le Mans, a city with a cathedral of dramatic flying buttresses located on the Sarthe River in the northwest. He paid for her military expedition against the Goddamns by selling many of his expensive Flemish tapestries. While not participating in the Hundred Years' War anymore, perhaps de Rais, because of his great affection for the Maid, felt any campaign she undertook necessitated his assistance. Even if he sensed this woman to be a false Joan, he wanted to believe in her so as to revive some link to a nobler time in his life. He had first fought the English around that area when he was a very young, brave warrior, as well.

After this Joan was proven false, Baron de Rais replaced her with one of his captains, the Gascon, Jean de Siqueville, a man no better than a brigand. Le Mans remained in the hands of the Goddamns for many years; similar to English looters, de Siqueville and his kind pillaged the French countryside instead of fighting the enemy. He tormented, raped, and killed all who would not give over their goods. He and thugs like him earned a stellar income from ransoms. Peasants trying to harvest crops paid dearly to be protected or left alone. These highwaymen, called *routiers*, obliterated villages with no defenses if they did not agree to their terms.

In November, 1439, Charles VII issued an ordinance which ended the arbitrary violence decimating his realm by these hooligans. He had the likes of de Siqueville slapped in irons and thrown into dungeons. Charles's statute proved so successful that it brought forth a more democratic, structured Europe, where the administration of law and order replaced violence and intimidation.[10]

Charles dispatched his son, the future Louis XI, to put an end to this kind of marauding throughout his realm. Louis, nicknamed the Universal Spider, a characterization befitting his sinister appearance and the insidious reach of his tentacles into various political intrigues, unexpectedly showed up at Tiffauges to arrest de Siqueville. Louis, condemning de Siqueville to death, imprisoned him in one of his own residences, the Chateau de Montaigu, just over nine miles from Tiffauges. De Siqueville escaped and slipped away very quickly, disappearing and then going on to rob and plunder more discreetly.

Louis's presence at the Tiffauges Castle made Gilles de Rais aware that his own pilfering would no longer be tolerated. His lordship constantly battled against his neighbors. Like his deceased grandfather, de Craon, Gilles used banditry to achieve his goals. Ironically, Louis, believed to have murdered his father's beautiful mistress after she rebuffed his sexual advances, insinuated to the Marshal of France that he was not above the law. (In addition to gorgeous women, the Spider had an appreciation for fine wines. After he conquered Burgundy when he became king, he immediately confiscated the entire vintage of the local Volnay Champagne for his own consumption. Louis also traveled everywhere with his own pot of Dijon mustard, a rare commodity at that time.)

Louis's visit yielded more unexpected and unpleasant developments for Gilles. He told his judges at his trial that he would have succeeded one day in transmuting the metals he and his alchemists worked with into gold if the "Lord Viennese Dauphin" had not arrived at Tiffauges. The Dauphin's appearance had caused de Rais to order the demolition of the alchemic furnaces used in these illegal experiments. De Rais kept the Dauphin waiting impatiently in the courtyard as his servants destroyed his precious laboratory, and also erased all traces of black magic, which included drawings of cabalistic signs and symbols invoking demons. He had no intention of letting the Universal Spider discover that he practiced these forbidden rites. Then he went to greet his guest, graciously escorting Louis into the castle to partake of a hastily prepared but lavish banquet, which the Universal Spider enjoyed so much it is presumed he even permitted Gilles to sample his prized Dijon mustard during one of the courses. While Louis informed Gilles that he must cease and desist from his banditry, he discovered nothing untoward at Tiffauges other than the presence of the hooligan de Siqueville. He reported these findings to his father.

As a consolation for his devastating losses, de Rais listened to lascivious tales of homosexual orgies which took place on the Island of Capri when Louis finally departed. He gulped down Hypocras as his Italian hangers-on colorfully recounted these graphic stories in detail at his request.[11] His accomplices also found some children for him to butcher.

* * *

Gilles discontinued his alchemic experiments after the Dauphin Louis left Tiffauges. However, he confided in his close homosexual companions—Eustache Blanchet, a forty-year-old priest from St. Malo (located near Mont St. Michelle); Gilles de Sille, knight and relative; and Roger de Bricqueville, nobleman and cousin—that he had no choice but to carry on with his forays into black magic. Since he was at the ragged end of his finances, Gilles informed them, Satan would surely bring forth the gold he craved if he gave him proper homage. De Rais was certain of this, but he needed experts who could communicate with Satan on his behalf. These three intimate advisors, themselves posturers who had only their own well-being at heart, did not object.

The Catholic religion regulated every aspect of medieval life. Its followers unquestioningly believed in an all powerful, omniscient God, along with an invisible but ever-present Prince of Darkness who constantly tempted the righteous by offering tangible, earthly rewards. De Rais accepted these tenets; his life was embedded within this doctrine. After his alchemic experiments failed, Gilles de Rais, suffering from his cascading mental problems and lacking moral support, could think of no other way of recovering his fortune than to turn to the Devil for help.

Many practicing the rites of black magic were charlatans. They made good money conducting their charades and came from all classes of society, with contacts in every European capital. They fooled large numbers of people desperate to speak with the Devil, even though some of their antics were farcical. De Rais epitomized those who were duped by these imposters. At his trial he admitted "he was never able to see the Devil or speak to him, although he did everything he could, to the point that it was not his fault if he could not see the Devil or speak with him."[12]

Jean de la Riviere of Poitiers, the first of these sorcerers to show up at one of Gilles's castles, promised to intercede with Lucifer forthwith. Gilles became ebullient. The night after he arrived at the Pouzauges Castle, de la Riviere, clad in white armor and toting his supposed magical sword, swaggered to the border of the forest outside de Rais's fortress. Gilles, with his heart thumping, along with his most loyal menservants, Henriet and Corrillaut, hesitantly followed, trembling in the black night. De la Riviere left them and disappeared into the thick verdure, promising to find Satan and commune with him on de Rais's behalf. After a short interval, hair-raising sounds echoed through the soupy darkness. Weapons clattered; shouts, then wails resounded. The paralyzed group spotted de la Riviere running toward them. He gasped that the Devil was in no mood to strike a bargain, for he had appeared in front of him disguised as a hideous leopard, "passing him by without a word." The petrified party, with Gilles being the most "frightened and terrified," raced back to the castle, where they consumed huge amounts of alcohol and feasted on a particularly fine dinner to compensate for their encounter in the woods.

Soon after the debacle, de la Riviere, who was also a doctor, informed Gilles that he would have to leave Pouzauges to retrieve more of his magical instruments, and that he needed money for his journey. De Rais readily obliged with twenty gold crowns, pleading with de la Riviere to hurry back. De la Riviere smiled broadly, bowed, and thanked de Rais, promising to return in the very near future. De Rais never saw him again.

A new wizard arrived, this one with dusty, silver hair and big shoulders. While Gilles de Rais and his cousin Gilles de Sille watched, with great pomposity and enormous self-importance he formed the familiar symbols and signs of the rites on the floor in one of the rooms at Tiffauges. The sorcerer sketched a circle with a long rod, then tossed powder onto some coals, muttering a formula in an unrecognizable tongue. He ordered de Rais and de Sille to step into the circle.

It was May, but outside, the sky suddenly burst forth with hailstones, and the valley of the Crum became a snowfield. Unnerved by these natural but rare occurrences, also scared by the machinations of this magician, Gilles de Sille refused to enter the circle. He crept near an open window, clutching a statuette of the Virgin Mary. Gilles became frightened as well, anxiously making the sign of the Cross. As he began his incantations, the conjurer warned de Rais to stop his Christian gesticulations. Unable to withstand the pressure, de Rais started to recite a familiar Christian prayer, the *Alma Redemptoris*, under his breath. The magician yelled at Gilles: "Get out! Get out of the circle!" Gilles de Sille, purported to be a brave soldier, leapt out the window; de Rais, the recent Marshal of France, sprang out the door.

Immediately thereafter, it appeared to de Rais that someone was "beating a featherbed." Dreadful sounds of flailing came from the room. The wizard was found unconscious with marks on his swollen limbs and large bumps on his head. De Rais insisted the man be carried to his own bed chamber, where a priest heard his confession and administered the last sacraments. He did not die from his wounds, though, and quickly recovered, which amazed those who had seen his bruises. But this experience greatly unnerved an already unstable de Rais.

Gilles, who found the conjuror obnoxious because of his callous commands and aggressive manner, replaced him with Jean of Picardy. The Picard suggested that if de Rais would sign a request in blood, Satan or one of his demons might be more willing to accommodate him. This was the established method of communicating with the Devil, Jean the Picard stated. He drew up a document on parchment. De Rais pricked his right little finger with a dagger, and with his own blood, inscribed his first name. The Picard then conducted the forbidden ritual within a wide meadow close to the village of Machecoul. The incantations in the circle and the signature on parchment were apparently not tempting enough for Satan. Nothing happened. Finally de Rais, his associates, and the Picard left the field for refreshments at a tavern. "Hocus pocus!" snorted the innkeeper, his description of the conjuror's antics. As he banged down drinks on Gilles's table, he told de Rais he knew the Picard, and he was a fake.

De Rais hired yet another Satanist, by the name of du Mesnil. Abbot Bossard hinted that this man might have been the imprisoned Angevin knight Gilles visited. If so, perhaps his arcane manual, which he lent to de Rais and which dealt with summoning the Devil, had been devoured by the hundreds of chiggers that had shared the knight's cell, the bright red mites feeding upon the only plant material available in the damp dungeon. With or without his manual, du Mesnil proved to be no more successful in his conjuring than any of the other quacks.

De Rais despaired. He was perplexed. Why could no one invoke the goat-footed Devil for him? He needed to talk to him so badly. Hypocras flowed as he pondered this question. Little innocents also lost their lives to him as he waited for someone to help him commune with Satan.

Then Gilles's mood suddenly changed. He became overjoyed when a twenty-three-year-old tonsured clerk named Francesco Prelati, very familiar with alchemy and black magic, arrived at Tiffauges, and more promising invocations of demons began.

At Gilles's request, Eustache Blanchet, a stocky, many-chinned priest with a receding hairline, one of de Rais's close associates and a bon vivant, had been scouring Italy hoping to find somebody well versed in the forbidden arts who would agree to return with him to de Rais's castles. Blanchet had first produced Jean de la Riviere, who turned out to be a charlatan, but de Rais still trusted Blanchet's judgment, and he spoke Italian. After a lengthy quest, the priest discovered Prelati in Florence, at that time the center of alchemy, especially its occult component.

Prelati, a young clerical student, was intrigued by the occult. He studied it seriously, became its devotee, and left the Church. When he bragged to the priest at one of their meetings that he had successfully communed with Satan a number of times, Blanchet became overjoyed, deciding he must persuade the Italian to enter Gilles's service. After he had been treated to many copious feasts and abundant libations at de Rais's expense, and having heard about the tempting lifestyle de Rais could provide, Prelati, a Tuscan by birth, readily accepted Blanchet's offer to travel to Tiffauges.

Later, at his deposition before the ecclesiastical court, Blanchet, hired by de Rais as a moral tutor, put himself at great risk when he admitted to the judges that he knew Prelati was familiar with the highly criminal art of invoking demons. Francois, he said, had assured him of it when he answered Blanchet's question regarding his expertise in black magic.

The slender, dark-haired Francesco Prelati, with his Roman nose, full mouth, and olive skin, was dazzling. Fluent in Latin, he also spoke some French, and had knowledge of poetry and geomancy. He exhibited such fluid grace, such irresistible charm, such elegant refinement, that he immediately bowled over de Rais. Also crafty, Prelati instinctively knew how to take advantage of Gilles's gullibility. A homosexual relationship quickly developed between the two, which appeared to be on a more lofty level for de Rais than most of his simple sexual liaisons.[13] De Rais positively adored Francesco, while Francesco cherished the opportunities his new situation afforded him.

During Gilles's confession to the canonical court in Nantes, he raved about Prelati, and his control over de Rais was obvious to the judges. "Interrogated as to the motive that made him keep the said Francois close to him and among family, he responded that the said Francois was exceptionally gifted and agreeable to converse with, speaking Latin eloquently and learnedly, and that he applied himself zealously to the affairs of the said Gilles, the accused."[14]

Prelati most definitely inserted himself into de Rais's affairs. He attended to Gilles's desire to commune with the Devil, for he wanted to ingratiate himself; he wanted to be a necessary part of de Rais's life in order to remain on his payroll, not unlike the many other sycophants who had recognized and taken advantage of his fragile mental state. While Prelati's attempts to invoke the Devil were better planned than his predecessors', his results remained unconvincing to everyone but Gilles. Prelati conducted many of his invocations in order to bring forth a gorgeous youth called Barron, an intermediary for the Devil. A master charlatan, Prelati tantalized de Rais with his description of Barron's incredible beauty.

"Barron is his name and fertile is his love. His eyes are poppy flowers polished in the rain. His mouth is ecstasy running down the wind. His mouth is ichor cascading in the sky. His mouth is liquid sex...Ah, the opiate of his hands! the feathers of his hands! the tongues of his hands. His body is white velvet marble. His hair is a drowsy god. He advances in a sonata of anemones impregnating the earth as he passes."[15]

Prelati had alluded to this demon when he met with Blanchet in Florence. He told Blanchet that he had actually seen Barron, who took the shape of a handsome young man, a flock of ravens accompanying him (ravens are often associated with Hell). Prelati had even spoken with Barron, and both had agreed on a pact of mutual assistance and collaboration.

Francesco Prelati performed his diabolical séances, like the others, in order to receive messages from Beelzebub on Gilles's behalf. Francesco held three important invocations. In these three attempts to communicate with Satan, Gilles's letter, which he had written to the Devil and signed in blood, was on hand.

The first invocation occurred in the summer of 1439 in the Great Hall at Tiffauges, overlooking the deep green-blue valley of the Crum River. After one of the libidinous nightly castle revels, Francesco Prelati, the conjuror, Gilles de Rais, the mighty lord, now thirty-five, Blanchet, the priest who convinced Prelati to come to Tiffauges, and Gilles's attendants, Henriet and Corrillaut, ascended the stairway, entering the large chamber as rain drops fell on the roof and ran down the windows. Henriet and Corrillaut had laid a fire there earlier in the evening. In addition to burning coals placed in an earthenware pot, they had also stocked candles, incense, and aromatic gums in the huge room along with two cages containing birds to be sacrificed. Sensing something unnatural about their environment, the birds were very agitated. At Prelati's bidding, the attendants lit wax torches and candles in the great hall.

Prelati then made several of the requisite circles and esoteric signs with the tip of his sword, which he had brought with him from Italy. Like all swords used in satanic rituals, it was welded in the form of a crucifix. The long, sleek blade made of unalloyed steel, which had been heated in a fire of laurel and cypress wood and cooled in snake blood, had cabalist symbols etched into it. Prelati mumbled satanic sentences, which he repeated verbatim at his deposition before the ecclesiastical judges at de Rais's trial. "I conjure you, Barron, Satan, Belial, Beelzebub, by the Father, Son and Holy Ghost, by the Virgin Mary and all the saints, to appear here in person to speak with us and do our will."[16]

Prelati dusted incense combined with myrrh, aloe, and powders onto the hot coals. Clouds of piquant smoke began to rise. When they were dense enough, Prelati made further mystical tracings on the wall, calling for the four casement windows in the room, arrayed in a cross, to be opened wide.

Following Prelati's ceremony, de Rais's associates, after swearing to keep the proceedings a secret and to maintain a vigil, were sent out of the great hall to his bedroom. Corrillaut, testifying before the canonical court in Nantes, mentioned that as he, Henriet, and Blanchet left the great hall, the priest, Blanchet, mumbled disparagingly in French "...Master Francois, in exchange for a jug of wine, would make the Devil appear."[17] Abbot Bossard also intimated that Prelati might have been an alcoholic, or at least an enthusiastic guzzler, similar to de Rais. Both Francesco and Gilles would drink an astounding amount of wine as they awaited the Devil.

When Prelati and de Rais were alone, they entered the circle for the solemn invocation. Gilles carried his note to the Devil written in French. It stated: "Come at my bidding, and I will give you whatever you want, except my soul and the curtailment of my life." At his trial, Gilles explained that Francesco told him it was important to deliver the note to Belial as soon as he revealed himself. Therefore, during the invocation, Gilles held the note constantly in his hand, as he awaited the pacts that Francoise and the Devil would formulate, and to learn what they had agreed Gilles would promise to do for Satan in exchange for bringing him gold.

The ceremony started with the two standing, then genuflecting, duplicating Catholic scripted prayers, invocations, vows, and promises. No demon responded. There was no sound, no wind, no flickering of the candles. Around one thirty in the morning, Prelati, in a parody of the Christian purification rite, slaughtered the birds, a turtledove, a pigeon, and a cock, one by one, shedding their blood slowly, mixing it with myrtle. (In the Christian religion the purification rite of immersion, or baptism, is done in the name of God, the Father, the Son, and the Holy Spirit for the cleansing of all sins.) Prelati then repeated his veneration. Still the dark spirits remained silent. The Devil refused to show himself.

An infuriated de Rais strode out of the circle with Prelati following after him to Gilles's bedroom, where the others waited. Corrillaut had fallen asleep. Blanchet and Henriet, both wide awake and keeping a vigil as they had been instructed, reported they had not seen or heard anything. However, in an effort to mollify the very perturbed Gilles and make him think the Devil might have passed nearby, they revised their comments; perhaps, they said, they had caught the sound of strange paws upon the roof.

The next morning, a still-annoyed Gilles demanded Prelati once again attempt to arrange the anticipated encounter with Satan. Prelati, with the valet Corrillaut, set out for a meadow near the village of Tiffauges, "about an arrow's flight from an old, uninhabited house." The two brought incense, a lodestone, and a book on black magic with them, along with the marshal's personal note to the Devil, inscribed in blood. The circle and signs were drawn. Prelati, pulling Corrillaut with him, stepped into the designated area. Corrillaut, horrified at taking part in the ceremony, unobtrusively crossed himself. Prelati directed Corrillaut, nicknamed Poitou, not to do so while entering the circle, nor while they remained there. He told Poitou such gestures would prevent the demon from appearing.

Prelati began his incantations and called out the name of Barron, the ravishing agent of Lucifer. The two waited, Corrillaut stiff with fear. There was no response at all except for an uncommonly strong, chilly wind which howled overhead. It became "pitch dark." Claps of thunder reverberated throughout the valley with "torrential" rain, heavier than the cloudbursts of the previous night, beginning to fall. After half an hour, Prelati and Poitou, drenched and shaking, returned to the castle. Corrillaut was extremely relieved to be returning without having encountered Lucifer. De Rais, who had been waiting impatiently in the grand hall, was exasperated when Prelati handed him back his very wet note. In his later deposition before the ecclesiastical court, Prelati sketched out the incident which cemented his own culpability.

Prelati convinced de Rais that when he was not present, Barron, the denizen of Hell, appeared to him at least ten or twelve times. In fact, Prelati said he successfully delivered Gilles's note on one occasion. Another time, Barron became so willful de Rais thought Francesco was in tremendous danger. De Rais heard horrible sobbing, sighing, and loud groans coming from a side chamber where Prelati spoke alone with the Devil's go-between. Gilles recognized these cries as the unmistakable sounds emitted by his sorcerers when Beelzebub beat them up. Too petrified to investigate the commotion himself, Gilles pleaded with the priest, Blanchet, to find out what was occurring.

The priest mustered up his courage and peeped through an interior window into the room. He could see Francesco, sprawled on the floor, motionless. Blanchet repeatedly called to Francesco, who did not respond, but moaned loudly. Gilles stood in the corridor outside, fretting about Francesco and squawking like a mother guinea hen. After an endless interval, Prelati appeared. He was utterly disheveled, and had large bruises on his forehead and extremities. (Satan had left similar marks on some of the other wizards Gilles hired.) De Rais, together with the priest, steadied him. In a weak voice, Francesco recounted how the Devil thrashed him mercilessly because Prelati belittled his authority. Prelati had derided Lucifer and his demons, including Barron, calling them a bunch of powerless bums.

Eustache Blanchet, so proud of his analysis regarding Prelati's beating, pointed out to Gilles that he had told Prelati the demons were inconsequential. When Prelati confronted the little devils, he used Blanchet's sharp characterization. Thus they became incensed and pummeled him, the priest blathered.

A. L. Vincent, in his early twentieth-century book on de Rais, had a more sophisticated, less subjective take than Blanchet. Like the priest, he did not believe Prelati's thrashing was mummery. He noted that "beating" by an invisible presence was the best authenticated form of a psychic phenomena, stating it was related to poltergeist activity, the most common among such manifestations, which could have transpired with Prelatis's invocation.[18] Abbot Bossard also remarked on this peculiar occurrence. He thought Prelati was deeply affected by his beating, even though he regained his health.

Gilles de Rais, so naïve, so mentally impaired, so determined to have a relationship with the Devil, believed Prelati's shenanigans, or perhaps his real communication with an "invisible presence." He became hysterical. His lover might die because of his brutal encounter with Belial. He could not lose one more person he loved. He looked for his black planet to approach the horizon once again as Prelati lay listless in his bed for many days, draped in a purple satin gown lined with white fox. The devoted marshal catered to all his wishes, nursing the Italian conjuror back to health. He would not let anyone else enter his room.

Shortly after Prelati recovered from his pounding, he told Gilles he needed to commune once more with Barron. De Rais remained apprehensive, fearing for his lover; he felt another invocation might risk tragedy for both of them. Prelati persuaded Gilles the meeting must take place so that he could find out when the Devil would make his appearance. In this second invocation on de Rais's behalf, Barron told Prelati, alone again, that Belial was disgruntled. De Rais upset him because he did not wait upon three indigent men who had showed up at his castle for a meal on All Saints' Day. Gilles had previously celebrated the solemn Office of the Damned on that sacred day and served paupers himself to honor the Devil, even washing their feet. Nevertheless, Satan wanted to demonstrate his magnanimity toward de Rais, Prelati told him. Barron steered Francesco to an immense stack of gold ingots hidden in the corner of the room where he and Francesco conversed. The spirit disappeared after he pointed out the welcome surprise to Prelati.

A jubilant Prelati found de Rais and hurriedly brought him to the room heaped with ingots. Francesco opened the door with de Rais behind him. Horrified, he spied a large, green, winged snake as big as a dog coiled up on the floor. He warned Gilles not to enter the room because of the snake. Gilles, in a fright, obeyed and started to run for cover with Prelati following. Both men bolted down the passageway. Prelati would testify to this event in his sworn deposition. De Rais corroborated Francesco's statement; in his impaired mental state, Gilles never imagined Francesco would have concocted this.

Gilles returned, brandishing a crucifix, and holding a relic he had acquired, a splinter of the Holy Rood, the True Cross. Prelati cautioned de Rais not to try dealing with Satan, who had taken on the form of the viper, by waving the utmost Christian symbol at him. But Gilles needed that gold and, undeterred, he entered the chamber, cross raised above his head, only to find yellow powder on the floor.

Gilles de Rais did not throw Prelati out of the castle after the adventure with the serpent. He permitted Francesco to conduct a third invocation, at Bourgneuf-en-Rais. Gilles went there to meet with Duke Jean V. At this point, Gilles recognized Duke Jean V's indifference to him. Few of his fine properties remained for the duke to buy or steal. Nonetheless, the once mighty Lord de Rais wanted to stay in the duke's favor, to keep his respect.

While he waited to see Jean V, de Rais begged Francesco to summon Satan. He needed some sign as he urgently wanted to discuss the guidelines for receiving the Devil's gold; he hoped for a marvel. Prelati humored him and attempted to entice Beelzebub, or at least his intermediary, Barron, to come forth as winds from the west whipped the building where they stayed. No demons or gold appeared. Belial did not bestow any gifts on Gilles, nor did the duke. There were only violent rushes of rain outside.

Gold, gold, gold! De Rais fixated on gold. He must find it. He became obsessed, convinced that the Devil would help him because of Prelati's personal contact with Barron, his ravishing assistant. Since God could enact miracles through the work of His saints, Gilles believed Lucifer with his great powers would come to the rescue of somebody showing him reverence. Francesco, always ready with an ingenious explanation, attributed his own failure in communicating with Belial to de Rais's pious observances, to the religious objects Gilles insisted on keeping around his castles. One form of his Christian veneration was the intricately and beautifully painted statuettes of saints, such as Michael, Anne, Catherine, Denis, that he had placed against the pillars of his fortresses. All French nobility of that era displayed such exquisite pieces in their castles.

Prelati persuaded de Rais that Satan desired greater proof of his allegiance. The Devil wanted human sacrifices. De Rais, so courageous on the battlefield, was not afraid to kill his enemy, but the former Marshal of France, like most fifteenth-century Europeans, feared demons. Prelati made light of de Rais's fright, insisting Gilles take an oath to kill five children. The pledge would be inscribed in Lord de Rais's blood. "The seeping virus of Prelati's mind had permeated Gilles's tormented brain, turned it into a leprosy."[19] De Rais reluctantly agreed to the sacrifice, but again demanded safety for his life and for his soul. Unbalanced as he had become, he thought he could commit blasphemy and murder and still remain without blame, as he only looked to Hell for temporary relief from his difficulties. This conviction assuaged his guilt. Then Joan of Arc, in white mail, appeared to him in a vision. He could not understand what she was saying, but he kept thinking something terrible was about to happen to her and to him. He desperately wanted her to know that he had always clung to his Catholic faith; he had never broken from his God. His heart was racing, pounding. He had difficulty breathing. He felt very dizzy. When his panic attack, one of the many from which Gilles suffered, subsided, Prelati demanded that de Rais give him some parts of a child. Gilles, still reeling from his ordeal, presented this depraved offering to Satan at Tiffauges in the approaching dusk.

Shortly thereafter, his servants Henriet and Corrillaut unexpectedly entered his private chamber. Corrillaut would say when interrogated that he found his master holding a linen cloth which contained "the hand, heart and eyes of a child killed by his order in the castle."[20] (He did not know whether it was the right or the left hand.) Discombobulated by his servants' entrance, Gilles quickly placed the parts in a glass chalice on the mantelpiece. The tiny corpse, still warm, lay on the polished tile floor. Aggravated by the interruption and not even glancing at his menservants or the bloody remains, Gilles suddenly took the container off the mantelpiece and carefully shoved it up his long sleeve. He fanatically strode around the room. Abruptly he dismissed his retainers, telling them he was leaving for an important engagement and that they should close and lock his chamber.

Then he hurried away down the corridor and ran toward a small cubicle in an unfrequented wing of the castle. Francesco Prelati eagerly awaited him there. He held up the offering of the child's parts to the Devil as soon as Gilles, quivering with anticipation, handed them over. Time went by; Satan did not emerge. The two diligently waited for an interminable duration, the container always raised. Satan still did not appear. In the hush of night,

Prelati hastily buried the baby's body, which he had retrieved from Gilles's chamber, along with its detached organs and hand, in sacred soil near the castle chapel with its gloomy crypt. Neither Prelati nor Gilles showed remorse for the killing; Satan was their justification for the murder. As perverse as it was, this act was unrelated to Gilles's psychopathic need to rape and butcher children. De Rais did not repeat this foray into the darker side of black magic.[21] Prelati never requested another sacrifice to Lucifer. But the murder and mutilation of innocents continued.

CHAPTER SEVEN

THERE BE MONSTERS HERE

AFTER HE LEFT THE MILITARY, GILLES DE RAIS, THEN TWENTY-eight, moved into Champtocé Castle in 1432, the year his grand-father died. He invited Gilles de Sille to reside at the chateau. A distant relation of Jean de Craon's second wife, de Rais knew him from their participation in the Battle of Lagny. With his cold eyes, his malicious smile, his hard, chiseled face, de Sille not only shared Gilles's homosexual proclivities, but also exhibited the same lack of moral integrity, the same barbarity de Rais displayed before and after he became Joan of Arc's valorous and loyal warrior. De Rais's cousin, Roger de Bricqueville, a bedfellow since his youth, who later married and had children after leaving Gilles's service, was already ensconced at the mighty fortress. The Lord de Rais appointed this man to take charge of his fortune during his theatri-cal sojourn to Orleans. De Bricqueville lacked scruples too, already demonstrated by his desire to steal large amounts of money from de Rais to amass his own fortune.

Up to the eleventh and twelfth centuries, gay life was accepted in Christian Europe and practiced openly. Homosexual art, poetry, and music flourished. The most popular literature of the day portrayed same-sex lovers, with clerics at the vanguard of this movement. The Cistercian abbot, Saint Aelred, a homilist and spiritual writer, provided the clearest, most detailed writing glorifying homosexual friendship. He described his youth as a time consumed with enjoying other men and being enjoyed by them. In his eulogy on the death of his homosexual partner, Simon, he wrote:

> "He was the refuge of my spirit, the sweet solace of my grief, whose heart of love received me when fatigued by labors, whose counsel refreshed me when plunged in sadness and grief…What more is there, then, that I can say? Was it not a foretaste of blessedness thus to love and thus to be loved?"[1]

However, pedophilia was never condoned, and after the twelfth century, Christian tolerance of homosexuality evaporated, for sexual deviants, it was believed, had lost their souls to the Devil. The French civil code dictated that the testicles be chopped off a sodomite for a first offense, his member be removed for a second, and that he be burned to death, his property forfeited, for a third. By the end of the thirteenth century, Christians feared God would smite any nation tolerating homosexual behavior, now linked to the molestation of children and the fornication of beasts.[2]

Even so, Gilles de Rais flaunted his homosexuality; perhaps he dared to do so because of his title and standing. He made sure no women resided at the Champtocé Castle. De Rais had so alienated his wife and young daughter when he returned from combat that they fled to the Pouzauges fortress, which belonged to Catherine's family. He made it absolutely clear he loathed both of them.

"Gilles appears to have despised the" female "sex ever since leaving the court...Like others whose ideal of concupiscence is deteriorated and deviated, he certainly comes to be disgusted by the delicacy of the grain of the skin of women and by that odor of femininity which all sodomists abhor."[3]

His feelings for Joan of Arc were an aberration; she remained Gilles's heroine. He believed God had somehow provided her with great physical and mental abilities so that she could successfully command an army of men who worshipped her.

But Joan was no longer Gilles's ceaseless companion on the battlefield. Now cousins de Sille and de Briqueville became de Rais's primary escorts, and also his bed partners. Needy parasites like so many of his retinue, they lived lavishly off of de Rais. Gilles de Sille even brought his brother, Michael de Sille, into de Rais's entourage as a captain of the castle. It is presumed he was paid handsomely for his services. Roger de Briqueville as well as Gilles de Sille made sure they ingratiated themselves by obsequious flattery, by condoning Gilles's frivolity and provoking his insanity, as de Rais's sibling, Rene de la Suze, pointed out in *History of the heirs*. Long nights of nonstop debauchery and abuse ensued at Champtocé.

There is no conclusive explanation for why Gilles de Rais began his depraved spree, killing hundreds of children; why he embarked upon the bizarre sexual rituals, the mutilations and murders. Possibly his severe PTSD so incapacitated him that he lost all control. His dammed-up sorrow, his rage, his guilt destroyed him. In his confused state, his underlying psychopathy emerged, and he started to murder for fun. (Regardless of any other motives, most serial killers carry out their crimes because they want to.)

Certainly, homoerotic endeavors did not provide enough satisfaction or entertainment for the drink-drenched trio of de Rais, de Bricqueville, and de Sille. With their senses aroused by alcohol and spicy food, they devised a game that led to unimaginable perversions: the capture, rape, torture, and murder of beautiful children. Disregarding both law and convention, de Sille and de Bricqueville, thoroughly twisted, totally unprincipled, goaded Gilles on to commit his savage acts. A salacious diversion at first, this sport soon turned into a compulsive activity for de Rais. His mind now frayed, he could not function without sodomizing and killing innocents. Driven by his strong penchant for pedophilia and murder, whatever conscience he still possessed was no match for his lack of self-control.

De Sille was the first to help de Rais slice up innocents at the Champtocé Castle. Soon de Bricqueville became an enthusiastic regular at the bloodletting. As Gilles moved on to the castles of Machecoul and Tiffauges, and the Hotel de la Suze, the sinister enterprise of finding children for him became more calculated and sophisticated, a common occurrence in serial killings, but in Gilles's case, many accomplices, not just de Sille and de Bricqueville, took pleasure in the orgies.

Gilles had numerous opportunities to participate in his deranged amusement, right at his chateaux. Amid their riches, fifteenth-century French nobility practiced charity. Food and money was dispersed to the poor all day at the gates of castles such as Champtocé, Machecoul, or Tiffauges to commemorate weddings, great days of the church, births, deaths, public rejoicings. Gilles's choice of victims for his psychopathic addiction was enormous, as paupers swarmed to his portals when alms were distributed. With hot, burning eyes, Gilles de Rais paced back and forth; he looked out unseen from a high window, desire bubbling. To satisfy his perverse craving, he selected the most delicious child, waiting expectantly for a gold coin. Stroking his penis, he ordered the child to be brought to him.

The youngster was told that if he entered the castle, he would receive meat and cakes to take back to his family. As soon as he set foot in the edifice, the little one was jumped. A flax cloth was quickly stuffed into his mouth, his wrists and ankles bound with leather cords. De Rais's cohorts surreptitiously carried the victim to Gilles's room or to a secret underground prison where they kept the child until de Rais was ready to ravish him.

Roger de Bricqueville and Gilles de Sille delighted in helping to pick which of the unsuspecting children would be the most suitable. Other conspirators soon participated in the selection process, too. If the marshal saw two children together, brothers and sisters, boys or girls, and he fancied only one, he still seized and killed both, so that the remaining youngster would not be able to identify the august Lord de Rais as a child molester and murderer. Gilles's manservant, Etienne Corrillaut, deposed by the ecclesiastical court of Nantes after the bloody crimes were uncovered, was the first to inform de Rais's judges about this practice.

In the villages near the Baron de Rais's castles, where he was known, his followers frequently dismounted from their horses, patted a child on the head, well aware he or she would be the next unfortunate to quench Gilles's carnal flame. De Rais's hirelings spoke kindly to the parents, mentioning that one as attractive as their lambkin should be living a far better life. It was not unusual to observe a little barefoot gamin heading toward Gilles's fortress accompanied by de Sille, de Bricqueville, or other de Rais henchmen. Families were ecstatic that their tot could be so blessed; they also had one less mouth to feed. Though the offspring did not return to show his family how he rolled in the lap of luxury now, suspicions were not aroused for some time. Parents told themselves the eminent lord could not do without their sprout's services.

Folk gave their children most willingly to Gilles's valets, Etienne Corrillaut and Henriet Griart, who were well dressed and rode beautifully harnessed steeds. They understood the two came from humble backgrounds like their own, prospering from their employment with the great Lord de Rais. Thus Macee de Velleblanche, a widow from the immediate surroundings of

Machecoul, pinched for money, readily handed over her child to Corrillaut after he told her the youth, with his luscious brown-black locks, would become Gilles's page and be clad in crimson. Another needy mother, Yvon Kergen, the widow of a stonecutter and parishioner of Sainte-Crois of Nantes, gladly entrusted to Corrillaut her delicately featured fifteen-year-old son. At the time of the hearings looking into de Rais's crimes, she would tell the ecclesiastical court that she never saw her son again.

In their confessions during de Rais's trial, both Henriet and Poitou conceded they were also able to take many innocents "from mothers and fathers they did not know." They assured these parents their children would be well educated, well dressed, well fed. They specifically remembered a very poor couple living in the tiny town of La Roche-Bernard, situated on the spur of the Garonne River near Vannes, who proudly allowed them to take their precious, bony-limbed blessing away with them. Henriet further admitted "that the said Lord sometimes gave him two or three crowns for the said children..."[4]

The reaction of parents whose children disappeared from roads, fields, or outlying villages was very different. They had terrible misgivings regarding the fate of their loved ones, and for good reason. It was too easy for Gilles and his bunch of undesirables to snatch a child at the gates of his castle or its environs. And killing was not enough. They looked forward to a more chilling form of entertainment. Following the evening routine of heavy drinking and feasting, numerous forays into the countryside, together with trips into remote areas occurred. De Rais and his companions hunted for victims in these locations, even in the gloomy moors of Brittany.

Great sport emerged for Gilles de Rais when small human bounty was spotted, chased, trapped. Gilles went cock-a-hoop watching his young prey try to outrun the collection of inebriates cantering after him on horseback. He became more elated the more the innocent struggled when caught, a characteristic shared with numerous serial killers. The child was gagged, thrown into a sack or tied up with ropes, and brought back to the castle for slaughter. Good-looking, curly-haired young shepherds turned out to be de Rais's favorite target.

Micheau Bouer and his wife, who lived near the windswept salt marshes bordering the Atlantic Ocean in Saint-Cyr-en-Rais, lost a thin-cheeked boy in this cruel way while he tended the family animals. During the inquest commissioned by the Duke of Brittany to find out if Gilles de Rais committed acts of violence against children, eighty citizens, including Bouer, testified about the disappearance of children, often as they tended to their beasts. The widow of Aimery Edelin and former wife of Jean Bonneau, a Machecoul resident, spoke very emotionally. At the end of her sworn statement she warned the duke's emissaries that the abductions were serious and many. "...she (even) heard a man from Tiffauges, whose name she has forgotten, say that for one child lost around Machecoul, seven were lost around Tiffauges."[5] (Her son had been snatched in Machecoul.)

If shepherds could not be found, other youths became the marshal's quarry. One cold afternoon in late December, Ysabeau Hamelin, residing in the borough of Fresnay, southwest of Machecoul, sent two sons, age fifteen and seven, off to buy bread with the little cash she possessed. They never returned to her small but tidy hut. On a starry summer night a wide-eyed orphan called Jamet, eight or nine years old, vanished from a leafy path outside the distant hamlet of Saint-Etienne-de-Montluc. Months later, another very shy, thirteen-year-old youth who inhabited that same secluded warren could not be found after his tutor left him alone at bedtime. In faraway La Boucardiere, two hemp gatherers came home well after sunset from backbreaking work in a field to find their lean-limbed eight-year-old, left to care for his infant sister, abducted.

Again the humble, including Ysabeau Hamelin, Jean Toutblanc, tutor, and the hemp gathers, Guillaume and Janette Sergent, conveyed their heartfelt concern over the missing children to the commissioners of the duke, setting forth when and where they had vanished.

Procurers, procuresses, old female go-betweens were also hired to lure innocents to the mighty de Rais castles as Gilles's libidinal urges and depravity increased. A particularly ghoulish figure, Perrine Martin, named "La Meffraye" (bird of prey) by the peasants, enjoyed nabbing children. Unbearably poor, this eerie crone, between fifty and sixty years old, lived in a tumbledown hovel, subsisting on wild roots and berries. Roaming around Nantes, Machecoul, and their vicinities, she was easily recruited into Gilles's service, as he paid her some silver marks for each victim. Always dressed in grey, she wore a black veil and hood to disguise her ruddy face. The description by common folk of La Meffraye to the commissioners remained as above. They also observed the "old, small woman" usually had "a young boy with her."

Perrine Martin provided more children for de Rais than any other attendant.[6] Her terrifying seduction was masterful. La Meffraye suddenly appeared in her mysterious attire. She stealthily approached little ones tending their cattle, or those with dirty hands begging for alms or crying as they were lost on roadways. She caressed them, she flattered them. Any bit of caution they demonstrated dissolved in the face of her kind, assuring manner. Her speech echoed the rhythms of the countryside. And when she lifted her veil, La Meffraye seemed to be a smiling little fairy to the trusting youngsters.

Playing upon their imaginations, Perrine Martin offered beautiful descriptions and tantalizing promises which piqued the innocents' curiosity and inflamed their fantasies. Those fancies could become realities if they merely took her hand, for she would lead them to a life of luxury, an existence of magnificence at a resplendent nobleman's castle. She not only tricked young children with her convincing promises, but also those in their teens and early twenties.

When the children arrived at de Rais's castles, a similar end awaited them. Nightmarish butchery, ghoulish bloodshed, demonic destruction, sadistic slaughter...a ghastly pattern occurred forty, eighty, one hundred, perhaps more than two hundred times at Champtocé, Machecoul, Nantes, Tiffauges, and elsewhere. At dusk a child was secretly brought to Gilles's darkened bedroom, where his lordship and his friends waited impatiently. With a hint of a leer on their faces, they playfully undressed the youngster, fondled him, forced him, and made him take different sexual positions, depending upon Gilles's fancy.

Suddenly de Rais's captive was grabbed and suspended by the neck with a rope or a hook attached to a pole. His eyes bulged as he dangled three feet off the ground in the corner of the large chamber. The terrified youth swung back and forth long enough that his vocal cords were damaged and he could not cry out. Then Gilles de Rais took the innocent off the hook himself. He held his prey in his arms, pretending to comfort the terrified little one. He said he had no intention of doing harm; he was having fun, making up a silly game. The infant dried the tears from his cheeks, smiling at his protector. Just when he thought he was safe, Gilles went in for the kill, first mutilating and torturing, then raping the child.

Occasionally de Rais ravaged a victim in his cavernous living quarters right after the child had been taken down from the pole. But the majority of innocents faced a similar ritual of agony and murder in all of de Rais's frightening fortresses: only after Gilles or one of his cohorts slit the child's throat with dirks and daggers, cut a vein in the neck with a knife, broke the neck with a club, or dismembered or decapitated the little one using a special short, thick sword called a braquemart, did de Rais sexually brutalize the youth.

As transcribed in the record of his trial, Gilles de Rais would admit to committing these crimes "because of his passion and sensual delight." He could not remember how many children he had killed after he committed sodomy, but he confessed that "he had ejaculated spermatic seed after their deaths as during it."[7]

His further testimony in front of the court contained more strange but revealing remarks about his state of mind. De Rais chillingly specified that he derived immense pleasure in the slashing and the bashing. He liked to observe the maimed innocents as he methodically carved them up. Gilles thrilled to the anguish of the children, with their mangled heads and limbs hacked to pieces. He basked in the splatters of their gurgling blood. Like other serial killers, the moans, the suffering of the boys and girls being gutted, aroused de Rais sexually. A lack of self-control leads most of these psychopaths to increase their brutality and perform such grotesque acts.

Baron de Rais pulled out the eyes of one youth, then casually crushed his skull before he had an orgasm. He smashed in another boy's chest, letting him bleed to death so that he could bathe his hands and beard in the child's small body cavity.[8] Smeared with blood, Gilles subsequently had an erection. Victims were also savagely thrown to the floor when they did not die quickly enough, or did not exhibit enough pain to stimulate Gilles's libido.[9] Occasionally they were just strangled.

Etienne Corrillaut later astonished the canonical court when he not only corroborated de Rais's testimony, but further indicated that after the children were tortured, de Rais regularly proceeded to "abuse these boys and girls in the heat of his lust in an unnatural manner according to his abominable custom: first he took his own penis or virile member in one or the other of his hands, rubbed it or stretched it out, then put it between the thighs or legs of these boys and girls while avoiding the natural vessel of the girls; he rubbed his penis or virile member on the belly of these boys and girls with great pleasure, ardor and depraved concupiscence until he emitted his sperm on their belly. …and shamefully abused the girls in the same ways as the boys, shunning their sexual organ, and that he often heard Gilles say that his pleasure was much greater in thus abusing the girls than in using their proper vessel in the normal way."[10]

Sometimes de Rais became so aroused by the gore that he raped a youngster a second time, as the innocent lay dying. In a few instances, Gilles had sex with broken, lifeless corpses. Usually the greatest stimulation for de Rais was to feel the child's death spasms during the heat of his own passion. He often sat on the bellies of mutilated youngsters after he cleaved them to bits and sodomized them or masturbated. Squatting on the entrails, he leaned forward, watching closely as the luster faded from their eyes. He grinned, even made fun of them while they slowly perished. In his own words during his trial, Gilles affirmed that "…very often, when the children were dying, (I) sat on their bellies and delighted in watching them die thus, and with the aforesaid Corrillaut and Henriet (I) laughed at them…"[11] As long as blood still flowed onto the floor, with some life in the small body, Gilles de Rais remained ecstatic, raving. The dark, red stains coming from his victims' violated anuses and oozing onto their buttocks and legs also mesmerized him.

The murder of children did not provide sufficient sexual stimulation to fulfill Gilles's needs. After the decapitation and killings took place, the Lord de Rais ordered the dismemberment of the bodies. "(I) had their bodies cruelly opened up and delighted at the sight of their internal organs…"[12] he admitted to his judges and spectators, who became unsettled by his remarks. He beamed while he examined the splattered brains and bones of his victims and smelled their crushed genitals and entrails. He gleefully probed the bleeding innards which spiraled and wiggled. The pouch, called the caecum, or blind gut, joining the large and small intestine, particularly fascinated him.

A macabre beauty contest ensued after de Rais's extensive study of the chopped-up remains. Having changed into a spotless, iridescent-lilac or garter-blue robe, de Rais savored looking at the many heads of the dead children, trimmed neatly at their necks by his fellow miscreants. Gilles chose the most appealing, and had those placed on the mantel above the fireplace in his bedroom, like statuettes of the saints. They brought some meaning to his now contaminated existence, for they were so lovely. He gently stroked these faces, whose tranquil expressions belied their last horrifying moments. He tenderly combed their hair. "Which children dead, (I) embraced them, and (I) gave way to contemplating those who had the most beautiful heads and members."[13] He subsequently turned to his servants and asked them which head they thought the most agreeable. After they made their choices, he held these up, ardently kissing the cold faces of the prettiest on display. He caressed their severed limbs. Devoid of any feelings or concern when he killed them, Gilles now referred to the victims as his "dear angels." Showering them with love, he affectionately told them to "go, go pray to God for me."

Gilles de Rais had reached the abyss.

But here was gruesome group evil; here was a lurid catalogue of perversions without restrictions too. Gilles de Sille, distant relative, councilor, bedmate, considered a hardened soldier lacking conscience as well as empathy, was the first to know of and participate in de Rais's unrestrained baseness. Roger de Briqueville soon connected with de Rais and de Sille, contributing to the grotesque murders at Champtocé. It is not clear why de Bricqueville decided to join his cousin in his acts of sexual violence against children, but it is likely that de Rais tapped a streak of depravity in his homosexual partner that had previously found only limited expression in his thievery. In addition, De Bricqueville presumably took part in Gilles's orgies, knowing this to be the surest way of consolidating his position. These two accomplices, Gilles de Sille and Roger de Bricqueville, derived sinister pleasure engaging in the savagery. They thrilled to the kill as much as de Rais, but they could control their desire to murder. They were more cruel than insane.

When de Rais moved to Tiffauges, Machecoul, and Nantes, his valets, Corrillaut and Henriet, loyal to the man that fed and clothed them, executing all his orders punctually, assisted in the massacres that de Rais presided over. Both were assumed to be thick-wits, but Henriet had enough of a brain to formulate the strategy of slicing victims' throats with a knife. Henriet *"forma alors la dessein de se trancher la gorge d'un coup de couteau..."*[14] At least five other hirelings, who expected considerable compensation for keeping Gilles's acts secret, participated as well. Because of his largesse, these hangers-on had no wish to upset de Rais by questioning why he performed such rituals. Perhaps Francesco Prelati, the conjuror of demons, the shameless fraud, also entered into the barbarity.

Gilles's own bedroom or an adjoining apartment became the slaughterhouse. The baron's suite, used for his orgies in the Champtocé Castle, formerly stored weapons. At Machecoul, the chamber of horrors was found in the portal of the fortress, and at La Suze, in Nantes, near the far end of the mansion facing the parochial Church of St. Denis.

After the murder, Gilles would fall into a drunken stupor with the remains of the child still in his chamber. His accomplices washed away the blood pouring onto the floor as well as the other body fluids. At Champtocé, de Silles and de Bricqueville methodically tossed the small, dead innocents into the bottom of a dungeon, where they remained undetected. Elsewhere, the tiny corpses of the victims were burned up in the room where they died. Thick, long logs and leaves were placed on andirons in the fireplace. Dried faggots thrown onto the bodies fueled the hot flames. The children's clothing, held above the fire to minimize the putrid stench, was gradually charred and destroyed piece by piece. Sometimes the castle latrines were used, as were the moats or any other secret place that could be found.

Frequently, when the mighty Gilles de Rais awoke after the murders, he experienced deep remorse. Clothed in worn fustian and serge, he restlessly roamed his castles, along the solitary halls, the long corridors, up the great stone staircase into the turrets. Tormented by dreadful visions of his victims, he spent desolate hours contemplating his plight. Plagued by images coming from his inner hell, he plunged into dementia: the enveloping silence of the night terrified him. Sometimes, when he listened closely, he could hear the low moans of the dead innocents. Distraught, he ventured beyond the outer walls of his castles in the cold, damp, early-morning hours. Crying or mumbling incoherently, he shuffled along the narrow cobblestone streets of Nantes, Machecoul, and Tiffauges, or in the countryside.

Passersby thought he was a crackpot, a loon. They admonished him for wandering around at odd hours, since he was sick, his mind fragile. They scolded him, telling him he dressed inappropriately for a nobleman; he should return to his fortress where his servants would take care of him. Falling to his knees, he begged God and the Maid of Miracles to help him. With trembling hands he prayed for his own redemption. His face was transparent, colorless. His eyes teared when he vowed to amend his evil ways: he would become a monk; he would make a pilgrimage to the Holy Lands.

His guilt passed as he immersed himself in maniacal gaiety and heavy drinking. By the time night fell, he had a relapse. As dogs return to their vomit (an analogy used by Gilles's prosecutor) his lust for blood recurred.

When a juvenile could not be found to satisfy the marshal's

abnormal desires, he sodomized the choirboys under his supervision. He never murdered them after he had sex with them, for they were his darlings and never tattled on him. He somehow controlled his impulse to kill, for he considered these aesthetic youths part of his household. They were not destitute outsiders with whom he had no prior relationship. (Serial killers usually murder strangers.) De Rais alone had chosen the boys for his chapel; he selected them because of their exquisite beauty and their superb singing ability. De Rais, passionate about music, felt God spoke through song. Gilles adored hearing his little cherubs burst with divine joy as they performed the breathtaking sacred Mass in four parts and motets, or church music for choruses, which he selected, as well as other pieces. The organ vibrated throughout his chapel, embellishing the mellifluence of the children. Gilles's body resonated with the sound.

De Rais overwhelmed these rosy-cheeked youngsters with gifts and dressed them lavishly, even giving them fur choir hats crowned with squirrel. The baron's pet, long-haired Perrinet Briand, along with his older brother, often frequented de Rais's bedroom. The Briand parents received substantial amounts of money in return for their sons' sexual favors to de Rais, and their own complicity.

While Gilles pampered his beloved sweethearts, France in the late Middle Ages presented a grim, unfriendly environment for most youngsters, especially those who wandered away from their homes. Beggars at the time killed and mutilated little ones. A group called the Caymans went to fairs for the specific purpose of seeking out children to slash and murder. Gypsies appeared in the country; they, too, abducted many innocents in the provinces before they were expelled from France.[15] Concern for a child who disappeared was almost futile in a tattered land crawling with the English, as well as the Burgundian enemy. Order and security did not exist. Michelet, the nineteen-century French historian who expressively described that era, wrote that the fear of God no longer acted as a deterrent against brutality. Because of the atrocities of war, the taste for blood was rampant. Life had little value for skeletal children or cadaverous adults. Miserable, bowed, docile, crushed by so many conflicts on French soil, they roved the land desperately looking for food. With their blank countenances scarred by smallpox,[16] their hollow eyes sunken in their heads, they could not defend themselves against this human viper.

Many French nobles, though, still lived a privileged existence of abundance and leisure, devoid of suffering or accountability. With their air of unbridled arrogance, their philosophy of entitlement, they remained the exception. In the midst of his gleaming castles, his glittering accoutrement, his enormous staff, Gilles de Rais was one of these sovereign lords. As the killing spree began during this era which knew little restraint, no one dreamt that Baron Gilles de Rais, a rich feudal chief, near enough to a minor monarch, would be involved in the cruel disappearance of innocent children. After all, the Lord de Rais gave assistance to the needy. He often partook of the sacraments in the Trinity Church in Machecoul and elsewhere, with his beloved poor regarded as extended family.[17] As a protector of his own flock, the perception remained that his Lordship de Rais kept them safe from the misfortunes of war inundating the country. Warnings signs regarding his behavior were ignored.

Only after the carnage in Gilles's territories increased significantly did the possibility of his culpability begin to be raised. Folk started to notice that when a child vanished, the nobleman de Rais or his henchmen had frequently been spotted skulking around.

While J. K. Huysmans in his novel *La-Bas* exaggerated the number of Gilles's victims, his depiction underscores how heinous de Rais's crimes were. He asked, "How many children did he disembowel after deflowering them?…The text of the times enumerates between seven and eight hundred, but the estimate is inaccurate and seems over conservative. Entire regions were devastated.

The hamlet of Tiffauges had no more young men. La Suze was without male posterity. At Champtocé the whole foundation room of a tower was filled with corpses."[18]

* * *

When Gilles de Rais and his pack moved on from Champtocé to Machecoul Castle, his twenty-six-year-old valet, Henriet Griart, inadvertently delivered a victim to Gilles. The child, the brother-in-law of a town painter, hoped to become one of Gilles's choirboys. He met one of de Rais's requirements for his chorus; he was gorgeous, with long, black lashes framing grass-green eyes. So that Gilles could determine whether he also sang well, Henriet led the pretty one into de Rais's bedroom. Henriet then left for Nantes to transact some simple business for his lordship. When he returned three days later, he did not see the boy around the castle and made inquiries. Henriet expressed great surprise when de Sille told him Gilles had murdered the youngster.

Henriet approached de Rais, curious to find out why he destroyed the little one. As soon as they were alone, the former Marshal of France, with a warped smile, described his insane, psychopathic addiction. After learning of Gilles's destructive practices, Henriet expressed no horror, no astonishment, nor outrage, just like other participants who displayed only indifference to the killings. Perhaps Henriet was so weak-minded he could not comprehend Gilles's deviancy, could not understand the severity of de Rais's vice. Certainly he did not comprehend the depth of de Rais's mental instability. In any case, Henriet willingly promised he would remain closemouthed about the confidences his master divulged to him. He told de Rais's judges: "Gilles had (him) swear to reveal nothing of the secrets that he would make him privy to."[19] The oath, extracted from Henriet, was administered by Gilles himself the next night by candlelight as the two slinked behind the high stone altar in Machecoul's Trinity Church.

Henriet subsequently became an efficient procurer of children. He blithely found thirty-nine youths to satisfy de Rais, assisting in their murders as well.

De Rais's twenty-year-old retainer, Etienne Corrillaut, also took a vow on the Gospels to keep mum about his lordship's unusual behavior. When he was twelve years old, Gilles performed carnal acts upon this youngster, originally from Pouzauges, a territory which bordered Brittany. According to Corrillaut, in his testimony before the ecclesiastical court of Nantes, Gilles "lasciviously" violated him after Corrillaut came into his household. Like Gilles's other victims, Corrillaut was hung on a hook in de Rais's bedchamber until he was nearly unconscious. Thereafter Gilles engaged in his "abnormal lusts."

As de Rais finished sodomizing Corrillaut, he became possessed. With eyes flaming, Gilles screeched deliriously in an ecstatic rage, and raised the shining tip of his serrated dagger. He attempted to slash Corrillaut savagely. Petrified, Corrillaut could not scream because his suspension on the hook had made him temporarily speechless and weak. Still, he frantically tried to escape de Rais's sharp blade.

For some reason, Gilles de Sille intervened and saved Corrillaut by pulling de Rais off him. De Sille persuaded de Rais that Corrillaut was so good looking he would make an exceptional servant. De Rais remained transfixed, utterly stunned. Finally his face no longer contorted; his composure returned. He not only agreed to make the sinewy and stunning Corrillaut his page, but de Rais also continued to have sexual intercourse with him for many years. Like Henriet, this loopy young man, Corrillaut, did not fully understand Gilles's abnormalities even after de Rais revealed his obsessions. And like Henriet, who never expressed any judgment of Gilles subsequent to the disclosure, Corrillaut, still devoted to the former Marshal of France, acquired thirty-six children for him to rape and kill.

Well into Gilles's killing spree his brother, Rene de la Suze, along with other family members, seized the Champtocé and Ingrandes fortresses to prevent Gilles from selling them to Duke Jean V of Brittany. After their lengthy negotiations, de la Suze returned Champtocé and Ingrades to de Rais, stipulating he could dispose of the castles. But Gilles had already signed over Champtocé to the duke, and now thought the removal of the little corpses he had dumped there needed immediate attention. In his lucid moments, like many serial killers, de Rais still knew that what he was doing was wrong.

Corrillaut and Henriet, along with Gilles de Sille and two other henchmen, Hicquet de Bremont and Robin Romulart, removed the evidence, hidden in one of the rear towers at Champtocé. With de Sille acting as supervisor, Corrillaut and Romulart were lowered into the bottom of a desolate dungeon where the remains had been discarded.

In their statements during Gilles's trial, his accomplices could not remember the exact number of decomposed victims they discovered, although they both recalled that they found an identical number of skulls. It is possible they were prompted to give particular responses to solidify the case against the Baron de Rais; it is also possible that their answers were accurate.

"The witness (Henriet) and others counted them by the heads and by other means so that they could find out the number of bodies which had been thrown there..."[20]

"Having been asked how he (Corrillaut) and others ascertained the number of bodies, he answers that it was by the count of the heads which they made then, but he does not remember the exact number, except that he is sure that it was either thirty-six or forty-six."[21]

Making sure no evidence was left behind, Corrillaut and Romulart carefully placed the small corpses in sacks and secured them with ropes. Hicquet de Bremont, together with Henriet, pulled up the sacks and crammed them into three large chests.

Under the cloak of night the coffers were carried to a wooden boat moored in the willows growing on the bank of the Loire River, forming a natural hedge that concealed the group's furtive actions. The marshal stood watch as his men loaded the bodies onto the boat, then returned to the castle and turned it over to the duke's representatives.

Next, the gang silently journeyed westward. Gilles de Sille had wanted to simply fling the children's remains into the Loire, but de Rais refused. Thus, the boat transported them to the outskirts of Nantes where the chests containing the little corpses were removed and hastily placed in a horse-drawn cart for a bumpy voyage to Machecoul.

De Rais became agitated by the disposition of the skeletons. In a manic state, his chest aching, extremities tingling, convinced he was choking, he frantically implored God to pity him. Eventually, his panic attack passed and he calmed down, ordering a Mass to be sung for the eternal souls of the departed children. Soon after, Gilles's companions matter-of-factly scattered the children's ashes over the moat.

Roger de Bricqueville made sure he was not involved in the clandestine disposal of the bodies. Sensing the murders would be discovered, he now wanted to distance himself from Gilles and his other accomplices. De Bricqueville had decided he needed witnesses to prove he played no part in these illegal acts, and secretly brought two noble ladies into Machecoul Castle. Women of rank at that time enjoyed observing gruesome spectacles. Many spent their days attending hangings and floggings. Corporal punishment was another form of entertainment for the rich and for the rest of the medieval population.[22]

Wearing their elaborate samite costumes of silk and gold, they peeked through a crack in the wall and watched the morbid occurrences in Gilles's room. De Bricqueville pretended to be stupefied by what was occurring. He told the ladies to say nothing until he looked in to the matter. No one knows why the women never reported the incident. De Bricqueville kept silent, too, until many years later when he described the murders in detail to Gilles's son-in-law, Prigent de Coetivy, whose service he entered.

De Bricqueville was never arrested or tried for the serial killings; he had saved himself by deflecting guilt. Sure of his innocence, de Coetivy sent letters written by de Bricqueville to the King of France. De Bricqueville in these letters was determined to absolve himself and stated that when the murders occurred, "he was then a young squire of little understanding." He went on to write that his master, Gilles de Rais, "killed and put to death" many innocents, forcing de Briqueville to find children for him to sodomize.[23] De Briqueville also brought out his family's patriotism and his service to the king during the war with England. In a detailed analysis of Gilles de Rais, Abbot Bossard labeled de Bricqueville "odious" and a "coward," because he lied, and convinced de Rais's son-in-law of these lies; the trial documents clearly proved de Bricqueville an eager accomplice.[24]

However, de Bricqueville's correspondence with Charles VII described in detail de Rais's extensive crimes and perversities. While he omitted his own role in the murders, de Bricqueville's letters offer the only evidence supporting the accusations of murder, sodomy, and blasphemy brought against Gilles de Rais by the ecclesiastical and civil courts in Nantes.[25]

De Bricqueville's deception was so believable that he received the pardon he sought, letters of grace from Charles VII. (*Lettres de grace accordees par Charles VII a Roger de Bricqueville, le 24 mai, 1446.*)[26] Describing Prigent de Coetivy, who secured the pardon for de Bricqueville, George Bataille and Jacques Heers both called him self-serving, rapacious, and devoid of honor. De Coetivy appears to have admired those same qualities in de Bricqueville, as he went on to become such an integral part of the de Coetivy family that Marie de Rais took care of his children from time to time.

Prigent de Coetivy was a nobleman of Brittany, and a well-known admiral of France. In 1441, the year after Gilles's execution, he married twelve-year-old Marie de Rais, with the blessing of her family and Charles VII. Upon her father's death, Marie's estate was considerable enough that her mother was incapable of maintaining her trusteeship over it; when the Duke of Brittany decided to confiscate the remaining properties, de Rais's family contracted the marriage between Marie and de Coetivy. The marriage was never consummated, but the king offered de Coetivy, then his chamberlain, the opportunity to rehabilitate Gilles, granting him a writ to that effect. The family chose instead to support the plea for Gilles's insanity. After hearing the argument that de Rais suffered from a mental disorder, Charles seized Champtocé from the Duke of Brittany and gave de Coetivy title to the chateau and its lands. Less than ten years later, in 1450, de Coetivy died outside of Cherbourg when a shot from an English arquebus struck him down. Charles VII quickly arranged for Marie to wed one of her respected Laval cousins.

Unlike Roger de Bricqueville, the priest Eustache Blanchet, who introduced the conjuror Prelati to Gilles, was not privy to the murders. Yet the longer he stayed at Tiffauges, the more suspicious he became. Time and again he saw children led into Gilles's chambers who never reappeared. Eventually, he purposely picked a fight with Corrillaut, pretended to be upset by the confrontation, and promptly left Tiffauges. He moved to a village inn, about three miles away, located in a different province, about three miles away. For several weeks, de Rais tried unsuccessfully to persuade the priest to return to the castle.

Another lodger at the inn befriended Blanchet, and when he found out that the priest was acquainted with Gilles de Rais, he told him about the talk going around. De Rais, people said, had murdered many children, and written a manuscript about black magic with their blood. De Rais called upon the Devil as well, and worst of all, de Rais had eaten the flesh of the missing innocents. The greater part of northwestern France believed Gilles de Rais had snatched those missing children, killed them, and devoured them, and this was discussed openly everywhere but in Gilles's territories. All referred to him as the monstrous Bluebeard.

In the rambling deposition he would later make, Blanchet described this incident:

"And in the interim Jean Mercier, the castellan of La Roche-sur-Yon…came to lodge with the said Bouchard, whom the witness asked for news about the regions of Nantes and Clisson. The said Mercier responded that, according to public rumor spread in the aforesaid region and elsewhere, the said Gilles de Rais was killing a large number of children, and having them killed, and that he was writing a book in his own hand with their blood. And that, with this particular book, the said Gilles, the accused, would take all the fortresses he wanted; and that with this said book, thus written, nobody could harm him." [27]

When child snatching continued unabated and mounting circumstantial evidence pointed toward Gilles, he became fodder for many grim stories. Brought up on the folklore of werewolves, vampires, and hobgoblins, the superstitious throng started to accuse Gilles of being an ogre, a cannibal, a Devil worshiper, a grotesque fiend; he became the mythical Bluebeard, "outsized, monstrous." [28]

Unlike fantasies of werewolves and vampires, the stories about Gilles were true. He might not have been eating them, but de Rais was a deranged pedophile who tortured, sodomized, and murdered hundreds of children in frightful rituals. He also called upon the fearsome Belial to help remake his fortune. For centuries after his death, just the mention of Bluebeard's name terrified the residents of Brittany. Charles Perrault modeled his sixteenth-century fairy tale, *Bluebeard*, on Gilles de Rais. In Perrault's chilling, fictional work, Bluebeard kills eight wives behind his castle walls. De Rais's crimes were real, and far worse, and those living in Brittany were doing more than whispering in hushed voices at night. They already decided to bring their grievances and suspicions about de Rais to the Bishop of Nantes.

Blanchet had vowed not to go back to Tiffauges, and when the goldsmith, Jean Petit, came to the inn with an order from the marshal that Blanchet must return to the castle, the priest refused. He still cared enough about de Rais, though, to repeat the stories he had heard about Gilles to the goldsmith. He urged Petit to pass them along to the marshal and warn him, which Petit did. De Rais flew into a rage when he heard the goldsmith's account. Instead of thanking him for his information, Gilles hurled Petit into the dungeon with its big, iron door at St. Etienne-de-Mer-Morte, a remarkable fortress Gilles still owned. The marshal bellowed that Blanchet was a "vicious gossip, fertile with idle remarks, who would squeal about the murdered children."[29] De Rais could not understand that Blanchet was trying to protect him, and determined Blanchet was too much of a risk to be roaming about.

A few days after the goldsmith's confinement at Mer-Morte, where he almost died, de Sille, Corrillaut, and Henriet, along with other muscular henchmen, all armed, showed up at the inn. They seized Blanchet as the other lodgers looked on in terror, too frightened to come to his aid. The priest, now certain of savage reprisals by Gilles, pleaded not to be taken to St. Etienne de Mer-Morte; he was sure he would die there in the wet dungeon, probably of starvation. Blanchet persuaded them to take him to Machecoul instead. They agreed. Machecoul would be a livelier place to guard Blanchet, and de Rais would soon arrive, which meant sumptuous banquets at the castle. There, they tossed him into a remote, dilapidated house, with Francesco Prelati, Gilles's conjurer, and the Marquis de Ceva, another Italian in de Rais's hire, as his guards. Even though Prelati and de Ceva were inebriated most of the time, they kept Blanchet incommunicado; no one got to visit him.

After Machecoul, de Rais journeyed to Nantes, staying at his Hotel de la Suze. He hoped to sell his mansion to the rich chapter of clerics at the cathedral there. During this trip he succumbed to murderous impulses and methodically massacred eleven more children. Subsequently, Gilles traveled to Vannes, in order to obtain money from the Duke of Brittany, and to discuss the transfer of his Bourgneuf-en-Rais real estate. The duke invited de Rais to be his guest at his castle, but the marshal preferred to stay at a hostelry run by a holy order of monks where he could come and go as he pleased. Not only did de Rais try to conjure up Beelzebub in this sanctified house, but one of his past attendants, then the duke's choirmaster, also procured another innocent for de Rais to enjoy. The mutilated body and severed head of this lovely ten-year-old boy was dumped into a lavatory after Gilles sexually abused him. Henriet, according to his statement, experienced much "pain and difficulty sinking the body to the depths of the latrine."[30]

The atrocities continued; Gilles remained unconstrained. As he dutifully accompanied Jean V to Josselin, Henriet, now de Rais's chamberlain, found three boys for Gilles to brutalize. Then Gilles, stopped at Bourgneuf-en-Rais on his way back to Machecoul from his excursion to sell his properties. When a striking fifteen-year-old Breton with high cheekbones, Bernard le Camus, who came to Bourgneuf to learn French, disappeared out of his rented room, leaving his shoes and clothes behind, Bernard's innkeeper questioned Poitou and Henriet, whom he had seen with the youth. They responded with a standard response all of Gilles's accomplices repeatedly used: Lord de Rais had asked the youngster to be his page and accompany him to Machecoul Castle. Le Camus would be one of the marshal's last victims.

Marguerite Sorin, chambermaid to Bernard's innkeeper, later described what occurred, when the commissioners of the Duke of Brittany were looking into Gilles de Rais's crimes:

"...she and the said child (Bernard) being after supper in the house of the said Rodigo where they were playing together, the said Poitou appeared, who asked them whether they played like that together (often). They answered yes, after which he took the child aside, laying one hand on his shoulder and holding his hat in the other, and spoke to him in a voice so low that she could not hear. Then, having thus spoken, the said Poitou left. Immediately, the present witness asked the child what Poitou had said to him, who responded that he had not said a thing; a little while later the child told her that he wanted to go away, and asked her to take care and arrange his affairs; then he left, unwilling to tell her where he was going even though she insisted. He left his garment, his shoes, and his hood, going out in his cloak. Since then, she has neither seen him again nor had any news of him."[31]

Poitou (Corrillaut) would elaborate upon this abduction:

"...that during Pentecost in 1439, he, the witness, together with the said Henriet, took from Bourgneuf...a very beautiful adolescent, approximately fifteen years old, who was staying with a man named Rodigo; and they led him to the said Gilles who was then lodging with the Cordeliers of the same place, where the said Gilles committed and exercised his lusts on the said child, in the aforesaid execrable manner."[32]

He and Henriet killed the child, brought his remains to the castle of Machecoul and burned them in Gilles's bedroom.

During a repentant period, Gilles de Rais erected his lavish

Machecoul Foundation, hoping it would be a monument to his piety, and protect his soul from damnation. He named it the Holy Innocents after the children slaughtered by Herod in Bethlehem, without any sense of irony. The foundation, with its sumptuous ceremonies and pampered clergy, did not protect Gilles from the consequences of his transgressions, nor did his lachrymose confessions to his priest at Holy Trinity Church on Easter Sunday, March 27, 1440. The priest, Olivier de Ferrieres, could not divulge Gilles's horrifying secrets. But did he wonder what fiend stole the soul of Gilles de Rais?

* * *

Why did such a many-faceted individual become a psychopath? George Bataille, who put much thought into the nature of crime and transgression, ruled that Gilles simply wanted to kill. He emphatically stated: "This fatal need to kill, to kill without reason, which no words could clarify, which had possessed him as a gallop possesses an overexcited horse… It was not important to the guilty party to learn or reveal the origin of his crimes. These crimes had been what he himself inherently was, what he was deeply, tragically, so much so he thought of nothing else."[33] Dr. M. Hablin Smith, Medical Officer of H. M. Prison, Birmingham, England, held similar views. Writing in his foreward to A. L. Vincent's work on de Rais, he remarked that psychology "realizes that neither society nor the offender understands the causes of their action."[34]

Wyndam Lewis, a new recruit to Catholicism in the early part of the twentieth century, offered a startling, almost medieval observation. He felt Gilles was possessed by the Devil: "That is to say, the Marshal's little victims were not crudely butchered for the mere sake of shedding blood; they were made to serve their executioner's pleasure in many ingenious ways, such as could be derived only by a man literally possessed of the Devil."[35] He also blamed de Rais's accomplices for not attempting to control him. Instead, de Bricqueville and de Sille, he said, spurred Gilles on because they relished participating in the brutality of the murders.

But perhaps there was more. De Rais later revealed something about his own state of mind in his comments to one of his judges during his out of court confession. In great pain and in a voice that cut right through those present in his chamber, he admitted that no one on earth could fathom how he suffered from a mysterious curse that forced him to commit such acts of brutality. He did not know why he should be so punished.

Michelet, the French historian, wrote that because of the atrocities of the Hundred Years' War, the taste for blood was rampant. When there is madness in a country, in a land plagued by death, destruction, and misery, it bursts forth in its mentally ill. They expose the dislocation of the nation as they go berserk. Gilles's serial killing was an act of madness, a heinous crime with the barbarity of war turning this decorated soldier into a monster.

Here was a man who accomplished great feats, a man of heartrending complexity; a hero haunted by flashbacks who, like so many present-day warriors, became mentally unbalanced after a comrade was killed. This fabulously wealthy French aristocrat, this Marshal of France, this celebrated warrior, this Renaissance man, shocked his country with his extreme depravity. His pedophilia, his necrophilia, his narcissism all led to his violent end. But as previously discussed, Joan of Arc's death played the major part in de Rais's mental collapse. When he could not save her, his world fell apart. He began to exhibit wild mood fluctuations, far more extreme than those he manifested in his youth, with his fits of dark despondency, his displays of great egotistical excesses, vanity, and inhumanity. At times he believed the universe existed for his pleasure, that he was invincible, in control; he tested fate to its limits. Then he would become angry and irritable, and want to harm others. He had trouble concentrating; he feared for his safety, all painful traits manifested by someone with an unsound mind. His abuse of alcohol exacerbated his mood inconsistencies. Severe PTSD, from which Gilles presumably suffered, can put an individual at greater risk of developing other mental-health problems, such as a bipolar affliction, depression, an antisocial personality disorder, or all of these illnesses and more. Certainly his unstable mental condition triggered his covert psychopathy which resulted in sadistic serial murders.

There are no tidy solutions. All that can be said about Gilles de Rais is that his thirst for unspeakable violence became insatiable soon after he left the military. His delight in cruelty was not restricted to the perverse acts of his youth. Spurred on by his drinking partners, he now enjoyed inflicting intense pain and shedding blood, which aroused him. He preyed upon the most vulnerable, a trait common to many serial killers. The slaughter of children intertwined with his pedophilia and developed into an obsession. Similar to Corrillaut's deposition before the canonical court of Nantes, Gilles's manservant, Henriet, would remark that he repeatedly heard "Gilles, the accused, say that he was born under such a star that, in his view, nobody could know or understand the anomalies or illicit acts of which he was guilty."[36] Broken psychologically, this fallen warrior had nothing more to lose when he committed his crimes.

CHAPTER EIGHT

THE BRAZEN BLUNDER: ST. ETIENNE DE MER-MORTE

WHITSUNDAY, 1440, NEAR TEN THIRTY IN THE MORNING, THE entire population of St. Etienne de Mer-Morte celebrated the High Mass of Pentecost in the parish church. Communion was already over. Mass was almost completed. Suddenly the huge oak door to the church was flung open; the congregation heard the sound of armed men entering, the clink of their spurs. Then they caught sight of Gilles de Rais, the former Marshal of France, brandishing his double-sided axe as he barged in and came straight toward Jean le Ferron, who was near the chancel assisting with the Mass. The baron screamed "Rascal! You have beaten and robbed my men. Get out, get out of this church and I'll kill you dead!" Le Ferron, petrified, falling to his knees, asked for mercy. The marshal continued his tirade. He demanded that le Ferron leave the church. Four heavily armed bodyguards, including Gilles de Sille and the Marquis de Ceva, attempted to calm de Rais, but he paid no attention. In an even louder voice de Rais menaced le Ferron, "Out! Out! I'll kill you!" De Rais threatened to decapitate the trembling le Ferron on the spot if he did not leave the church. The congregation remained paralyzed. Speechless, the priest celebrating Mass stopped the Communion. (Then as today, a priest must finish his Mass in almost any circumstance.)

Le Ferron finally agreed to step outside. Gilles, still bristling, seized him by the neck. He then hauled le Ferron to the Castle of St. Etienne de Mer-Morte, where at sword's point the marshal ordered le Ferron to lower the drawbridge and hand over the keys to the fortification. Next de Rais dumped le Ferron and another attendant of the Duke of Brittany into the dungeon, where water dripped from the ceiling and made puddles on the stone floor. The fuming Gilles shoved the terrified men against the foundation with all his might. He ordered them manacled to the moldy walls and beaten, and left them there. (He had railed against his tutor, Michel de Fortenay, in a similar manner in his Machecoul prison.)

A decision against de Rais in a lawsuit precipitated his demented, uncontrollable rage. Thirty-five–year-old Gilles, ever short of funds and with de Bricqueville's consent, had sold the impressive Breton Castle along with its dependencies of St. Etienne de Mer-Morte to Geoffroy le Ferron, the new Treasurer of the Duchy of Brittany. He was the brother of Jean le Ferron, who was assisting at the Mass on Whitsunday. Soon after the documents were signed, Gilles de Rais decided he wanted the properties back. He learned that Geoffrey le Ferron had only acted as an intermediary for the Duke of Brittany, the beneficiary of the sale, transacted at a very low price. Gilles concluded the duke had cheated him. In anger and exasperation, he decided to retaliate against the duke by reclaiming the lands and kicking Jean V's representative out of Mer-Morte. He then intended to resell this valuable feudal estate.

Before Gilles initiated his plan, Geoffroy le Ferron, anticipating de Rais might attempt to take back Mer-Morte, brought a lawsuit against Gilles and won a judgment. De Rais was not permitted, under any circumstance, to reestablish ownership of Mer-

Morte. In addition, the verdict obligated Gilles to pay the cost of the suit, but he refused. Thinking himself invincible and above the law, he decided to settle the score as he had originally planned, by physically taking over the castle. He led sixty of his armed household troops to the outskirts of Mer-Morte on Whitsunday. These men remained in the woods ready to assist de Rais when he charged into the church.

Gilles de Rais's irresponsible actions along with the impoundment of St. Etienne de Mer-Morte led to his undoing. By bursting into a holy place of worship with a drawn weapon, Gilles committed a sacrilege against the Catholic Church, a capital offense. Moreover, his hostile gesture toward Jean le Ferron, the tonsured clerk who wore the habit of a minor Christian order, demonstrated de Rais's intent to kill a representative of the Church if he were not obeyed. On top of these infractions, de Rais disregarded clerical immunity when he intimidated le Ferron, throwing him into the Mer-Morte dungeon.

Gilles also committed three offenses against Duke Jean, his suzerain. The King and Dukes of France had recently issued a joint order: nobles could not conscript or use a military force without special permission from the Crown or the Dukes of France. This regal and ducal decree was initiated because rival lords had been using the confused state of the country to raid each other's properties, settling their disputes by force. Even the upright brother of the duke, Arthur de Richemont, as well as de Rais's cousin, the corpulent Georges de la Tremouille, benefited from the lack of central authority. Both conducted extensive private wars. To end the anarchy, the king and dukes attached severe penalties to the new law.

Gilles had not obtained Jean V's permission to lead his armed men into the Duchy of Brittany. To make matters worse, de Rais manhandled two of the duke's subjects, Jean le Ferron and the official the duke had specifically sent to Mer–Morte to prevent de Rais from collecting any taxes from the property. In addition, Gilles took over Mer-Morte by coercion when he imprisoned the two men.

Retribution came swiftly. Jean V called for the immediate release of the prisoners and the restoration of the fortress of St. Etienne de Mer-Morte to le Ferron. De Rais was assessed fifty thousand gold crowns for his insubordination. In defiance of the duke's order, de Rais sent le Ferron and the ducal functionary to his Machecoul prison. He then gave instructions that anybody Jean V sent to Mer-Morte to collect the fine was to be beaten, then shoved off the castle drawbridge. When the duke learned of de Rais's disobedience, he deployed half of a brigade to recapture St. Etienne de Mer-Morte and arrest his vassal, Gilles de Rais. Before the duke's soldiers arrived, de Rais fled to Machecoul, then to Tiffauges, carting his prisoners along with him, out of Jean V's territory.

Infuriated, the duke declared Gilles a rebel, and Jean appealed to Charles VII to dispatch a military force to Tiffauges. The king quickly agreed, a rare departure from his usual dawdling, and sent his constable, Arthur de Richemont, the duke's brother, to lead the sizeable force.

Years earlier, when de Rais had frequented the Chinon court, Arthur de Richemont had taken notice of de Rais because of his seriousness, determination, and military acumen. He became an admirer of the young man. Later, he and de Rais had ridden to battle together with Joan of Arc. Now a close confidant of the king's, the moral and energetic Count de Richemont approached Tiffauges Castle ready to capture it along with the once-revered warrior, de Rais. The instant Gilles saw de Richemont and the large force behind him, he relented. He set the captives free and promised to pay the fine as soon as he could. De Rais embraced de Richemont affectionately before he left Tiffauges. De Richemont must have found Gilles sadly changed.

Supposing his civil disputes over, de Rais visited Jean V at

Vannes and then Josselin as a gesture of reconciliation. Determined to display a semblance of his past opulence, Gilles brought along his entire, splendidly dressed choir; they sang for the duke at Vannes on a sun-bathed Christmas morning.

Before the journey, which also brought more guileless victims his way, Gilles discussed the trip with Francesco Prelati. Like many afflicted with PTSD, Gilles feared for his life. A worried Gilles asked Prelati to consult with Satan to find out whether the forthcoming excursion might be dangerous to him. After a short interval, Francesco happily informed de Rais that he had held a successful conversation with Barron, the Devil's demon. Prelati told Gilles how the erotic Barron, enveloped in a filmy, violet-silk mantle, had assured him the voyage would be uneventful. A delighted Gilles looked forward to meeting the enticing Barron in the very near future; perhaps Prelati could arrange a visit when he returned from Vannes. But for now, with a guarantee of safety, Gilles departed for the capital of Brittany with his still-colossal entourage.

Oblivious to the riptide of troubles teeming around him, de Rais continued his daily bacchanals after his voyage to Vannes. He did not realize that his followers had begun to talk about his secrets, that many of his most trusted accomplices, including Gilles de Sille (never to be seen again) and Roger de Bricqueville, had wriggled away like worms, taking a fortune gleaned from the marshal with them. Prelati, who did not have the wherewithal to race back to Italy, rented a room which he shared with Blanchet in one of the poorer quarters of Machecoul. He assumed no one would be clever enough to discover him there.

Also unbeknownst to de Rais, the Bishop of Nantes, Jean de Malestroit, had made inquiries throughout his diocese in Brittany before the fracas at St. Etienne de Mer-Morte. He wanted to find out if there was any truth to the rumors and complaints that had surfaced about Gilles's shocking behavior. At first the bishop had paid scant attention to the dark allegations about his Lordship de Rais, brought to him by those living on de Retz lands. He thought they must be no more than the ridiculous gossip of the jealous and superstitious masses. When the nephew of the Prior of Chemere disappeared from the de Rais household, however, where he had been sent to learn how to sing, the bishop had second thoughts. At that point, though, the allegations were based on hearsay, and without sufficient direct information, the bishop felt he could not arraign Gilles de Rais, a man of such high rank.[1]

The transgressions against the Catholic Church at Mer-Morte afforded the bishop the opportunity to conduct a more thorough investigation of de Rais. Ecclesiastical law dictated that he travel to areas where there were claims that a crime had been committed. If there was evidence of criminal behavior, the bishop could begin proceedings against the wrongdoer.

With his officials at his side, Jean de Malestroit listened in horror to the people who came forward wanting to testify. The bereft felt secure divulging their nightmare to the bishop, representing God's goodness, God's justice on earth. Long, pitiful laments spilled out; the accumulated testimony of the stories he heard grew more and more shocking. There were grieving peasants whose priests vouched for their character; weeping laborers; toothless grandfathers and grandmothers; others belonging to religious houses; laymen of gravity. All told the same wrenching account of losing their children and pointed to de Rais as the culprit. Attention focused on Gilles's henchmen. When a child disappeared, one of de Rais's staff was always lurking nearby.

The bishop appointed deputy commissioners who obtained more complaints and recorded all the depositions. Among the many who testified were: Agathe, the wife of Denis de Lemion; the widow of the late Regnaud Donete; Jeanne, the wife of Guibelet Delit; Jean Hubert and his wife; Jeanne, the wife of Jean Darel; the widow of the stonecutter Yvon Kerguen; Tiphaine, the wife of

Eonnet Le Charpentier, butcher; the wife of Pierre Couperie, Jean Magnet. Their mourning echoed that of hundreds of others. The commission compiled more than enough evidence to make out a prima facie case against the Baron de Rais.

Just a month after the incidents at St. Etienne de Mer-Morte, as the baron was murdering another victim at Vannes, de Malestroit issued a formal indictment, a Declaration of Infamy, against de Rais. The bishop alleged in the declaration, the first paper forming part of the ecclesiastical record, that Baron Gilles de Rais, a subject and "justicable," first took advantage of and then killed a number of children. The indictment continued "...we have become convinced that the nobleman, Milord Gilles de Rais ...with certain accomplices did cut the throats, kill, and heinously massacre many young and innocent boys, that he did practice with these children unnatural lust and the vice of sodomy..." The bishop further stated in this declaration that de Rais performed "the dreadful invocation of demons, did sacrifice to and make pacts with the latter, and did perpetrate other enormous crimes within the limits of our jurisdiction." [2]

It was not clear how many ecclesiastics and dignitaries received this indictment, as the inquiry was still ongoing, with the prosecution searching for more corroboration. The French historian, Emile Gabory, who studied the life of Gilles de Rais, believed this document was not circulated widely out of fear of de Rais's reaction to it. However, the bishop presented his initial findings to Duke Jean, and also sent these papers on to the king. If the duke refused to put a man of Gilles's rank and stature on trial, de Malestroit trusted that Charles VII would feel compelled to take action after he read the indictment.

He need not have worried; the duke embraced the bishop's declaration and rhapsodized over the idea of Gilles's arrest. He demonstrated little outrage regarding the suspected murders, but according to an agreement between the duke and Gilles, de Rais had the option of redeeming his properties if he came up with the money within a six-year period. If de Rais could be successfully prosecuted, that would never happen.

After reading the Declaration of Infamy, Jean V immediately began his own inquiry. He designated Pierre de l'Hopital, Chancellor of Brittany, to head up this investigation, titled an *Inquest by the Commissioners of the Duke of Brittany*. The duke's commissioners interviewed witnesses from all over Brittany. His emissaries heard dreadful accounts regarding Gilles de Rais, similar to those Bishop de Malestroit had collected: "…the said plaintiffs lost their children and that they suppose that the said Lord and his men snatched them, or caused them to be taken, and put them to death"; "The said plaintiffs requested sorrowfully, with tears and loud cries, that justice be done… and the said inquiries having proven the guilt of Gilles de Rais, the latter" be "charged with the death of these small children and many others…"[3]

The evidence from both the bishop's and the duke's inquiries, some given by the same complainants, became overwhelming. The duke requested the prosecution of de Rais in a civil court. Certain of his vassal's crimes and a forthcoming guilty verdict at the trial, Jean V signed an order that took all of Gilles's lands away from him three weeks before any formal proceedings began. The properties transferred to Jean V's eldest son. The duke's rapacity was evident; he was eager for his share of the marshal's immense holdings. He also acted to prevent the de Rais family from claiming Gilles's properties by force at the end of the hearings.

Because of his past alliance with the English, the duke wondered how the King of France would react to the arrest of Gilles; de Rais was Charles's vassal as well as his own. On advice from Arthur de Richemont, the duke's brother and counselor to the king, Jean V moved the proceedings along. He sent his captain, Jean Labbe, with a heavily armed troop to Machecoul on September 14, 1440. He carried a ducal warrant for the imprisonment of Gilles de Rais and his main accomplices, Gilles de Sille and Roger de Bricqueville.

Six weeks after his initial charge against de Rais, Jean de Malestroit circulated a second indictment to all clergy, notaries, and anyone else who dealt with legal matters in his diocese, as canon law demanded. It called for the apprehension of Baron de Rais, ordering him to appear before ecclesiastical officials in Nantes on September 19, 1440. Therefore, a notary of the Catholic Church accompanied the duke's men to Machecoul Castle.

The group arrived at the drawbridge of Machecoul near daybreak, the outline of the somber castle barely discernible. Captain Labbe ordered a trumpet to sound, and a porter to shout that "Baron Gilles de Rais must give the duke's men access to the castle: the past Marshal of France, de Rais, was under arrest; the ecclesiastical and civil courts called for his lordship to answer to his wrongdoings forthwith in Nantes."

A long silence ensued. No one dared move; no one knew what to expect. The sun remained low on the horizon. Finally Labbe had the trumpeter blow again, louder. Again, there was no response from inside the castle. Jean V's soldiers feared the celebrated Marshal of France might be staging a defense. They felt the unholy atmosphere of the stark, silent stronghold; they remained uneasy in the frigid dawn. As it grew lighter, they became a little more courageous. The trumpet sounded forcefully for a third time, while the military assemblage glanced around. A grey-plumed sparrow hawk, with its short wings and long tail, swooped down among them, to carry off a rabbit. The bird's sudden assault on its struggling prey jangled their nerves.

Then, after a seemingly interminable period, the heavy, wooden castle gate opened very slowly. The duke's soldiers stood battle ready, but did not dare advance. Without warning, de Rais appeared. He was alone, bedecked in Cyprus gold, fine periwinkle silks, long fuchsia hose. He gallantly led the group inside. At first he joked with the captain of the troop about his name. *L'abbe* means a priest in French; "Labbe," Gilles said. "I myself want to become a monk." Gilles laughed about his predicament until the official of the ecclesiastical court served Gilles with the summons explaining the gravity of the citation, and mandating his appearance before the bishop's tribunal. The baron became more serious, and in his most grandiose manner, directed Henriet to give the man some gold pieces.[4]

If the Lord Gilles de Rais resisted arrest, he would appear guilty of serious crimes; such conduct would provide a reason to act against him. Fleeing the country meant the confiscation of his remaining fortune. His only recourse was to submit to the authorities. He supposed that a trial would involve accusations of heresy and sacrilege, and while these were serious offenses, he could make reparations without losing his freedom or ruining his reputation. He permitted the castle and its grounds to be searched, knowing Labbe's men would find nothing. But a bloody shirt and the carbonized remains of one of Gilles's last victims were found in a nearby dwelling used by his servants. These discoveries were further evidence of his misdeeds.

Gilles, as well as his only attendants present in the castle, Corrillaut and Henriet, were arrested and transported to Nantes that evening. Frightened by the prospect of what awaited him, Henriet considered killing himself.

Nantes, together with its surrounding villages, vibrated with the news of the baron's arrest. People lined the roadway, watching agape as Gilles, Baron de Rais, Lord of Laval, Marshal of France, Lieutenant of Brittany, the companion of Joan of Arc and Constable de Richemont, the friend of Charles VII, was marched into town in chains. He still carried himself haughtily, with disdain.

Befitting his stature, Marshal de Rais was locked up in a well-lighted, comfortable chamber in one of the upper stories of the fortress in Nantes, the castle of the Dukes of Brittany. He received all the privileges accorded a prisoner of rank. Henriet's and Corrillaut's confinement was far less elegant. They were thrown into putrescent prison cells riddled with bedbugs, rodents, and excrement. Within days, other accomplices were arrested and brought to the same disgusting place.

CHAPTER NINE

TRIAL: THE ADMINISTRATION OF MEDIEVAL JUSTICE

THE BARON DE RAIS'S TRIALS WERE SHOCKING, SENSATIONAL. TWO tribunals presided in judgment over the former Marshal of France. The ecclesiastical court was headed by two men: Jean de Malestroit, Bishop of Nantes, a close relative and counsel to the Duke of Brittany; at his side was Jean Blouyn, the forty-year-old Vice-Inquisitor for the Inquisition in France. The charges for which his Lordship de Rais was arrested fell primarily within the jurisdiction of this court. The tribunal convened so as to make a judgment regarding the invocation of demons, sorcery, and sodomy performed by Gilles de Rais, and to study the affair of Saint Etienne de Mer-Morte for violations against the Church.

The ecclesiastical court's decision influenced the outcome of the civil tribunal headed by Pierre de l'Hopital, Chancellor of Brittany, and one of the most powerful officers of the duke. This secular court would determine whether Gilles de Rais was guilty of the most serious crime of murdering children, and whether de Rais revolted against Duke Jean of Brittany when he captured Mer-

Morte. The two tribunals were conducted at the same time. The ecclesiastical trial lasted over a month; the civil trial took place within forty-eight hours.

While the Duke of Brittany coveted Gilles's property, and the courts were packed with his confidants, the judges and the prosecution behaved impeccably. Unlike the trial of Joan of Arc, Gilles de Rais received utmost consideration. Since the late thirteenth century, the obligation to protect a suspect and ensure a fair trail had been followed in French courts. However, in Inquisitorial tribunals searching out heretics, the accused was culpable until proven innocent, the antithesis of due process and contrary to any concept of a defendant's rights. Even though de Rais received great respect, as the proceedings progressed, it became apparent they were conducted in order to obtain a guilty plea.

The dry, legal phraseology of the courts still conveyed the horror of the atrocities his lordship committed. In its fifteenth Article of Accusation, the ecclesiastical court alleged that:

> "… boys and girls had been seized, had had their throats cut in a cruel manner, had been butchered, then dismembered and cremated and had been otherwise treated cruelly and shamefully by Gilles de Rais, the defendant; …and…Gilles de Rais, the accused, had damnably sacrificed the bodies of these innocents to demons; …that he had horribly and vilely committed the unnatural sin of sodomy with these children, as many boys as girls, sometimes while they were living, at others after the death of these innocent children and sometimes while they were expiring, and that he abused both sexes; …disdaining the girls' natural vessel…"[1]

The number of victims was debatable. The canonical prosecutor, in the twenty-third Article of the Bill of Indictment, asserted that Gilles de Rais had murdered 140 or more children, boys as well as girls. The secular court stated that:

"The said Lord took many young children, and had them taken, not merely ten, nor twenty, but thirty, forty, fifty, sixty, one hundred, two hundred and more, such that the exact number can not be certified; he had sexual intercourse with them, taking pleasure unnaturally and committing the detestable sin of sodomy, the horror and abomination of every good Catholic..."[2]

The manner in which the children all died was similar and bestial. Gilles's crimes were considered so horrendous that his confession and the depositions of his accomplices were transcribed at a later date from the French into Latin, a language that only the most educated of that time understood. In his letter summoning de Rais before the ecclesiastical tribunal, Jean de Malestroit alluded to these transpositions. He stated that de Rais's sins against nature were so "abominable" and "execrable" they would only be expounded upon in Latin at an appropriate time.

Interrogated apart, the testimony of Henriet and Corrillaut was similar. The official account reflects that they talked freely, without coercion, or torture, referred to as "the Question." These frightful methods had been devised to make the recalcitrant acknowledge his or her guilt. Generally, torture was only held out as a threat at first. If the accused did not own up to his evil deeds, he was led to see the instruments to be used, including the rack, the wheel, the pillory, screws, and scourges. Joan of Arc had been brought to the torture chamber at the Rouen Castle to observe such tools so that she would admit to her supposed heresy. In case that sight did not result in a confession, the prisoner was stripped. For one still unwilling to talk, he would be bound to the rack nude. If the desired response was still not forthcoming, a winch on the rack was rotated manually, stretching the defendant's limbs, beginning the process that would tear his muscles apart and snap his bones.

Water torture, today known as waterboarding, was another means of obtaining an admission of guilt. The "...prisoner was tied to a ladder that was sloped downward, so that the head was lower than the feet. The head was held fast in position by a metal band, twigs were placed in the nostrils, and ropes winched tightly around his appendages. The mouth was forced open with a metal piece and a cloth placed over the mouth. Then a pitcher of water was brought, and poured over the cloth. With each swallow, the cloth was drawn deeper into the throat, until in gagging and choking the victim nearly asphyxiated. The terror of suffocation was extreme, and the process was repeated endlessly, bloating the body grotesquely until the victim was ready to confess. If the suspect was still uncooperative, his body was turned over, causing unimaginable pain to the heart and lungs." [3]

The strappado was another deadly Inquisitorial device. If a prisoner would not talk, his hands were tied behind his back and attached to a pulley. He would be yanked off the ground and then dropped halfway down with a jerk. This method of persuasion resulted in brutal internal injuries.

Breaking on the wheel proved fatal. A prisoner's arm and legs were placed across two heavy beams, his bones broken with a large hammer. Alternatively, each limb would be fractured multiple times, with the mangled appendages from either ordeal threaded through the spokes of a large wheel. The wheel was hoisted on the top of a tall pole so that birds could eat the accused alive.

The record of de Rais's ecclesiastical trial concealed the chilling terror of these Inquisitional tools available to the court, but everyone living at that time knew of their existence. Neither Henriet nor Corrillaut wanted to endure the suffering caused by these mechanisms. Accordingly, they willingly detailed the crimes Gilles de Rais had committed, though they could not remember all the children they had seized for him. They described graphic, grisly, gut-wrenching incidents. Etienne Corrillaut in his deposition elaborated about how children were hung by the neck, with ropes or cords, on pegs or hooks, so that they could not cry out.

Henriet Griart outlined the manner in which the children died, which included severing their heads, lopping off their appendages, slitting their throats, and breaking their necks using a cudgel. He further described how de Rais would cut the vein in the neck so that youngsters bled. He told the court that sometimes Gilles would then sit on the bellies of the innocents while they died, and carefully observe them. He would sodomize his victims at different times, before beginning to kill them, as he killed them, and after they were dead...as long as the "bodies were still warm."[4]

Henriet and Corrillaut also gave incriminating evidence against Gilles de Sille and Roger de Bricqueville, who fled Machecoul and vanished before they could be arrested. They implicated some of Gilles's other hangers-on as well, who were detained.

The tribunal forced Francesco Prelati, Gilles's lover and spurious conjuror, to testify. To save his own neck, he offered considerable evidence against his former employer, which placed the marshal in a perilous situation. Prelati disavowed planning the horrors that went on in de Rais's castles, skillfully portraying himself as the obedient servant of a deranged tyrant. Prelati, though, could not dodge the charge of practicing alchemy and sorcery, of which he had been accused. The verbose priest, Eustace Blanchet, jabbered away, corroborating this fact in his lengthy, discursive deposition. After he admitted his guilt, Prelati then boasted to the ecclesiastical court that he could successfully conjure and speak to Barron, the Devil's alluring demon. He even hinted he could bring forth this sexy apparition for the judges if they were so inclined.

Possibly, out of arrogance, he thought his intelligence superior to that of the judges. By artful deception, he thought he could tantalize the tribunal, which he must have believed to be gullible and sex-starved, like de Rais. The judges would pardon him so that he could bring forth his erotic spirit for them. Instead the tribunal sentenced Prelati to life in an ecclesiastical prison, as his clerk's tonsure necessitated, for committing heresy, sacrilege, diabolism, and apostasy. He was not charged with murder. However, his sentence involved a bread and water diet and periodical scourgings.

A few months after this sentence, Rene, Duke of Anjou, an ardent admirer of alchemists, who had listened to some of Prelatis's testimony at de Rais's trial, facilitated Prelate's escape from jail and protected him. Undoubtedly Prelati impressed the duke with his claims that he was just one step away from producing gold, for Rene appointed Prelati to the lucrative post of Governor of La Roche-sur-Yon some time later. There, Prelati imprisoned Geoffrey le Ferron, Treasurer of Brittany, when he passed through the village, and held him for ransom. Gilles's "elegant" Francois believed Ferron was responsible for his misfortune, which he saw as beginning with the incident at Mer-Morte. Upon his release, Ferron retaliated. He in turn had Prelati arrested and called upon the Privy Council, the supreme court of France at that time, to render justice by hanging him. The council put an end to Prelati's nimble-wittedness.

Since Blanchet was not accused of being an accessory to the murders, and neither Gilles nor his accomplices mentioned the paunchy priest in their descriptions of their crimes, he did not receive a prison sentence. But he was banished from France for life, and fined three hundred gold crowns for his association with de Rais. No one knows where he spent the rest of his days.

The depositions of many other witnesses who lost loved ones shed light on how the simple folk of that era lived. Beggars, bakers, cobblers, furriers, grape pickers, haberdashers, shoemakers, tailors, and farmers testified. With their shoulders heaving in grief, they wept as they described what happened to their children.

"Guillaume Hilairet and his wife Jeanne, living at Machecoul, declare a twelve-year-old child, the son of Jean Jeudon, was living with" them "to learn the furrier's trade. And the said Guillaume Hiliaret declares that in the presence of Roger de Bricqueville, around the aforesaid time, Gilles de Sille requested that he lend him his said valet to carry a message to the said castle of Machecoul, and the said Hilairet lent him the valet and sent him to the said castle." He and his wife "had not seen the said helper again nor heard that anyone else had seen him. And much later that same day the said Guillaume Hilairet asked the said Sille and Bricqueville what had become of his said valet: they told him that they did not know, unless he had had to go to Tiffauges, and into such a place, the said Sille said, where thieves had snatched him to make him a page."[5]

"Andre Barbe, shoemaker, living at Machecoul, deposes under oath that since Easter he has heard that the son of Georges Le Barbier of Machecoul had been lost, that on a certain day he had been seen picking apples behind Rondeau's house and that he had never been seen since; certain neighbors of his had told Barbier and his wife that they ought to watch over their child, who was at risk of being snatched, and they were frightened about him; in fact the witness had even been at Saint-Jean-d'Angely, and someone asked him where he was from, and when he responded that he was from Machecoul that person was shocked, telling him that they ate little children there."[6]

"Jean Roussin, of Machecoul, declares that about nine years previously a child of his, nine years old, was to watch the animals one particular day, on which day he never returned home; and he and his wife were greatly astonished by this, not knowing what happened to him. And thereafter, after the complaints and outcry of his wife and family, two of his neighbors, who are now deceased, told him that they had seen Gilles de Sille, wearing a tunic, his face thinly veiled, speaking with the said child, and that the said child left for the castle, going through the back gate. What is more, he says his child, who was living close to the castle, knew the said Gilles de Sille well and occasionally carried milk to the castle for those who wanted it. And he declares that he has heard no more talk of his said child since then." [7]

Malnourished, the people craved food. At first a loaf of bread, brought home to parents as a gift from his lordship, made them think their ragamuffin youngster would be eating and living well. He had been asked to join the La Suze household of the mighty Baron de Rais. Their delight changed to despair when they never saw their son again. The wife of a weaver in Nantes stated that her eighteen-year-old nephew, living with her and her husband, sometimes frequented La Suze. One evening, about a year and a half prior to her testimony, while Lord de Rais was resident in his mansion, one of his servants requested that the nephew take him to the house of the Archdeacon of Merles. He also promised her a loaf of bread if she agreed, which she did. She stated she never received the bread, and the child vanished.

Money proved to be an incentive, too. Peronne Loessart gave up her handsome son to the marshal's men for the price of a new dress. Upset that they cheated her out of the full amount promised, she stated that Corrillaut only brought her four crowns for the dress. She told him twenty ecus were missing, which he denied, saying they had settled upon four crowns.

The lower classes were not supposed to speak to the nobility. Nevertheless, the same mother had second thoughts about letting her son go to live with de Rais after his servants tricked her. She confronted de Rais as he led her boy away on a little pony. So that the woman could hear his retort but not addressing her, Gilles remarked to his men that the child would be well cared for. He found the young one to be "as beautiful as an angel," the terminology he used to describe his dead victims. The mother's fears were not baseless, for Gilles murdered the boy at Machecoul

Castle. A few weeks later, Peronne Loessart spotted another young one on the same animal her son had ridden. She asked de Rais's henchmen what happened to her child. They said he drowned in the Loire when strong crosswinds caused him to fall off the pony into the river.

Perrine Rondeau, the wife of the innkeeper Clement, clutched herself as she spoke to the Court about the senseless brutality of two of de Rais's hangers-on who lodged with her. While she grieved for her husband, who had just received extreme unction, Prelati, Gilles's "decorous" Francesco, and the Marquis de Cerva kicked her in the lower back, then punched her. They next tried to throw her down a staircase, irritated that she had been in their chamber. They showered her with insults as one carried her by her feet, the other by her shoulders to the staircase and sent her flying. Her old nurse who lived with her, hearing the commotion, dashed to save her from the fall and caught her by her dress.

* * *

In its first preliminary encounter with de Rais, the court disguised its ambition to prosecute him to the absolute measure of the law, to use torture if necessary to obtain a guilty plea. Gilles at this point believed the only charge against him involved heresy. He thought he would be able to vindicate himself. However, the accusation of heresy mandated the inclusion of the Vicar of the Inquisition in the tribunal, for "… according to the apostle Paul, the fault of heresy spreads like cancer and secretly kills the simple unless it is weeded out by the diligent hoe of the inquisition…"[8] With heresy implied, the accused also forfeited the privilege of having an attorney present during the procedure.

At first de Rais agreed to appear before the Vicar of the French Inquisition as well as the rest of the ecclesiastical court. The marshal even bragged he was ready to prove his innocence. He did not take the proceedings seriously, blithely refusing the right to establish a defense. When the canonical court adjourned, Gilles spent time in the well-appointed quarters accorded him in the new tower of the Castle of Nantes. He heard Mass from his own household priest. (Joan of Arc would have savored this privilege, which had been denied her.) Nevertheless, the tribunal forbade de Rais from taking the sacraments or drinking Hypocras. Gilbert Proteau, in his novel, *Gilles de Rais*, painted him as an alcoholic, imagining that his sudden, forced withdrawal from the huge daily quantities of Hypocras he consumed caused him to act irrationally at his inquiry.

The ecclesiastical trial against Gilles de Rais began at nine o'clock in the morning, the hour of Terce—the third hour of the canonical day—on October 8, 1440. This first court session, open to the public, took place in the grand upper hall in the Castle of Nantes. A large, dark room, its walls were of heavy stone, and the rounded arches and massive vaulting were supported by thick Romanesque pillars. Amidst those soaring columns, Jean de Malestroit, "mitred, wearing his purple robes and purple ring, sat on a raised throne."[9] The Vice-Inquisitor of France, the bishops, and their assessors also sat in a row of tall chairs on the long, raised dais. Notaries and secretaries took their places below the bishops. The public prosecutor's table faced to the right of the notaries, with the space directly before the tribunal assigned to de Rais and his guards. Behind de Rais two-thirds of the hall held the spectators eager to hear the trial.

Every available space filled up long before the appointed hour. Peasants, artisans, gentry, nobility, burgesses, nuns, priests, and monks jammed into the courtroom. Many of the uneducated Bretons present could not speak Latin or French, but they understood the importance of the event at hand.

An unpleasant shock awaited de Rais. The ecclesiastical court, drawing upon its own report as well as accounts from the civil court, which had established an independent inquiry, had accumulated a great mass of evidence regarding his abnormal conduct. Thus, the Act of Accusation brought forth that day included murder and offenses against nature. These crimes would be formally presented in writing in forty-nine articles of a Bill of Indictment at a later session. On October 8, though, the entire accusation was read in Latin, then French, with de Rais expected to respond to the many charges.

Listening to the accusation, de Rais realized he had been tricked when the judges implied he would only be indicted for committing heresy. Furious at being hoodwinked, he was determined not to let the prosecution have its way. He declined to answer the charges, thus disrupting the hearing. De Rais also attempted to stall the proceedings as he hoped the King of France might rescue him by disbanding the tribunal because of Gilles's rank and his record of bravery defending his country.

In a most insolent, disdainful manner, de Rais insisted on being examined by his peers. The defendant declared he was appealing the hearings, for he questioned the legal competence of the present judges. He also wished to void his initial consent to be tried. The Bishop of Nantes overruled his demand, deeming it frivolous because it was not presented in writing and the nature of the case was very serious. The Church along with the state, not the accused, appointed judges, de Malestroit instructed the prisoner. Surly, Gilles rudely refused to take an oath to tell the truth.

The court adjourned upon this dramatic note, with the ecclesiastical tribunal withdrawing for refreshments. (Custom dictated that its members fast from sunset of the previous day in order to have clear minds when they presided over a case.) De Rais was sent back to his spacious chambers. In his depressing solitude, he pondered whether to admit to his guilt and beg for mercy from the court or shamelessly deny the charges. Should he use his nobility as a defense? He did not know how much the judges knew.

The Palace of the Bouffay, where the civil court convened,

stood one hundred yards away from the Castle of Nantes. De Rais acted imperiously there too, three days after his clash with the ecclesiastical tribunal. First the baron urged the judges to make haste with their proceedings, since he wanted to give himself over to the service of God. As the court digested this statement, he proclaimed he wanted to donate a large amount of money to a particular church in Nantes and most of his belongings to the poor. The dour judges remained unimpressed. Scowling, the president of the civil tribunal, Pierre de l'Hopital, told de Rais that while he reflected upon his soul, he still had to answer to the justice of man; the civil hearings regarding de Rais's infractions would continue. After this short exchange, guards shuffled Gilles back to his living quarters.

The ecclesiastical court sat two days later to proceed with its trial and render a verdict. A priest from the Church of St. Nicholas of Nantes, Guillaume Chapeillon, became the promoter or public prosecutor of the case. Besides the Bishop of Nantes and the Vice-Inquisitor for France, the tribunal consisted of the Bishops of Le Mans, Saint Lo, and Saint Brieuc. Pierre de l'Hopital represented the secular authorities.

Throngs curious to lay eyes upon the prisoner jammed the approaches to the Castle of Nantes. The trial of such a famous man was astonishing, his appearance high drama. Gilles de Rais did not disappoint his audience. As he came in to the immense courtroom, there was a dim hum that turned into an anxious silence.[10] The Lord de Rais, head held high, arrogantly acknowledged his grim-faced judges while he awed the spectators, dressing for the occasion from head to toe in white. He wore tight-fitting, oyster-white stockings, a snow-white silk shirt, an eggshell-white vest, flake-white boots. His pearl-white silk doublet was embroidered with gold stars. His cap had ermine borders, the sign of a very high feudal lord of Brittany. A dagger in a red velvet sheath hung from a scarlet sash tied around his waist. He exhibited all his military and official orders on his breast. A gold chain around his neck displayed a reliquary.

The proceedings began with the written charges. They comprised the forty-nine articles of the Bill of Indictment, which characterized his lordship as a murderer, a heretic, an apostate, a magician, a sorcerer, a seer, a cutter of throats of innocents, a sodomite, an evoker of evil spirits, a diviner and a violator of the Church, a criminal, a backslider, and an idolater.

The tribunal, the prisoner, the tightly packed crowd of spectators, heard the entire document. Articles fifteen through forty-nine detailed the crimes of which Gilles was accused. Very specific, they covered the abduction and murder of the children. Article fifteen stated that:

> "...the prosecutor says and intends to prove...Gilles de Rais, touched by an evil spirit and unmindful of his salvation, seized, killed and murderously slit the throats of many innocent boys and girls, which things he himself did as often as he had his accomplices do them; that he caused them to be seized, murdered and also to have their throats cut; that he had the bodies of these innocents burned and reduced to ashes..."[11]

This particular charge also alleged Gilles de Rais had evoked demons and made sacrifices to evil spirits.

The next two accusations dealt with the explicit invocations of the Devil on Gilles's behalf. These took place over five years in a basement room in the Tiffauges Castle or in a grove near the castle. The indictment singled out Prelati, since he boasted of his skill in the forbidden art of geomancy. It also mentioned Jean de la Riviere, as well as other magicians and evokers of demons "who made divinations or conjurations and assisted de Rais in entering into a pact with evil spirits in order to acquire knowledge, power and wealth."

Articles seventeen, eighteen, nineteen, and twenty-six described the places where the invocations took place: in a meadow about a quarter of a league from the fortress at Tiffauges; in a meadow near the walled town of Josselin; in the house of the Franciscans at Bourgneuf-en-Retz; in the La Suze house in the city of Nantes; at the inn with the sign of the golden Cross in Orleans; as well as in the castles at Machecoul and Tiffauges.

The thirtieth count linked Gilles's sin of sodomy to his vast consumption of fine wines and to his gluttony. It stated that he daily ate rich foods and drank strong wines, mainly Hypocras, claret, and other drinks, in order to become more sexually stimulated and to enjoy performing sodomy "fully" on boys and girls.

Article twenty-seven considered Gilles's transgressions of sodomy and murder to be "cruel and horrible." It revealed that he committed these "abominable" sins before and after the death of his victims, "which shames the heavens." He abused the children unnaturally in order to satisfy "in a damnable manner his illicit carnal desires."[12] The twenty-ninth accusation asserted that the sin of sodomy caused "earthquakes, famines and plagues...here on earth according to the disposition of divine justice."[13]

Displaying no emotion as he read all forty-nine articles, the prosecutor, a skilled canon lawyer, now turned to the judges and forcefully demanded that Gilles de Rais be found guilty of the crimes in the indictment, be excommunicated, be punished as the law and canonical sanctions required.

De Rais's composure left him. When it was his time to respond, he again refused to submit to the authority of the tribunal. Shaking his fists, he screamed that he was insulted to have to appear before a court of "simoniacs and ribalds." Two court officials tried to restrain him, but he broke lose from them. His tantrum continued as he hurled further abuse. The bishop and the vice-inquisitor were unfit to judge him. He stomped his feet. He would rather be hung by a rope than tolerate breathing in the same room with them. De Rais's voice filled the courtroom. The high walls amplified and distorted his words. He spun towards Pierre de l'Hopital of the secular court. Raising his left hand above his head, then smashing it down on his thigh, Gilles berated de l'Hopital for permitting the ecclesiastical judges to make such infamous accusations. Still fuming, the Baron de Rais, arms flailing, eyes flashing, raged at Jean de Malestroit: "I will do nothing for you as Bishop of Nantes."[14]

Total disorder reigned in the high hall; wild confusion gripped the spectators. Finally, there was silence. Master Chapeillon, an experienced prosecutor, rose. In a measured voice, he calmly requested that the tribunal inquire whether the accused wished to respond to the charges orally or in writing. De Malestroit asked Gilles four times to answer to the charges read to him in French and Latin by the prosecution. The nobleman Gilles ignored the bishop. Still hoping to block the way in which the proceedings were heading, de Rais continued his diatribe.

"I tell you again, I have nothing to say! Don't I know the Catholic Faith from end to end? Do those who say I have betrayed it know who I am? I am a perfect Christian and good Catholic!"[15]

The court held the prisoner in contempt, immediately excommunicating him. The tribunal also denied Gilles's immediate verbal appeal of the sentence.

During the Middle Ages, all Christians feared excommunication. Those who transgressed presumed they would be condemned forever, going straight to Hell when they died. The medieval Church devised a fiery, detailed catalogue of endless torments and punishments for the damned. They lived "in flaming fire,"[16] "half-starved" in pits, or were "chained on the burning lake" of Hell, "...there to converse with everlasting groans, unrespited, unpitied, unreprieved."[17]

Article twenty-seven in the canonical trial of de Rais expressly mentioned Hell. "As often as someone usurps the Creator's office by destroying a creature, the angels do not desist from shouting out in the presence of the Divine Judge until punishment is inflicted upon the murderer, who will burn forever in eternal fire."[18]

Here on earth, the Church did not permit the censured to attend services, be married, be buried, or receive the last sacraments. No one could have anything to do with those cut off from the Catholic rites. If anyone helped the excommunicated, he or she too would be completely removed from the community and be doomed for eternity. In the Middle Ages, community in Europe meant Christianity, which meant most of society. Thus this stiff sentence immeasurably changed the Baron Gilles de Rais.

De Rais behaved very differently two days later at his fourth appearance before the tribunal. Perhaps he might have become more lucid, since he had been forbidden to drink alcoholic beverages. In any case, clothed in somber garb, Gilles tearfully accepted the jurisdiction of the court with downcast eyes. He beseeched the judges, attired in their richly embroidered golden copes, to pardon his insults and quash the Writ of Excommunication, which they did. He readily took the oath to tell the truth, granting the court authority over him. He admitted to all the crimes of which he had been charged, except he refused to acknowledge that he invoked demons.

While the court swore in Baron de Rais, the prosecutor produced Gilles's valets, Henriet and Corrillaut; the priest, Blanchet; the conjurer, Prelati; and the procuress, Perrine Martin (La Meffray), as witnesses. All took the oath to tell the truth. The prisoner consented to abide by their depositions, along with those of any other witness for the prosecution. He agreed to accept further accusations put forward by the court.

As jailors led his accomplices away, the Baron de Rais fell to his knees, sobbing. Clasping his hands and swaying backward and forward, he implored the bishop and the vice-inquisitor to lift the sentence of excommunication upon him in writing. The court had no idea that the man writhing in front of them had mentally disintegrated. Instead, the judges saw a Christian in pain, stricken by conscience and were overjoyed to help him. They instantly agreed to de Rais's wish, even though the sentence had already been removed orally. The court subsequently adjourned.

The ecclesiastical tribunal reconvened a few days later, again at the hour of Terce, in the great upper hall of the Castle of Nantes. The bishop and the Vicar of the Inquisition, at the prosecutor's request, asked Gilles if he had any objections to the indictment. He had none and consented to the publication of all of the testimony. The marshal's acknowledgement amounted to a confession. Nevertheless, since de Rais did not know what his accomplices had divulged, his avowal departed from ordinary procedure. The prosecutor continued to follow the rules established by the court. He requested that the judges apply torture in order to assure the sincerity of Gilles's admission, and to learn more about the crimes of the accused. The judges conferred with experts in Church affairs, including lawyers versed in canonical procedure. All agreed that torture should be used.

The tribunal adjourned, but assembled again in the lower hall of the castle at nine o'clock the next morning and sent for the prisoner. As soon as he entered the room, the nobleman Gilles pleaded with the judges to put off the torture. He would confess forthwith; however, he insisted that his full disclosure be heard far from the dreaded chamber. The judges agreed.

That same day, at two o'clock, the baron detailed all his crimes in a precise and lengthy statement to the Bishop of Saint Brieuc and to Pierre de l'Hopital in his sumptuous living quarters in the tower. He admitted to the horrors of which he had been accused. Totally overwhelmed, totally perplexed by the marshal's staggering testimony, given in Latin, de l'Hopital pressed him. He tried to ascertain why, how, and where the baron conjured up such unfathomable atrocities. De Rais, reading de l'Hopital's expression of disbelief, now responded in French. He persisted in claiming he alone thought up the acts, purely for his own pleasure, for his carnal delight. As both his valets stated in their deposition, de Rais now told de l'Hopital he believed he had been born under the curse of the blackest of stars. It maliciously influenced him, made him commit undertakings devoid of morality and beyond reason. In great pain and in a voice that cut right through those present in his chamber, he admitted that "No one in this world is capable of understanding my life's deeds; no one on this earth is able to act as I did."[19] No one on earth at that time could fathom that he suffered from an antisocial personality disorder which compelled him to commit his serial killings; no one understood how PTSD or some other mental illness had destroyed his life.

Six prison attendants escorted Prelati, the conjuror of Satan and Gilles's lover, into the marshal's chamber. As soon as de Rais saw Prelati, he started to weep. After de Rais had controlled himself, the two gave the same account of the invocations made to the Devil. They also detailed the offering of a little baby's hand, eyes, and heart. At a recent hearing, Prelati had acknowledged taking part in the offering, but continued to insist he had nothing to do with the murders. Disgusted with their testimony l'Hopital ordered Prelati taken away. Gilles embraced his co-conspirator and the object of his desire, passionately kissing Prelati on the mouth. Gilles bade Prelati a mawkish farewell and began to sob again.

"Good-bye, Francis, my friend! Never again shall we see each other in this world; I pray that God gives you plenty of patience and understanding, and be sure, provided you have plenty of patience and trust in God, we will meet again in the great joy of paradise! Pray to God for me, and I will pray for you!"[20]

While considered extrajudicial, de Rais's avowal to Pierre de l'Hopital satisfied the judges. They did not mention torture again.

The next day Gilles gave his judicial confession to the tribunal.

After its transcription, men-at-arms ushered him into the courtroom. He dressed appropriately for the proceedings in an all black ensemble; ink-black fur trimmed his ornate, corbeau-damask doublet; a rich blue-black velvet hood rested below his shoulders. As daylight disappeared from the small panes of leaded-glass windows in the courtroom, the judges commanded the former Marshal of France to proclaim his guilt. Thereupon Gilles de Rais read his public testimony, the culmination of his trial, to the immense crowd that had gathered in the late afternoon at the hour of Vespers.

De Rais began speaking tearfully in French, his voice very weak. The packed gathering, straining to hear the nobleman, listened in stunned silence. With chilling precision he traced his tortures, sexual violations, and murders. He admitted that he committed these offenses solely for his evil pleasure and evil delight, in accordance with his imagination. No one had urged him to commit these heinous acts. His murderous impluses started at the fortress of Champtocé, the year his grandfather died, the year he returned from military service. He said he killed a large number of children at the castle.

De Rais refined his previous testimony, his tale of horror. He offered more specifics regarding the various kinds of abuse the children suffered. He could not recall the exact tally of all his victims, even though he volunteered graphic remembrances of the lurid murders. The audience, appalled, listened intently to the various tortures he and his henchmen applied to the victims: amputating or separating heads from bodies with daggers and knives, striking heads with violent blows of a club or some very sharp instrument, binding other victims and hanging them from a portico on an iron hook or spike so that they would be strangled or languish there. He named those who participated: Gilles de Sille, Roger de Briqueville, Henriet, Poitou, Rossignol, little Robin, and a few others.

Gilles then confessed that he sodomized these children, sometimes before, sometimes during, and sometimes after their deaths. He further baffled the spectators when he said that while the children were languishing, he took pleasure in sitting on their bellies and watching them die. He told these spectators, already aghast at his comments, that he even laughed about the children's suffering with Corrillaut and Henriet. He kissed those already dead and liked to decide which of them had the most beautiful head. He also enjoyed opening their bodies or having them opened so that he could look at their internal organs.

At the end of his confession, including admitting to the evocation of demons, which he had previously refused to acknowledge, and the sacrilege at Mer-Morte, he urged the people, especially the churchmen, "who were present in great number," to revere the Church. Had he not remained faithful to the Church, he stated, the Devil would have stolen his soul because of the enormity of his misdeeds and sins.

De Rais spoke to all the parents in the great hall with intense emotion. He told them to be strict, to bring up their children with virtue, with religion. They should not follow the example of his youth, when he went unchecked as he wallowed in luxury and idleness. He attributed his sins to gluttonous eating along with intemperate drinking, which spurred him on to commit every unimaginable, illicit act. He exhorted fathers to dress their children modestly and not tolerate laziness. He noted that laziness as well as excessive eating and drinking caused many sins. He emphasized that his laziness, his insatiable desire for delicacies, and the frequent consumption of mulled wines kept him perpetually excited and led to the perpetration of his crimes.

Gilles's avowal conformed to the ecclesiastical court's explanation for his perversions in its Articles of Accusation. His out-of-court revelation to Pierre de l'Hopital exposed a man poised on a knife's edge between sanity and insanity. It pointed to deeper and more complex psychological factors at work than indolence and heavy eating and drinking. It portrayed a man felled by deep mental anguish, a decorated soldier shattered by the trauma he experienced in combat, which led him to commit unimaginable psychopathic acts.

Gilles de Rais's confession paralyzed the assemblage. Even the judges and priests listened with incredulity. Gilles's admission that killing children gave him more pleasure than having sex with them stupefied the audience. During the most demonic part of de Rais's disclosure, the Bishop of Nantes rose, crossed himself with his right hand, then covered the face of Christ on the crucifix behind him.

After his testimony, de Rais wept uncontrollably. He asked for pardon from God and for charity in the prayers of his victims' parents. His supplications made him a fellow sinner who needed help. Fifteenth-century Christians believed that the worst transgressor could receive God's mercy if he truly repented. Gilles's contrition was accepted as his ultimate transformation from an evildoer to one who would be with God. There was no mention of his insanity. The Bishop of Nantes embraced de Rais after his passionate outburst. He told de Rais he hoped the Almighty might be pacified by Gilles's remorse, that his tears might purify his soul. De Rais's visible suffering moved the entire room. Caught in the spirit of the Lord, all knelt to pray.

It is not known whether Gilles de Rais truly felt guilt in his heart or whether like some other serial killers who have been apprehended, his confession was more calculated. Possibly he still was capable of understanding the sorrow, the misery that gnawed at the hearts of families who lost little ones. Or perhaps he cunningly crafted and uttered platitudes of the times to play on the sympathies of the court, thus softening his fall from grace, averting a condemnation. His admission could have simply eased his own guilty conscience.

Nevertheless, confession was Gilles de Rais's method of influencing how the court would determine his fate. He used abject remorse to gain sympathy from the Church, from God, from the duke, from the populace, from his accomplices. As will be seen, his perceived penitence was so persuasive that the court overturned his sentence of excommunication and even permitted him to direct his own execution.[21] Not unlike his theatrical ventures, a large audience would attend this dramatic event.

October 25, onlookers again crammed into the great upper hall of the castle. In a quiet, flat voice, the prosecutor asked the Bishop of Nantes and the Vicar of the Inquisition to conclude the trial, to render a verdict "immediately" against the Lord Baron Gilles de Rais. The court first considered and diligently examined all of the records, arguments, letters, minutes, proceedings, confessions of Gilles, depositions of witnesses, and any other documents they had obtained.

The tribunal found the prisoner guilty of heresy, apostasy, the invocation of demons. He was also convicted of performing sodomy on children, as well as violating ecclesiastical immunity. The court excommunicated de Rais once again. However, the judges instantly lifted this last sentence, admitting Gilles de Rais back into the Church. They granted his request for permission to confess. Scribes recorded the verdict. The trial ended.

* * *

Gilles de Rais faced the civil authorities that same evening. The enormous hall in the Bouffay, where the secular court sat, overflowed with spectators as the sun set. They came from Nantes, from the countryside, on foot, in carts, by horseback. Peasants, gentry, nobility stuffed themselves into the oppressive stone room. Duke Jean V attended. Some of the Baron de Rais's noble kin watched the trial, though not his brother or his estranged wife.

While the ecclesiastical court had been in session, the civil authorities waded through the charges of murder and rebellion by de Rais against his suzerain, the Duke of Brittany. Pierre de l'Hopital directed the inquiry with eighty witnesses testifying, most giving painful accounts of the disappearance of their children. The civil proceedings were conducted in French, with a synopsis of Gilles's final confession to the ecclesiastical court also offered as evidence.

In an effort to appear independent, not just a rubber stamp of the ecclesiastical judges, the civil court appointed a lawyer, Henri Mechinot, to make a plea on Gilles's behalf. De Rais was not present at the proceedings. He stayed in his chambers reading from his *Book of Hours*, one of the finest manuscripts he brought with him from his library at Machecoul. The *Book of Hours*, a popular prayer book in the Middle Ages, offered stunning, illuminated images and a stirring religious text devoted to the Virgin Mary.

De Rais's defense attorney faced a herculean task as he attempted to prove the past Marshal of France had become mentally unsound. He tried to convince the court that Gilles was crazy, that only an insane person would have done the things he did. This heroic warrior had snapped, Mechinot said, no longer remaining the captain of his soul. The nobleman could not be held accountable for his pride nor for the inner demons that surrounded his psyche. After his fervid argument, its psychological insight remarkable in the fifteenth century, Mechinot asked for leniency for his client.

The civil judges paid no attention to Mechinot's entreaty. A unanimous guilty verdict had been a forgone conclusion. Possibly Mechinot's argument had also been ignored because there was great unease about madmen at that time. (Before insane asylums existed, lunatics, if their families could not take care of them, were gotten rid of by putting them on vessels to sail the seas for years in ships filled with "fools.") In any case, the judges did not consider Gilles mentally ill. Convinced that he had been possessed

(Grandfather de Craon had been similarly persuaded), they felt justified sentencing de Rais to death for the murder of the numerous innocents. The court only disagreed on how to carry out the sentence. A lengthy debate ensued, with some on the panel pressing for de Rais's decapitation. Finally it was decided that the nobleman be hanged and burned. The order was confirmed in the *Records of Gilles de Rais's Final Days*. A scribe further wrote: "So that he might beg God's mercy and prepare to die soundly with numerous regrets for having committed the said crimes, the said Gilles would be executed the following day at eleven o'clock."[22] In addition, a fine of 500,000 gold crowns was awarded Duke Jean for Gilles's insurrection stemming from his unlawful, armed attack on Saint Etienne de Mer-Morte.

Pierre de l'Hopital informed Gilles of the court's decision. The marshal received the verdict calmly and thanked de l'Hopital. Possibly, after his wrenching confession, Gilles was at peace for the first time in many years. De Rais had three requests: that Henriet and Corrillaut, already sentenced to death by the civil court, be executed with him so that they would not think they alone paid for his crimes; that his body be taken out of the flames before he was reduced to ashes (according to doctrine, this allowed the possibility of resurrection on the final Day of Judgment) and be buried in the Carmelite Church in Nantes, a choice resting place for the nobility and the dukes of Brittany; and that the Bishop of Nantes order a general procession of citizens to pray for his soul before his demise. His wishes were all granted, as the scribe noted in the *Records*, specifying that because of his profound contrition the president, de l'Hopital, acceded to his requests.

No one of political or social prominence attempted to rescue de Rais. His relatives never petitioned Charles VII. So easily persuaded by others, the king was not counseled to save his onetime marshal, for Gilles de Rais's deeds had made France weep.

* * *

Hooded priests in black, white, grey, and brown robes emerged from the Castle of Nantes at the hour of Terce reciting psalms for the dying. In the bleak, chill morning, they solemnly walked behind a very big, ebony crucifix, four to five abreast, holding flickering candles. Nuns and monks wended their way behind them, chanting penitential songs: "*Domine, Deus meus, in conspectu tuo viam meam.*" "Direct, O Lord, my God, my way in thy sight."[23] The townsfolk of Nantes as well as a multitude from the country-side followed, intoning dirgelike prayers in their own tongue. If he heard the laments, it is possible de Rais might have enjoyed the antiphonal music filling the streets.

The somber funeral procession slowly crossed a bridge spanning the muddy Loire River and reached a large meadow on the other side. On that fall day, October 26, 1440, an enormous assemblage, including the silent, inscrutable Duke of Brittany, his entourage, judges from the two tribunals, nobility, and simple people gathered for the execution of Baron Gilles de Rais, who had just turned thirty-six that month. The whole city, awash with pity, comradeship, Christian piety, and beneficence, flocked to the tract of grassland not far from the bridge. Curious as well, all watched dumbfounded as a heavy guard brought de Rais there in chains, along with Henriet and Corrillaut, taken from their dirty cells. The route took them past the marshal's treasured property, the Hotel de la Suze, near the cathedral.

Three high gibbets had been erected above three unlit pyres of brushwood. This backdrop, nowhere near as grand as de Rais's theatrical productions, proved more riveting. Genuflecting, Baron de Rais prayed nonstop during the few moments left him. As the final preparations began, Gilles gave encouragement to his accomplices. He told them God in his infinite goodness would pardon sin if the sinner was repentant. "And they ought very much to desire to be out of this world, where there was nothing but misery, so as to enter into eternal glory."[24] A scribe recorded these remarks in *The Records of Gilles de Rais's Final Days*. Henriet and Poitou tearfully promised their master they would rely on God's mercy. They in turn reassured de Rais.

On his knees again, Gilles asked for God's leniency. He stood and addressed the crowd shivering in the cold. With outstretched arms, the Baron de Rais begged for forgiveness. He crossed himself. Then he gave his soul to the apostles, St. James and St. Michael, as his heroine, Joan of Arc, did before she was burned at the stake. De Rais gripped his hands together tightly, bent his head, and prayed to God once more.

Then Gilles signaled that he was ready to die. The hangman motioned to the onetime Marshal of France, who nodded and approached the gibbet, erect like a soldier. As iron-grey clouds concealed the sun, he climbed the ladder to a tall stool where an attendant bound his hands behind his back. The hangman adjusted the noose of rope he placed around de Rais's neck. The funeral pyre was lit, rapidly becoming intense. The stool was taken away and Gilles de Rais dropped many feet as the rope tightened around his neck. His agony was short. He died quickly.

As flames from the dry branches engulfed de Rais, his rope caught fire, dropping him into the burning blaze. In recognition of de Rais's full confession, the order to reduce him to ashes had been rescinded. Six women from his extended family and six nuns wearing immaculate white habits were able to snatch his body from the fire, wash it, and place it in a closed casket. They subsequently transported his remains in a cart to the eminent Carmelite Church where, as hundreds of candles glowed on the altar, they assisted with his internment. He rested next to the past dukes of Brittany.

Thirty-six years before, church bells had pealed with joy at Gilles's christening; now cathedral bells tolled slowly, signifying his death. All who witnessed Lord de Rais's demise began to sing the mournful "*Dies Irae*," a hymn used for the departed, describing the Day of Judgement. While the three funeral pyres continued to smolder, workers threw the ashes of Henriet and Corrillaut, ordinary reprobates, hung and burned, into the wind.

* * *

Baron Gilles de Rais's trial astonished those who lived in fifteenth-century France. That a man of such power could be sentenced for crimes against God and the people was unheard of; that a wealthy, esteemed feudal aristocrat, from such a lofty family, could be found guilty by the Church because of testimony given by simple folk was unthinkable. God and justice had prevailed. Hateful feelings against the wicked nobleman evaporated. Moved by medieval charity, the humble did not gloat over the grand lord's death. Rather, in keeping with Catholic morality of the time, the people rejoiced. They cried and blessed de Rais, who showed remorse, for his soul would not be damned to roam in Hell eternally. Gilles's ultimate contrition transformed him from a sinner to one who would be with God.

Gilles de Rais's execution by the banks of the amber-colored Loire made an unimaginable impression on the crowd. Many with tears in their eyes prayed vehemently and fasted for three days, according to custom, for the salvation of the heinous, terrifying Bluebeard, the murderer of hundreds of their children.

* * *

Because of the Christian piety de Rais displayed at the end of his life, Bishop Jean de Malestroit, conforming to the wishes of Gilles's daughter, authorized the erection of a memorial to commemorate the site where he died. It consisted of a tall crucifix with three religious figures—Mary; Gilles's patron, Saint Gilles; and Saint Laud of Coutances—resting at its base. The statue, known as Our Lady of the Milkmaker, La Vierge Cree-Lait, became a place where pregnant women from all over Brittany came to pray for good nourishment for their unborn children. That a monster who committed infanticide could be so sanctified seems ironic, but to these women, that was not who Gilles was. To these women, Gilles only existed as Gilles the Pentinent, Gilles the Saved, Gilles the Exemplar, who could intercede for them with Heaven. Bluebeard was a different character.

EPILOGUE

GILLES DE RAIS'S DEATH ON THE SCAFFOLD WAS WARRANTED. As he admitted to Pierre de l'Hopital in his out-of-court confession, "I've told you...enough to kill ten thousand men."[1] This errant warrior, with his melancholy visions of despair, became a fiend, intoxicated, like many psychopaths, by the sense, sound, and touch of pure evil. He gleefully slaughtered innumerable children as his grip on reality grew weaker.

Descendants of de Rais still agonize over his murders and do not want to be reminded of the sordid details surrounding the life of this serial killer. Distantly joined to Bluebeard by marriage, this author tried to probe de Rais's kinsman. Polite, accomplished, strikingly handsome, some with cobalt-black hair, they remain reticent; they run away when asked to divulge any facts they alone might be privy to regarding Bluebeard, or feign to know nothing about his life.

Despite his family's taciturnity, the legend of Gilles de Rais has been kept alive in France. His crimes still have the power to appall. Nevertheless, citizens of France today who ogle the crumbling remains of Bluebeard's castles and demonstrate outrage about his bloody acts are not profoundly affected by Gilles's monstrous misdeeds; many other atrocities that have occurred in France and around the globe since then are much more present to them. Until the end of the nineteenth century, that was not the case. Folk in

Brittany and the neighboring Vendee lived in fear of Bluebeard. Gilles de Rais bequeathed such a dreadful legacy in that part of France that the very mention of his name made the hair on the back of necks stand up. He controlled them from the grave, for they thought he might rise up out of his tomb and snatch them away. In 1885 Abbot Bossard wrote:

> "Four centuries separate Gilles de Rais from us: the people who suffered such cruelty by this man still recall without interruption the places where he committed his crimes. What vivid memories the populations of Tiffauges, Pouzauges, Nantes, Champtocé, Pornic, Bourgneuf and Machecoul preserve of this beast of extermination...Their recitations of him are unanimous. There is not a mother, not a nurse, who does not know where Bluebeard lived... how he committed his crimes. For the populace, the terrible baron still exists today (but) he does not look like Gilles de Rais...instead he possesses the somber, legendary, depraved physiognomy of the grotesque Bluebeard."[2]

The world recognizes the Marquis de Sade as the father of cruelty, of perversion. The term "sadism" is derived from his name to evoke licentiousness. This bisexual aristocrat lived a salacious, libertine existence during the French Revolution, then the Reign of Terror, when he carnally and physically abused employees of both genders on a regular basis, as well as prostitutes he procured. On a few occasions he was arrested for sodomy. While the Marquis de Sade receives instant acknowledgement, few can identify his predecessor, that trailblazer of savagery and sexual transgression, Baron Gilles de Rais. De Sade never validated de Rais as a role model, perhaps because de Sade did not kill his victims. Except in France, De Rais abides in relative obscurity, though his sins remain some of the most odious in the history of mankind. Today in America, for example, the public thinks of swashbuckling pirates of the Caribbean when Bluebeard's name is mentioned. They are more familiar with and affected by the bloodthirsty acts of their own numerous serial killers: John Wayne Gacy, Ted Bundy, Charles Manson, Jeffrey Dahmer, Donald Harvey, and Richard Ramirez, to name a few.

From time to time within France uncertainties about Gilles de Rais's guilt arise. Voltaire as well as the Benedictine Monks of Saint-Maur, highly respected for their devout lives and their extensive activity in the field of literature, wondered about the legitimacy of the verdict against Gilles. They argued that the nobleman de Rais associated himself with magicians and diviners who fabricated the horrors he could never have committed.

The French archaeologist, Salomon Reinach, also questioned de Rais's culpability. In the early part of the twentieth century he posited in *Cultes, Mythes et Religions* that the judicial errors in the Dreyfus Affair which occurred in the late nineteenth century paralleled those committed during the trial of Gilles de Rais in the fifteenth century. Alfred Dreyfus, a French artillery officer of Jewish descent, was dismissed from the army and sentenced to Devil's Island for life, charged with selling military secrets to Germany. (The French used the notorious Devil's Island located in French Guiana to house political prisoners because of its unpleasant climate. Few survived its hot, wet weather. Most contracted malaria or other tropical fevers and died.) Dreyfus's case was reopened when some of the papers in evidence against him proved to be forgeries. His supporters, including Emile Zola, demanded a new judicial examination. But the feeling in the army against Jews remained so bitter that a second trial proved a mockery; testimony favorable to Dreyfus was barred. A guilty verdict was again returned. Champions of justice, in France and other countries, protested the unfair decision. Finally the case was reviewed by the highest French court. Declared innocent, Dreyfus was reinstated as a major in the French army. Reinach claimed that the documents against the Marshal of France, Baron de Rais, had likewise been falsified.

Serious historians, including Georges Bataille and Jacques Heers, who studied the transcripts of both the canonical and secular courts (Reinach only read the ecclesiastical documents) disagreed with Mr. Reinach's conclusion about the outcome of the case. The distinguished scholar, Reginald Hyatt, while translating the de Rais trials from the old French and Latin into English in *Laughter For The Devil*, also decided that the facts of Gilles's crimes were established in the documents of his trials.

The French writer from the Vendee, Joseph Rouille, wondered whether all 110 of the individuals offering sworn statements to the canonical court about the disappearance of children could have been bribed to lie. Rouille further argued that de Rais had ample opportunity to declare his innocence before the large crowd that gathered to witness his demise. Instead, as he looked at the hangman, de Rais begged God to forgive him for his crimes in a loud voice. Rouille concluded if the de Rais family had objected, the outcome of his trial would have been thrown into doubt. Not a single relative uttered a peep. When Gilles's brother, Rene de la Suze, wrote *Memory of the heirs* twenty years after the trial so that Charles VII would permit him to recoup the de Rais inheritance, he made reference to de Rais's irresponsibility, his prodigality, his repentance at his death, but he never spoke about Gilles's innocence.[3]

Michelet, the noted expert on the Middle Ages who resided in Nantes in the nineteenth century, studiously reviewed both canonical and secular documents relating to Gilles's as well.

De Rais lived in a brutal, unsettling time. He was part of the passion, the drama, the horror which took place in fifteenth-century France. He engaged in the country's wars, theatrical events, religious pageantry, and chicanery. De Rais, like so many of the nobility, participated in the life and death upheavals of that era, and in the greed, betrayal, and murders, seeking greater prestige as well as possessions. These desires outweighed the need to act chivalrously, to behave decently, with de Rais's own demented massacres reflecting the worst of France's deep pathologies. At the beginning of, and well into the fifteenth century, the nation remained ruptured, because of, among other things:

The Hundred Years' War continuing, with the French rapidly losing their land to the English, who subjugated them unsparingly;

The Duke of Burgundy assassinating his uncle, the Duke of Orleans, younger brother of mad King Charles VI, in order to rule France and turn the country over to the English; Orleans's and Burgundy's followers consequently unleashing a brutal civil war;

Queen Isabelle of France arranging for the death of two of her sons, heirs to the throne, and exhibiting no guilt after their extermination;

The Duke of Brittany, Charles VII's brother-in-law, often changing his allegiance between England and France, depending on which country he believed would win the Hundred Years' War;

De Rais's cousin, George de la Tremouille, killing the Dauphin's favorite chancellor so that he could assume that position and personally benefit from the advice he gave the Dauphin;

The man she helped to anoint king standing silently by as Joan of Arc, the savior of France, burned at the stake because a suspicious Catholic Church in league with the English enemy wanted her dead.

During his short, tragic existence, Gilles de Rais came in contact with many of the above personalities, participating in their bloody, ruthless conflicts, which they equated to games, albeit deadly ones. De Rais easily inhabited this privileged feudal universe submerged in war. Until he went crazy, his values, supported by a tradition of violence, remained on par with those of his compatriots. He earned a reputation as a courageous, fearless warrior, an outstanding commander, surpassing many other knights because he craved the adrenaline produced in warfare and performed brilliantly in combat. His fame spread even after his death. Others would have parlayed the glory he originally won as a soldier into something more. Instead, his success drove him to exercise an immoderation that ruined him. Thus he differed from other gallants in that he remained a man prone to excess, not only in his battles, but also in his luxury, his ostentation...and then in his drinking, his sex, his crimes, his repentance—telltale signs of some mental disorder, perhaps PTSD, which exacerbated his latent psychopathy.

With his inheritance and mind rapidly drifting away, avaricious nobles, dukes, clergy, family, and household retainers rushed to take advantage of de Rais's desperation. But they did not accuse de Rais of murdering innocents. Most did not know of his crimes. Only his close associates, many being his bedfellows, participated in his slaughter; they kept silent about his iniquity for a long time, because they depended on his largesse. If the nobility had suspected Gilles of a few murders, they would not have been concerned. Savagery played too great a part in all of their lives. Furthermore, they considered common children and their glum-eyed adult relatives subordinate, one step above chattel.

At first, even the Bishop of Nantes, Jean de Malestroit, perceived as the Holiest of the Holy by the humble, did not take seriously the simple people's complaints about de Rais. His sacrilege against the Church at Saint Etienne de Mer-Morte forced the bishop to conduct further hearings regarding the conduct of de Rais. The astonished bishop listened to the multitudinous grievances coming from the so-called invisible folk. Their overwhelming testimony of the staggering horror that struck them, so poignantly described to de Malestroit, could not be ignored, despite the presumed aristocratic immunity of that day. Thus it turned out that public rumor instigated by the plain folk, those faceless masses disdained by the nobles, brought Gilles de Rais down.

Then, just as incredibly, those same, regular people who thought of de Rais as a monster asked God to forgive him once he tearfully apologized for his transgressions during his moving trial.

Jacques Heers acknowledged the difficulty for modern-day readers in understanding such unbounded faith in God's love from those who had been so wronged. Present beliefs must be suspended, he suggested. Abbot Bossard concurred:

"Strange morals of that time...By a change which seems impossible to us, the same people who reviled (de Rais)...all of a sudden began to pray for the Christian and no longer saw him as their mortal enemy, but as a fallen brother who sincerely repented his crimes."[4]

George Bataille pointed out:

> "What gripes us is the compassion. It seems that this criminal moved his audience to compassion; in part by reason of his nobility and...on account of the piety which Gilles de Rais gave proof of during (his) last moments."[5]

In the *Record of Gilles de Rais's Final Days*, the diligent scribe who chronicled de Rais's death, like those who witnessed his hanging, also believed in his transformation. He wrote: "Gilles de Rais died in this state of contrition."[6]

Some writers admonish the plain people for caring about the redemption of a lost, depraved soul more than they did for their dead children. Possibly those observations are true. But because of Baron de Rais's power, these so called "commonplace boors" that the aristocracy disdained would never have dared seek out the Bishop of Nantes if they had not been desperate. They felt compelled to tell the Bishop their woeful stories about the loss of so many of their children, and accuse Gilles de Rais of their abduction.

Reginald Hyatte, in *Laughter For The Devil*, offered a perceptive analysis of what transpired:

> "If the judges and others at Gilles's trials seem moved by his contrition and appear to believe in his ultimate salvation, it is certainly because the role he played so well in public conformed to popular morality and theater....Gilles took the story of his evil life and transformed it into an example of the miraculous intervention and boundless compassion of God. Several times he referred to his arrest as a sign of the intervention of the Church and divine providence....it is clear that he created and staged his own *miracle* along the same lines as many of the popular legends of miracles and martyrs."[7]

The people cared about the children they lost. They were also mesmerized, overwhelmed by Gilles's own medieval performance during and after his trial.

What most distinguishes our world from the Middle Ages is that our life is not as simple. We have little time to rely on miracles and revere martyrs, for we have gained sophistication. We have invented ever-changing, complex technologies, some that are helpful, some that are treacherous. The Kalashnikov AK-47 rifle can be fired more rapidly than the crossbow, for example, which also maimed and killed. Similar to modern-day efforts to ban the AK-47, there were attempts to restrict the use of the crossbow because of its power and lethal accuracy. It could pierce chain mail at a range of over four hundred yards.

Psychiatry, an unknown discipline in the Middle Ages, now plays a prominent role in our understanding of human nature. In fifteenth-century France, ordinary folk who forgave de Rais did not analyze why he snapped. They did not talk about the loss of his parents at an early age, his solitary childhood, his cruelty as a young boy, his latent psychopathy, the probable PTSD he suffered after Joan of Arc's death. Five hundred years later, Jeffrey Dahmer's attorney, Gerald P. Boyle, could point to similar characteristics in his shrewd defense explaining why a handsome former tennis player, the son of middle-class parents, a member of the US Army, turned into a perverse serial killer whose unthinkable acts shocked America in 1991[8] and, like de Rais, left grieving families behind.

Polish-born child-psychologist Alice Miller proposed in a groundbreaking study of the origins of violence, *For Your Own Good,* that all instances of mental illness, crime, and falling victim to religious cults are ultimately caused by childhood trauma and inner pain. Dr. Miller, writing at the end of the twentieth century, maintained Adolf Hitler became a monster because of his terrible youth. She postulated that he never received love from any quarter. Among other things, he felt abandoned by his mother, as she did not allow him to confide in her. He wanted to tell her about his true feelings of powerlessness. Hitler dreaded his brutal father, who beat him every day. This cruel man exposed Hitler to constant fear. Hitler's distress, his desperation as an abused child, turned into fury later on in his life.[9]

The renowned neuroscientist David Eagleman has explored other causes of mental illness in his provocative book *Incognito: The Secret Lives of the Brain.* He suggests brain damage produces some criminal acts. He noted that Charles Whitman, another soldier, an ex-Marine who in August, 1966, shot and killed thirteen people and wounded thirty-three from an observation deck at the University of Texas Tower in Austin, requested in his suicide note that an autopsy be performed to determine if something had changed his brain; Whitman suspected it had. When a medical examiner lifted Whitman's brain from his skull, he discovered that a tumor had compressed his amygdala, a region of the brain involved in emotional regulation, especially fear and aggression. Eagleman pointed out that Whitman's case is not isolated. Among others, he referred to a forty-year-old man he called Alex. After twenty years of marriage, his wife noticed that Alex suddenly showed a very active interest in child pornography, and was alarmed by the change in his behavior. At the same time, he complained of worsening headaches. A neurologist performed a brain scan on Alex, which revealed a massive tumor in his orbitofrontal cortex. After the brain tumor was removed, Alex showed no interest in child pornography.[10]

Might Gilles de Rais have been confined to one of his castles instead of being hung had his judges listened to his astute defense attorney, Henri Mechinot, who claimed de Rais was not responsible for his deeds because he was insane? What if these judges had been able to read the novelist William Styron's description of his own disturbing bout with madness in his book, *Darkness Visible*? Would they then have attributed de Rais's crimes to his mental breakdown, which manifested a possible post-traumatic stress disorder? Styron's painfully honest personal account lends credence to Alice Walker's theory of early abandonment as the cause of mental problems that sometimes lead to violent outcomes. Styron, a brilliant writer and not a murderer, poignantly spelled out how he went insane, falling victim to a crippling, almost suicidal, depression.

"But after I returned to health and was able to reflect on the past in the light of my ordeal, I began to see clearly how depression had clung close to the outer edges of my life for many years...The morbid condition proceeded, I have come to believe from my beginning years—from my father, who battled the gorgon for much of his lifetime, and had been hospitalized in my boyhood after a despondent spiraling downward that in retrospect I saw greatly resembled mine....I'm persuaded that an even more significant factor was the death of my mother when I was thirteen; this disorder and early sorrow—the death or disappearance of a parent, especially a mother, before or during puberty—appears repeatedly in the literature on depression as a trauma sometimes likely to create nearly irreparable emotional havoc. The danger is especially apparent if the young person is affected by what has been termed 'incomplete mourning'—has, in effect, been unable to achieve the catharsis of grief, and so carries within himself through later years an insufferable burden of which rage and guilt, and not only damned-up sorrow, are a part, and become the potential seeds of self-destruction."[11]

While many individuals experiencing the loss of a parent never endure depression or become serial killers, Styron's portrayal of his tumble into madness is one more confirmation that Gilles de Rais suffered from a mental breakdown, depression playing a major part in his illness. His wrenching comments to his co-conspirators as they awaited death, like Styron's assessment of his own illness, were very dark. To Corrillaut and Henriett he blurted out that they should be glad they were leaving this world that contained nothing but misery. Life had become more difficult than death for him.

His was a tortuous progression toward lunacy, from losing his mother and father at an early age, and then his idol, Joan of Arc, culminating at his trial. De Rais's perverse, shocking confession to the judges and spectators was, perhaps, courageous in its sordid detail. The judges, the assemblage, the crowd listening to his supplications right before he died, never understood the horror of the underlying insanity afflicting de Rais during his emotionally naked account of his wrongdoings. They did not sense that the psychopath standing before them probably suffered from PTSD; nor did they fathom that they might have wound up like de Rais, but for God's grace and their genes. They only saw de Rais as a sinner who asked for their help, for God's mercy. Without hesitation they were willing to forgive him, to call on God for him, to pray for him so that he could escape his terrible pain, his appalling shame. When he died they had faith this tormented soul would joyfully meet his Maker.

With all our modern advances, the planet remains "darkened by miseries"[12] and populated with butchers. Innocent lives are still swallowed up in absurd conflicts. Lawlessness prevails in many parts of the world. Insane serial killers torment and torture their victims. And...we have lost that benevolent, unwavering religiosity which inspired a selfless populace to build breathtaking flying buttresses and jewellike stained-glass windows to honor their God...that innocent spirit, that compassionate spirit which permitted parents with broken lives to pray to their God for the salvation of Gilles de Rais, the murderer of their slain children.

This medieval account of total forgiveness for a fallen warrior, for a crazed reprobate, and absolute faith in his redemption is uncomfortably humbling in its simplicity and in its grandeur.

CHRONOLOGY

1404: Gilles de Rais is born in October in the black tower of Champtocé to Guy de Laval, whose distinguished family owns extensive properties in northwest France, and Marie de Craon, of the foremost houses of Machecoul and de Craon.

1407: Rene de La Suze, a brother, comes into the world by the same parents. Joan of Arc is also born that year.

1415: Both of de Rais's parents die. Thus Gilles, eleven, succeeds his father and his mother to become one of the richest barons in France. Gilles's uncle, Amauary de Craon, is also killed during the Battle of Agincourt. His grandfather, Jean de Craon, takes over his and his brother's tutelage.

1420: Gilles and his grandfather abduct Catherine de Thouars after the sudden death of her father. They whisk her off to a priest who marries de Rais, sixteen, and Catherine, the same age, so that de Rais can inherit her vast fortune. These consist of: rich lands in Poitou including the great fortresses of Tiffauges and Pouzages.

De Rais and his grandfather assist in liberating the Duke of Brittany from a rival faction claiming the lands of Brittany who hold him prisoner. Gilles successfully executes his first battles in the Duke's defense.

Treaty of Troyes: The beloved but mad King Charles VI signs this treaty in which he gives France to the English and disinherits his son, the future Charles VII.

1422: Gilles and Catherine are formally bound in matrimony by the Bishop of Angers after de Craon sends a nice token to the Church of Rome.

1427: De Rais's cousin, the Grand Chamberlain of France, Georges de la Tremouille, hoping to use Gilles as an informant at the Dauphin's court and on the battlefield promotes de Rais for his extraordinary military abilities. He persuades the Dauphin, Charles de Ponthieu, to appoint Gilles de Rais, age twenty-three, to a significant military post.

Gilles along with renowned Angevin brothers-in-arms win some impressive victories over the English. Those fighting with de Rais affirm Gilles splits the English commander in charge of the Lude fortress in two.

De la Tremouille chases the Dauphin's upright and astute commander, Arthur de Richmont, from the Chinon court.

Jean of Brittany abandons the French cause and instructs his Parliament of Brittany to ratify the Treaty of Troyes.

1428: The English besiege Orleans, a strategic town for both the English and the French. The English feel they can easily overrun the rest of France if this town capitulates. The French see it as a bulwark against further English aggression.

1429: March: Joan of Arc arrives at Chinon. She tells the Dauphin who has been hiding behind his lords that she will make him king. While many of the nobility are skeptical of this uneducated peasant girl and her prophesies, de Rais, present at the meeting, believes she is sent from Heaven.

April: Charles agrees to send Joan of Arc as his commander in chief to Orleans. She requests and he agrees that his liege subject, Gilles de Rais, will be responsible for her safety. De Rais takes Joan's troops back to Blois in order to enter Orleans safely. She is met by enthusiastic crowds upon her entrance into Orleans.

May 8: The English retreat from Orleans. Joan of Arc at seventeen has accomplished one the greatest military feats in history with this capitulation. Gilles de Rais is cited by chroniclers of the time for his bravery at Orleans, especially in helping to secure Les Tourelles for the French.

May 11: Joan and Gilles inform the Dauphin at Loches that Orleans no longer suffers from English rule.

June 17: Beaugency is restored to the French. Gilles is honored for his fighting abilities here as he is the next day at Patay where the English are decimated and their commander, John de Talbot, taken prisoner.

July 17: Charles becomes the lawful King of France at Reims. De Rais and Joan are present at this impressive ceremony. The king soon appoints de Rais as one of his Marshals of France. Gilles is not yet twenty-five years old.

September 8: Joan of Arc, along with the newly appointed king's supporters, attacks Paris. Just as victory seems assured, Joan is wounded and requests that Gilles de Rais remain with her, as she thinks she is dying. Charles VII, following the advice of his chamberlain in league with the English, orders a retreat. He sends a mandate for Gilles to leave for his court.

Marie de Rais, the daughter of Gilles de Rais and Catherine de Thouars, is born sometime in the fall.

1430: Spring: Joan is ready once again to battle the English as the treaty to halt the fighting between the French and English expires. The citizens of Melun throw out their English captors and hand the town over to Joan and the army she has assembled. She then gains access to the Seine River. She also is warned by her voices here that she will be captured.

A delegation from the town of Compiegne begs Joan of Arc to help with its defense against the English threatening that town. She is captured outside its closed gates by the Burgundians who amass a great fee when they sell her to their English allies.

At the end of the year Gilles de Rais surfaces near Rouen, where Joan is held prisoner.

1431: During the winter, Gilles along with other captains, La Hire and D'Alencon, skirmish with the English in Rouen and attempt to free Joan from her captors. Neither endeavor is successful.

May 30: Joan of Arc is burned at the stake in Rouen as a witch and sorcerer by the English. Charles VII of France does not interfere. De Rais despairs.

December 16: Young King Henry VI of England is crowned King of France at Notre de Dame-de-Paris. Now there are two Kings of France, one English, the other French.

1432: August 10: A great battle takes place between English and French forces at Lagny. Gilles de Rais, now twenty-eight, is instrumental in obtaining a French victory here, which insures its control over an area outside of Paris. Gilles's reputation for military prowess is further cemented at Lagny.

Shortly thereafter: Gilles retires to his Champtocé fortress. The first of his child murders begins.

November: De Rais's grandfather, Jean de Craon, dies. Alarmed by the excesses of violence and debauchery de Rais has begun to display, he leaves his sword and breastplate, the sign of manliness, to his younger grandson, Rene de la Suze.

1433: The son of Queen Yolande of Aragon, also the Duchess of Anjou, along with Pregent de Coetivy, an important lord who will marry de Rais's daughter, kidnaps la Tremouille, Charles VII's favorite. De la Tremouille must swear that he will not be involved in court politics after their assassination attempt is unsuccessful. From then on, Yolande of Aragon virtually rules. She reinstates Arthur de Richemont, who assumes command and slowly destroys English dominance.

Children continue to be tortured and murdered by Gilles and his accomplices at his Champtocé Castle.

1434: King Charles demands that de Rais, thirty years old, leave military service as he is not fulfilling his duties as Marshal of France.

Children continue to be tortured and killed by Gilles and his henchmen.

1435: De Rais's theatrical endeavors become magniloquent presentations with *The Siege of Orleans*, commemorating the battle which freed Orleans, the most elaborate. His expenditures for the events at Orleans outrun his resources. His finances slide precipitously thereafter.

De Rais gives his cousin, Roger de Bricqueville, power of attorney for his entire estate. Moreover, de Bricqueville can set the dowry of Gilles's only child, a daughter, at any amount he pleases.

When the bills mount at Orleans and de Rais cannot pay them, he moves on to Montlucon. He can only come up with half of the money he owes for his stay in this sleepy village. He must leave two servants behind as collateral when he leaves.

July 2: Disturbed by de Rais's expenditures at Orleans and his style of living, Gilles's brother, wife, and cousin request that the king issue a Royal Edict forbidding the sale of any further possessions of de Rais. The king obliges but nobility and clergy, including the Duke of Brittany, the Bishop of Nantes, Gilles's cousins, and bourgeois ignore this fiat. Charles VII bans Gilles de Rais from his court for disobeying his edict.

Despite his overwhelming expenditures at Orleans, De Rais establishes a grand Chapel at Machecoul called The Holy Innocents. Its grandeur equals that of a collegiate church or cathedral.

The immense liquidation of his property begins in earnest. He also pawns many objects.

The faithful knight, Guillaume de la Jumeliere, who had been at his side since the battle of Orleans, leaves him, feeling de Rais no longer cares about public service.

Children continue to be tortured and murdered.

1436: Jean V of Brittany falsely swears to the Duke of Anjou that he has no desire to buy Champtocé, the fortress that Gilles owns located at the gateway into Brittany.

Gilles kidnaps his old tutor, Michel de Fontenay, in Angers and imprisons him.

Jean V commences negotiations with de Rais to buy his Champtocé and Ingrandes properties.

October: Gilles's brother and relatives take over Champtocé, Ingrades, then Machecoul.

December: The family reconciles with de Rais after he gives them some of his properties.

Children continue to be tortured and murdered.

De Rais begins his alchemic experiments and starts practicing black magic. His endeavors are not productive. The Devil does not respond to him.

1438: De Rais hands over Champtocé to Duke Jean V's assistants but not before his servants remove some forty skeletons of children from an abandoned tower.

More murders occur.

Invocations of the Devil by conjurors are unsuccessful; so are alchemic experiments.

1439: The false Joan of Arc shows up at Tiffauges. De Rais sends her to Le Mans to recapture that town from the English. She is unsuccessful and soon after is discovered to be a fake.

End of April: Francesco Prelati arrives at Tiffauges.

June or July: Prelati performs the great invocation in the hall of the castle of Tiffauges with no success. Then the invocation takes pace the next day in a field, again with no success.

Between May and November Prelati is beaten by demons.

August: A serpent appears rather than the gold the Devil promised Gilles through his intermediary, Barron, who had conversed with Prelati about this matter. Gilles also meets with Jean V at Bourgneuf-en-Rais to sell him more of his properties.

Children continue to be killed after they are tortured.

Around the end of the year: De Rais, at Prelati's command, sacrifices his first and only child to the Devil so that he will bring him gold. This ritual is different from Gilles's compulsion to maim and murder innocents for pleasure.

1440: March 27: The priest at the Machecoul Church hears Gilles's tearful confession on Easter Sunday.

More children are tortured and murdered.

May: The Blunder at Saint-Etienne-de Mer-Morte takes place.

After Gilles promises to pay the fifty thousand gold-crown fine imposed upon him for his insurrection at Mer-Morte, he visits Duke Jean V at Josselin, and more infants are slaughtered there.

July: Jean de Malestroit, Bishop of Nantes, issues the results of the secret inquest he started after de Rais's infractions at Mer-Morte.

The Duke conducts his own inquiry about de Rais's nefarious conduct.

September 13: Gilles is indicted by the canonical court of Nantes for murder and invoking demons.

September 15: The Duke's men arrest Gilles at Machecoul. A

representative of the ecclesiastical court accompanies these troops.

September 19: Baron Gilles de Rais's trial begins at Nantes.

October 8: The prosecutor cites all the charges against Barron de Rais. When Gilles's appeal is rejected, he madly denies all the accusations.

October 13: The list of crimes and charges are formally read. They consist of: crimes against children, heresy, and the violation of ecclesiastical immunity. After hearing the charges, Gilles will not recognize the authority of the court and is excommunicated.

October 15: Gilles submits to the authority of the court. He asks for pardon but denies he evoked evil spirits

October 16 & 17: Gilles's accomplices offer overwhelming evidence against the former Marshal of France.

October 20: Gilles acknowledges the charges. The prosecutor asks for Gilles to be tortured so that the court can ascertain whether his remarks are true. He is to be tortured the next day.

October 21: De Rais begs the judges to avoid torture. He will admit to all his crimes. He does so in his comfortable chambers to two of his judges.

October 22: Gilles dramatically confesses to his crimes again in front of all the judges and a large crowd.

October 23: Henriet and Corrillaut receive death sentences from the secular court.

October 25: Gilles is found guilty of the charges brought against him in the ecclesiastical court. That same night the secular court also sentences him to death for the murder of the children. In addition he receives a fine of fifty thousand gold crowns for his insubordination against Jean V.

October 26: Along with Henriet and Corrillaut, Baron Gilles de Rais, just thirty-six that month, is hanged and burnt to death.

CAST OF CHARACTERS

Marie d'Anjou - Daughter of Yolande of Aragon, wife of Charles VII and mother of Louis XI.

Arthur III, Count de Richemont – Brother of Jean V, Duke of Brittany. Captured by the English at Agincourt (1415), a grand ransom was paid for his release. Yolande of Aragon had him appointed High Constable of France. When George de la Tremouille removed him from that position, he still remained one of Charles VII's staunchest supporters and rode to battle with Joan of Arc. After Tremouille's fall from power, he solidified many of Joan's wins which permitted France to rid itself of English subjugation. Impressed with Gilles de Rais as a young soldier, he marched against Tiffauges later in the name of the king when de Rais imprisoned two of the Duke of Brittany's functionaries there.

Barron – the ravishing demon Francesco Prelati supposedly communed with when Gilles de Rais was not present.

Bedford (John of Lancaster, Duke of) – Henry V of England appointed him regent of the kingdom of France (1422). Defeated by Gilles de Rais and his companions at the Battle of Lagny (1432), he had trouble governing after that time as his ally, Philip the Good, Duke of Burgundy, signed a pact with Charles VII at Arras in 1435 to support the French.

Beelzebub – The Prince of Darkness. Francesco Prelati tried to summon Him to produce gold for Gilles.

Blackburn – The English captain in charge of Le Lude. Gilles de Rais reportedly hacked him in two.

Eustache Blanchet – The priest employed by Gilles de Rais who found the conjuror, Francesco Prelati, in Florence, Italy. Blanchet left Tiffauges when he suspected that de Rais murdered children there. De Rais's henchmen found him and kept him at Machecoul, thinking he might squeal on de Rais. He was arrested on September 15, 1440 along with de Rais. He gave a rambling, incriminating deposition at de Rais's trial and was exiled from France for the rest of his life.

Jean Blouyn – Vice Inquisitor of France. He and Jean de Malestroit oversaw the ecclesiastical trial of Gilles de Rais.

Roger de Bricqueville – Norman cousin of Gilles de Rais. Arrived penniless as a teenager at the de Craon-de Rais Castle of Champtocé. Took over the management of de Rais's entire estate when he and Gilles were adults. Homosexual companion and accomplice of de Rais. He escaped from Machecoul Castle before he would have been arrested. He surfaced a few years later in the service of Prigent de Coetivy, Marie de Rais's husband, who won a pardon for him from Charles VII. De Bricqueville to save himself detailed the crimes of Gilles de Rais, stating de Rais forced him to act as a procurer and slayer of children.

Andre Buchet –Choirmaster for de Rais. Later he held the same position under the Duke of Brittany. He procured victims for Gilles, one being the lovely young boy whose body was stuffed into a latrine at Vannes.

Pierre Cauchon – Bishop of Beauvais. Chief prosecutor during the trial of Joan of Arc. An ardent English sympathizer, he hoped to become Archbishop of Rouen by successfully convicting Joan.

Guillaume Chapeillon – Parish priest of Saint-Nicholas (Nantes). He became the prosecutor during Gilles de Rais's ecclesiastical trial. Seasoned and adept, he never deviated from his goal to find de Rais guilty of the forty-nine articles of the list of charges he presented.

Odette de Champdivers – Mistress of Charles VI. Looked after him when he became unhinged (1392) and his family shunned him.

Charles VI - The beloved King of France (1380-1422) who went mad. He could not prevent the further ravages of the Hundred Years' War, which commenced before his monarchy, in which England attempted to conquer France. Because of his insanity his country also suffered from a brutal civil conflict between his nephew, the Duke of Burgundy, and his younger brother, the Duke of Orleans, each wanting to rule France.

Charles VII - Crowned King of France in 1429 after Joan of Arc liberated Orleans and numerous areas along the Loire with the assistance of Gilles de Rais plus other warriors. Charles then made de Rais one of his marshals. Charles never rescued Joan of Arc after she was captured by his enemies. But, by 1436 Charles reorganized his army and strengthened his rule over his vassals, providing a more organized government in France and ultimately permitting him with the great assistance of the Count de Richemont to throw the English out of his country.

Regnault de Chartres – Archbishop of Reims. He officiated at

Charles VII's coronation. A churchman of high rank, he only cared about personal aggrandizement and with George de la Tremouille was in league with the English.

Prigent de Coetivy – Well-known admiral of France and nobleman of Brittany. He married Marie de Rais the year after Gilles's execution with the blessing of the family. He sought and received letters of pardon from the King for de Bricqueville's participation in de Rais's crimes. He died outside of Cherbourg in 1450 when a shot from an English arquebus struck him down.

Olivier de Clisson – Famous warrior who became High Constable of France upon the death of Bertrand de Guesclin, Gilles's highly esteemed military relative. He attempted to reorganize the army but lost his popularity after Charles VI became insane.

Etienne Courrilaut ("Poitou") – Page and personal servant to Gilles de Rais. Entered Gilles's household when he was twelve. Had sex for many years with the baron after de Rais raped him and almost killed him at their first encounter. He became one of Gilles's most loyal accomplices in murdering innocents; he procured thirty-eight children for Lord de Rais. Sentenced to death along with his master, he was hung at the same time as de Rais.

Amaury de Craon – Only son and heir of Jean de Craon. Killed at the Battle of Agincourt (1415).

Jean de Craon – Gilles de Rais's maternal grandfather. Took over his guardianship with little oversight when Gilles's father died. Important vassal to the Dukes of Anjou and Brittany. Only lived to acquire possessions.

Marie de Craon – Mother of Gilles de Rais. Daughter of Jean de Craon.

Bertrand Du Guesclin - Uncle of Guy II of Laval, Gilles de Rais's father. Esteemed warrior who battled the English at Poitou, Normandy, Guienne, and Saintonge.

Jean Dunois - Count of Longueville. Handsome, illegitimate son of Louis, Duke of Orleans, identified as the Bastard of Orleans. In charge of the defense of Orleans before Joan liberated the town, and became one of Joan of Arc's commanders at the Battle of Orleans. He and Gilles de Rais along with other compatriots also liberated the village of Patay. After Joan's death he, like Gilles, participated at Lagny, a decisive victory for France against the English. Afterwards, he helped to reconquer Normandy and Guienne.

Eugene IV (Gabriele Condulmer) – Thrifty Pope, former Augustine friar, who refused Gilles de Rais's request to establish a chapel on a grandiose scale. Patron to Ghiberti, Pisanello, Donatello, Fra Angelico. He prevailed over factions which tried to depose him.

Olivier des Ferrieres - Priest at Machecoul. Listened to Gilles de Rais's tearful confession on Easter Sunday, 1440, regarding his massacre of children.

Nicolas Flamel – Parisian who purportedly fabricated alchemical gold. When he died in 1418, he left substantial gifts to churches and hospitals.

Michel de Fontenay – Gilles's tutor when his father was alive. Later he posted Charles VII's Edict at Champtocé prohibiting citizens from buying de Rais possessions. A furious de Rais imprisoned him but then freed him due to numerous official objections.

Jacques Gelu – Archbishop of Embrun. Wrote an impassioned letter to Charles VII after Joan of Arc was captured suggesting Charles do everything in his power to obtain her release. An ardent supporter of Joan, he was one of the first prelates to recognize the supernatural vocation of the Maid.

Henriet Girart – Personal assistant and participator in de Rais's murders. Born in Paris, he entered Gilles's service around 1434. Arrested with Gilles, he was put to death with his master.

Pierre de Glac – Favorite counselor to Charles VII when he was Dauphin. De Glac was detested by the court. Georges de la Tremouille kidnapped him, drowned him, and married his rich wife, replacing him as Charles's grand chamberlain.

Guy II de Laval-Montmorency – Father of Gilles de Rais. Feudal knight. Lord of Blaison and Chemille. He married Marie de Craon to enhance his wealth. In 1415 a wild boar gored him while he was hunting, and he died a slow, painful death from his wound.

Amboise de Lore - Head of the Angevin resistance. A knowledgeable, spirited powerhouse. His troop of men included remarkable scouts and skirmishers.

Henry V – King of England (1413-1422). When Charles VI of France became insane, Henry attempted to usurp the French crown. After his victory at Agincourt (1415), he conquered Normandy, proclaiming himself regent. Because of the Treaty of Troyes (1420) and according to its provisions, he announced he was heir to the French throne. He also married Catherine of Valois, the daughter of Charles VI.

Henry VI - King of England. Son of Henry V who died when he was one year old. His uncles ruled in his place with the Duke of Bedford controlling most of France. At ten he was crowned King of France in Notre Dame Cathedral. When the Hundred Years' War ended, he faced many challenges in England including the unpopularity of his government and his French wife, Marguerite of Anjou. He became embroiled in the War of the Roses. Dethroned by Edward IV (1461), he regained his throne (1470), then lost it again to Edward IV, who murdered him (1470).

Pierre de l'Hopital – President (Supreme Judge) of Brittany. He officiated at de Rais's secular trial in Nantes and sentenced Gilles to death. He heard the out-of-court confession of Gilles de Rais as well.

Nicholas de Houppeville – Priest who objected to Pierre Couchon's tactics in his prosecution of Joan of Arc. Cauchon threw him into prison.

Isabelle of Bavaria – Unpopular Queen of France, daughter of the Duke of Bavaria, Etienne II. After Charles VI lost his mind, she became regent, favoring Charles's younger brother, Louis of Orleans, also her lover, over John the Fearless, the King's nephew. John assassinated Louis, resulting in a feud between the Armagnacs, loyal to Louis, and the Burgundians, who favored John. Isabelle switched her allegiance, siding with John the Fearless and his English allies. Complicit in the death of her two firstborn sons, left in John's care, she also denounced her third son, Charles VII, as a bastard, and by the Treaty of Troyes (1420) she disinherited him.

Jeanne d'Arc (Joan of Arc) – The Savior of France. A young peasant girl believing in the voices of her saints, who instructed her to help the Dauphin liberate France from the English. She persuaded the fearful Dauphin, the future Charles VII, that he was the rightful heir to the French throne and that she would crown him king. Without any prior military experience, she led the French troops at Orleans, winning one of the most decisive battles in history. The French went on to regain their land from the English, and Charles VII became their king. Joan was captured by the Burgundians, who sold her to the English. In league with the Catholic Church that thought her communication with her voices suspicious, the English burned her alive in Rouen (1431). Charles, who never tried to save her, established an inquiry in 1450, which found her death unjust. Beatified in 1909, she was canonized in 1920.

Jeanne des Armoises (Joan of Artemisias) – The false Joan of Arc. Convinced many French she escaped the flames of her English captors and was indeed Joan of Arc. Gilles paid for her military expedition to Le Mans before Charles VII unmasked her, declaring she was his half sister.

Jeanne Chabot, the Wise (la Sage) – Last of the baronesses de Rais, she adopted Guy II of Laval, Gilles de Rais's father. He took over her name and her immense fortune, quadrupling his wealth when she died in 1406.

Jean Juvenal (des Ursins) - Notable French chronicler and historian. He wrote *Histoire de Charles VI Roy de France*, one of the main sources of information regarding the Battle of Agincourt.

Jean V de Montfort – Duke of Brittany (1399-1442). Brother-in-law to Charles VII. He switched his allegiance between France and England often during the Hundred Years' War. A faction called the Penthievres also laid claim to the right to rule Brittany. Ensnared by the Penthievres, Jean V was imprisoned. A civil war between the Penthievres and the Montforts subsequently broke out during the Hundred Years' War, with Gilles de Rais and his grandfather, Jean de Craon, fighting for the victorious Montforts. As Gilles de Rais's debts mounted after he went insane, Jean V bought many of his landed possessions at rock-bottom prices. During the inquiry by Jean de Malestroit, Bishop of Nantes, into the allegations that Gilles murdered scores of children, Jean V launched his own investigation. Certain de Rais would be found guilty, he confiscated de Rais's remaining lands, bestowing them upon his own son.

Jean de la Riviere – First conjuror of demons hired by de Rais. He was also a doctor.

Jean sans peur (John the Fearless) – Duke of Burgundy (1401-1419). Nephew of Charles VI. When Charles VI became insane, he thought Charles's younger brother, Louis of Orleans, would claim the throne, so he murdered Orleans (1409). A feud ensued between those who favored Louis, called the Armagnacs, and those loyal to John, the Burgundians. John mercilessly killed anyone who did not support him as he tried to control Paris and the governance of France. He allied himself with the English, intending to give Henry V the French Crown. He was hacked to death by followers of the Dauphin, the future Charles VII.

Jean Labbe – Breton captain-at-arms working for Duke Jean V. He arrested Gilles de Rais at Machecoul. Present during de Rais's extra-judicial confession at Nantes.

La Hire (Etienne Vignolles) – One of Gilles de Rais's band of brothers, fighting at Orleans and Patay. Later won many other victories against the English in Northern France.

Rene de La Suze – Gilles de Rais's younger brother, born in 1407.

Jean de Craon left his breastplate and sword to this grandchild rather than to de Rais as a signal that he disapproved of Gilles's conduct. In an attempt to reclaim de Rais's squandered property, he wrote *Memory of the heirs*, detailing Gilles's prodigality.

Georges de la Tremouille – Baron of Haut Poitou, Lord of Talmont, Mareuill, and other seignories. He was Gilles de Rais's cousin on the de Craon side. Twenty-two years older than Gilles. High Chamberlain and favorite of Charles VII. He signed a pact with Gilles so that he would report on events at court and on the battlefield. Jealous of Joan of Arc, he did every thing he could to destroy her. He collaborated with the English. He fell from the King's favor in 1433.

Geoffroy le Ferron – Treasurer and principal tax collector of Brittany. Acting for Jean V, Duke of Brittany, he bought de Rais's Saint-Etienne de Mer-Morte property. Brother of Jean le Ferron.

Jean le Ferron – Tonsured cleric. Threatened by de Rais in the Church of Saint-Etienne-de Mer-Morte with decapitation if he did not give back the Castle of Mer-Morte to de Rais. After le Ferron obliged, de Rais threw him into the dungeon there for four months. This act led to de Rais's undoing as it was considered a violation of ecclesiastical immunity.

Louis XI – King of France (1461-1483) Son of Charles VII. In 1439 he unexpectedly showed up at Tiffauges and arrested one of Gilles de Rais's captains. His visit also forced de Rais to destroy his alchemical equipment and his signs of black magic. Nicknamed the Universal Spider, Louis's tentacles reached into many political intrigues.

Jean Louvet – Served in the Angevin finance chamber. Advised

Charles VII when he was the Dauphin about monetary matters at Yolande of Aragon's request. The Breton and Gascon factions at Chinon brought formal allegations against him, citing financial improprieties. They did not like him as he had plotted to murder the Duke of Burgundy, had been romantically involved with Queen Isabelle of France, and supported a rival group to rule Brittany. The Dauphin dismissed him from his court on charges of peculation.

Guillaume de Malestroit – Bishop of Le Mans, one of the judges rendering a verdict at Gilles de Rais's ecclesiastical trial.

Jean de Malestroit – Bishop of Nantes (1419-1443). Also president of the Chamber of Accounts and Chancellor of Brittany (1409-1430). Because of de Rais's sacrilege against the Church at Mer-Morte, he began an inquiry regarding de Rais which resulted in a prima facie case against de Rais for the murder of many children. He presided over the ecclesiastical court which found de Rais guilty of sodomy, heresy, and other crimes.

Perrine Martin alias La Pellisonne or La Meffraye –Nicknamed "Bird of Prey" by villagers, this old, impoverished woman found numerous children for de Rais to deflower. She produced more unsuspecting victims than any of Gilles's other henchmen. Arrested and brought to Nantes during de Rais's trail she gave evidence against him, which was transcribed but has been lost.

Martin V (Oddonne Colonna) – 204th Pope. After Jean de Craon contributed to the Catholic Church, Martin V granted a pardon to Gilles de Rais and Catherine de Thouars, sanctioning their tying the knot even though they were fourth cousins. (The Catholic Church forbade marriages between such close relatives in the fifteenth century.)

Guillaume Merci – Grand Inquisitor of heresy in France. He granted Jean Blouyn authority to preside over Gilles de Rais's ecclesiastical trial as Vice Inquisitor of Nantes.

Jacques Meschin de La Roche-Aireault – Second husband of Beatrice de Montjean, Catherine de Thouars's mother. An impoverished knight but able chamberlain at the court of Charles VII when he was the Dauphin.

Jules Michelet – Regarded by many in France as the country's greatest national historian. He completed his nineteen volume *Histoire de France* in 1867. His most compelling and picturesque pages deal with the Middle Ages. He is believed to present the best of all romantic interpretations of Joan of Arc.

Beatrice de Montjean – Mother of Catherine de Thouars. Jean de Craon captured her and brought her to Champtocé insisting she relinquish her marriage settlement claims to Tiffauges and Pouzauges. De Craon threatened to drown her in the Loire if she did not give up her dowry.

Antoine de Palerme or the Marquis de Ceva – In Gilles de Rais's service. This Italian alchemist along with Francesco Prelati kept the priest, Eustache Blancet, incommunicado at Machecoul after the latter informed one of Gilles's hires that the greater part of northwest France believed de Rais murdered children. Present at St. Etienne de Mer-Morte when Gilles threatened the tonsured cleric, Jean Le Ferron.

Jean Petit – One of the first to assist de Rais in his unsuccessful alchemical experiments. A goldsmith who left Paris to work with de Rais, he diligently tried to produce gold for de Rais.

Jeanne Peynel – First fiancé (1417) of Gilles de Rais. Daughter of Foulques, Lord of Hambe and Briquebbe, a very wealthy Norman. The marriage would have made de Rais the richest baron in France. The Parliament of Paris forbade the union as Jeanne, an orphan, was too young, under the age of fourteen, to marry.

Philip the Good - Became Duke of Burgundy after his father was hacked to death by the Dauphin's allies. A patron of the arts, his Burgundian court flourished during his rule. An English sympathizer, he persuaded the newly crowned King Charles VII to abandon his Paris offensive commanded by Joan of Arc. He fathered twenty-four illegitimate children with his nineteen mistresses.

Jean Pregent - Bishop of Saint-Brieuc. One of the judges presiding at de Rais's ecclesiastical trial. He along with Pierre de l'Hopital listened to Gilles's out-of-court confession.

Francois (Francesco) Prelati – Italian priest and conjuror of the Devil. Hired by Gilles in 1439 to intercede with Beelzebub on his behalf. De Rais's lover. He exerted a profound influence over Gilles even persuading him to offer a child's body parts to Belial. Arrested and brought to Nantes, September, 1440, he was sentenced to life imprisonment. He escaped, ending up at the Court of Rene 1ST of Anjou, called Rene the Good. Rene was also duped by Prelati, who promised the Devil would produce gold for him. While serving as a captain at La Roche-sur-Yon, he arrested Geoffroy le Ferron, the Duke of Brittany's Treasurer. Once le Ferron was released from prison, he used the auspices of Duke Jean of Brittany to hang Prelati in 1445.

Marie de Rais – Daughter of Gilles de Rais and Catherine de Thouars, born in 1429. After Gilles's death, this daughter's estate was so immense that her mother was incapable of handling it.

When Jean V of Brittany demanded that her lands be confiscated two years after de Rais's death, relatives of de Rais married Marie to Prigent de Coetivy, one of Charles' VII's important counselors. The marriage was never consummated and a year after de Coetivy's demise the king mediated a second marriage between Marie and a de Rais cousin, Andre Laval-Leheaoc (1453). Marie died childless in 1457.

Rene 1st, the Good – Duke of Bar, Lorraine, Anjou and Count of Province. Second son of Louis of Anjou and Yolande of Anjou. He was loyal to Charles VII. A patron of the arts, he tried to emulate Gilles de Rais's presentations but lacked the money and the wherewithal. Rene hired Prelati and probably facilitated his escape from prison so that Prelati would intercede with the Devil to produce gold for him.

Beatrice de Rohan - Niece of the Duke of Brittany and de Rais's second fiancé. Betrothed to Gilles in November 1419, the nuptials never occurred even though a marriage contract was agreed upon at Vannes.

Jean Rossignol – Choirboy in de Rais's chapel and one of his pets. De Rais granted him a prebend and gave him the property of La Riviere close to Machecoul. His parents were recipients of a contribution of considerable land as well.

Anne de Sille - Jean de Craon married her around 1420. She was Catherine de Thouars's grandmother and the cousin of Gilles de Sille, de Rais's bed partner and compatriot in murder.

Gilles de Sille – Military acquaintance of de Rais and his distant cousin. First to assist in the rape, torture, murder of children, he also procured victims for de Rais. Fled Machecoul before de Rais's arrest and was never heard from again.

Michael de Sille – Brother of Gilles de Sille. Captain at one of de Rais's Castles.

Jean de Siqueville – Another one of Gilles de Rais's captains. No better than a brigand, the Dauphin, Louis, son of Charles VII, arrested him at Tiffauges as the king attempted to end the rampant pillaging within the country perpetrated by such men. Louis imprisoned de Siqueville in his own residence at the Chateau de Montaigu. De Siqueville escaped and disappeared into the French countryside.

Agnes Sorel – Beautiful mistress of Charles VII. He so adored her that he gave her a chateau for every child she bore him. There were four chateaux and children, Loches being the largest chateau. After she rebuffed his many advances, Charles's son, Louis, slapped her, drove her out of the court and is thought to have had her murdered. She is the first recorded official mistress in French history.

John Talbot, Earl of Shrewsbury – Renowned English warrior. Along with the other English military leaders, he could not prevent Joan of Arc from retaking Orleans. Captured during the French success at Patay in 1429, he paid for his release. He subjugated Guienne to English rule in 1452, but during the battle of Castillon the next year he was defeated and cut down.

Catherine de Thouars – Only child of Milet de Thouars and Beatrice de Montjean. Gilles de Rais and his grandfather abducted her after her father died. She was forced to marry Gilles even though she was his fourth cousin and there were bans against nuptials between such close relatives in the fifteenth century. One of the wealthiest heiresses in France, her considerable dowry included the mighty fortresses of Tiffauges and Pouzauges. This match provided the de Craon-de Rais family with the opportunity to possess lands from the Atlantic Ocean to the Anjou Province, a territory called the basse Loire. When de Rais snapped, Catherine fled to her fortress at Pouzauges with her small daughter, Marie.

Jean de Touscheronde – A clerk. As commissary of the Duke of Brittany, he prepared the testimony from families regarding the disappearance of their children and presented them in written form at Gilles's civil trial. He was also present during de Rais's out-of-court confession to Pierre de l'Hopital and Jean Pregeant, the Bishop of Saint-Brieuc.

Catherine de Valois – Married to Henry V of England, she was the daughter of the beloved mad king Charles VI of France. Sister of Charles VII of France.

Xaintrailles (Jean Ponton, Lord of) – Fierce warrior loyal to Joan of Arc and Charles VII. Along with Gilles de Rais he was instrumental in the victory at Patay, where he captured John Talbot, and at the battle at Lagny (1432). He retook Guienne in 1453. Like Gilles de Rais, Charles VII appointed him a Marshal of France.

Yolande of Aragon – Ruled Anjou province after the death of her husband Louis II of Sicily. Mother of Louis III, Charles of Anjou, Rene 1st, and Marie of Anjou, who became the wife of Charles VII of France. Yolande courageously saved the Valois Dynasty when the English in league with the Duke of Burgundy and the then Queen of France, Isabelle of Bavaria, tried to hand over the throne to the King of England. She was instrumental in the governance of France during the reign of Charles VII.

RELEVANT SITES
(*) Properties belonging to Gilles de Rais

Ambrieres – * A seignory of Gilles de Rais located 60 kilometers west of Alencon and connecting with the seignory of Saint-Aubin-Fosse Louvain. The English take over these two properties in 1423.

Ancenis – Located in Yolande of Aragon's Anjou province. In 1430 as Yolande rides near this tiny town on the right bank of the Loire River, Jean de Craon and his men returning to Champtocé rob her as well as her escorts, taking jewelry, baggage and horses. In 1436, the Duke of Brittany also meets with Charles of Anjou at Ancenis telling him that he has no intention of acquiring Champtocé from Gilles de Rais. Shortly thereafter he buys the beautiful Chateau at a rock bottom price.

Angers – Gilles encounters an imprisoned knight in this city who lends him a book on the art of alchemy and ways to conjure the Devil. In addition, the city's cathedral with its grandiose religious ceremonies inspires Gilles. He imagines that his own cathedral chapter can be as great. 1436 Gilles kidnaps Michel Fortenay, his former tutor, a well respected member of the faculty at the University. Fortenay handled the publication in Champtocé of the Edict prohibiting any French citizen from purchasing de Rais's properties.

Auzance – * A seignory of de Rais located 5 kilometers north of Poitiers.

Agincourt – A village 80 kilometers north of Amiens. On October 25, 1415 one of the great defeats of the French in the Hundred Years' War occurs here with the loss of a large portion of their nobility.

Beaugency – June, 1429 this fortress on the Loire, 25 kilometers southwest of Orleans, is retaken by Joan of Arc. The Duke of Alencon directs the battle. Gilles de Rais and Arthur de Richemont participate in the struggle.

Benate –* Seignory belonging to de Rais which encompasses 13 marshes in Brittany and 13 in Poitou. Jean V, Duke of Brittany, attempts to purchase the properties but Anne de Sille, de Craon's second wife, objects

Blaison –* A seignory of de Rais 20 kilometers southwest of Angers and in close proximity to Chemellier, another fortress owned by Gilles's family since the 13th century. First of the unfortunate sales he conducts. Gilles parts with this patrimonial property in 1429.

Boucardiere (La) - A hamlet near Machecoul. The Sergent family's son is abducted from their home as the parents tend to their hemp crop.

Bouin –* Half seignory of de Rais located 10 kilometers south of Bourgneuf.

Bourges - Residence of Charles VII after he fled Paris. De Rais also spends some time in this city.

Bourgneuf-en-Rais –* Village where Gilles owns another Chateau. 15 kilometers northwest of Machecoul. Gilles abducts the handsome child, Bernard Le Camus, a native of Brest, from his living quarters, then sexually assaults and kills him. Arthur de Richemont receives this fief from his brother, Jean V of Brittany, after he storms Tiffauges to liberate Jean le Ferron, the tonsured Priest from St.-Etienne-de-Mer-Morte whom de Rais holds at this stronghold.

Breuil Mingot - * More lands belonging to Gilles de Rais, 5 kilometers east of Poitiers.

Briollay - * A de Rais Barony consisting of a chateau, 20 kilometers north of Angers.

Brissac -* A dependency of de Rais, 25 kilometers southeast of Angers.

Broceliande or Paimpont) -* A dependency of de Rais, 40 kilometers west of Rennes situated in forestland.

Chabanais -* Seignory with a Chateau belonging to Gilles about 40 kilometers east of Angouleme.

Chalonnes – After Rome receives an extensive gift from Jean de Craon despite a ban of fourth cousins' tying the knot, Gilles de Rais and Catherine de Thoaurs are formally married here in the Church of St. Maurice-de-Chalonnes, located 25 kilometers southwest of Angers.

Champtocé –* Exquisite fortress 25 kilometers west of Angers where Gilles is born in the Black Tower. He inhabits this chateau well into the 1430's. Jean V of Brittany salivates over the property.

So do many of de Rais's family including his brother, Rene de la Suze and his cousin, George de la Tremouille.

Chateau Morant –* Seignory Gilles owns in Anjou.

Chemere – The prior of this village, 8 kilometers north of Bourgneuf, sends his nephew to Machecoul Castle to learn how to read music so that he can become one of de Rais's prized choirboys. The prior never hears from the boy after he enters the Castle.

Cheneche –* Another seignory belonging to de Rais. Located 20 kilometers north of Poitiers, it contains a chateau.

Chenes (Les) –* An additional seignory of Gilles de Rais, 90 kilometers south of Nantes.

Chinon – Charles VII and his Court reside here even before he became King. The future monarch meets with Joan of Arc at this Chateau where she promises to bring succor to the French cause.

Cloue –* Seignory of de Rais 25 kilometers south of Poitiers.

Compeigne – City in Champagne that asks Joan of Arc for her assistance delivering it from the English. Joan is captured outside its closed gates by the Burgundians and sold to the English.

Confolens –* Seignory of de Rais with a chateau 50 kilometers northeast of Angouleme.

Coustumier (Le) -* Fiefdom of de Rais 10 kilometers southwest of Machecoul

Crecy, Battle of – The first major land battle of the Hundred Years War and a crushing defeat for the French. Fought August 26, 1346 near Crecy-en-Ponthieu located in northern France.

Falleron -* Seignory of Gilles de Rais located 45 kilometers south of Nantes.

Fief Macqueau –* Seignory of de Rais 85 kilometers south of Nantes.

Florence – The Priest, Eustache Blanchet, scouring Italy to find an alchemist and conjuror for Gilles de Rais, encounters Francoise Prelati in this Tuscan city. Blanchet persuades Prelati to journey to Tiffauges and work for Gilles.

Fontaine Milon –* Seignory and chateau belonging to de Rais, 20 kilometers northeast of Angers. Gilles sells this seignory in 1432.

Fosse-Louvain –* This seignory of de Rais with its chateau is situated 70 kilometers west of Alencon.

Fresnay-en-Rais – A village 5 kilometers northwest of Machecoul. Ysabeau Hamelin's two sons disappear from this site at Christmas time, 1439, after they leave their small home to buy bread for the family.

Grancy – A town belonging to the Duke of Bourbon located 45 kilometers north of Dijon. The Duke of Burgundy besieges the town in 1434, and the Duke of Bourbon seeks assistance from the Crown who dispatches Gilles de Rais to aide Bourbon. After de Rais takes out an extensive loan from his cousin, George de la Tremouille, he uses most of the money to present his spectacle at Orleans rather than assist the Duke of Bourbon. He gives over his command to his brother, who brings some of de Rais's troops to the fierce battle that is raging. The town surrenders to Philip the Good, the Duke of Burgundy, in August of that year.

Grattecuisse –* Another of Gilles's small seignories, 40 kilometers north of Angers. The Bishop of Angers buys it from de Rais in 1433.

Grez –* 20 kilometers northwest of Angers, this seignory belonging to de Rais contains a chateau.

Hugetieres –* Located 15 kilometers south of Nantes, this is a vassal chateau and lands which Gilles possesses.

Ingrandes –* A beautiful seignory of Jean de Craon and then de Rais. 5 kilometers from Champtocé. Built on the right bank of the Loire River, like Champtocé. Jean V of Brittany desires to own this property.

Jammonieres (Les) –* An additional small de Rais seignory in the Saint-Philbert-de-Grandlieu parish 15 kilometers northeast of Machecoul.

Jargeau - A town located 17 kilometers east of Orleans occupying the left bank of the Loire. Joan of Arc, with the assistance of Gilles de Rais, recaptures it from the English on June 12, 1429. According to Abbot Bossard in his chronicle detailing the life of Gilles de Rais, Charles VII awards this victory to de Rais because of his exploits there.

Josselin - A small town 120 kilometers northwest of Nantes where Jean V of Brittany owns a country residence. Gilles accompanies Jean there from Vannes. His servant, Henriet, procures three children which de Rais murder in a meadow.

Lagny – A village 35 kilometers north of Compiegne. On August 10, 1432, Gilles along with other renowned knights, Dunois, Xaintrelles, de Gaucourt defeat the English in a decisive battle which ensures control for the French of the lower Marne near Paris.

Lamballe – Located near Mont St. Michel in the Gulf of St. Malo. De Rais planned and, then successfully executed an audacious siege on the fortress. It was his first battle.

Loches - 40 kilometers west of Chinon where Charles VII likes to stay. Joan of Arc accompanied by Gilles de Rais informs Charles on May 11th, 1429 of the French victory at Orleans.

Lodunois –* 80 kilometers southwest of Angers, this is a tenancy of de Rais.

Loroux-Bottereau (le) –* 20 kilometers east of Nantes, this seignory of de Rais has a village and a chateau. Beatrice de Montjean, the mother of Catherine de Thouars, is imprisoned here before being transported to Champtocé where de Craon and de Rais insist she give up her dowry, or they would drown her in the Loire River. In 1436 Jean V of Brittany worried about plots and sneak attacks against him, demands an oath of loyalty from the captain of the fortress.

Loubert –* De Rais's seignory 40 kilometers northeast of Angouleme.

Louviers - Located on the Eure River, 16 kilometers south of Rouen. De Rais stays here when Joan is imprisoned at Rouen. Some chroniclers believe a note of indebtedness by Gilles signed in that village implies he tried to amass troops from that vicinity so as to free the Maid.

Lude (Le) – In 1427 de Rais invades the fortress situated in this village which is occupied by the English and executes an astonishing victory. In addition de Rais's comrades-at arms proclaim that Gilles splits Blackburn, the English captain in charge of the stronghold, in two.

Machecoul –* 30 kilometers south of Nantes, Gilles moves into this stronghold located on the southern marshes of Brittany after he leaves his Champtocé residence. The fortress becomes the second of his major Castles where Gilles murders children. Gilles along with Henriet and Poitou are arrested at this stronghold on September 15, 1440.

Mans (Le) – 1427, Gilles partakes of his first military action against the English around this town, but French forces are repelled. 1439, de Rais dispatches the false Joan of Arc and then one of his unsavory captains to again attempt to defeat the Goddamns at this site. This breathtaking town and its surroundings remain in English hands until 1448.

Mauriere (La) –* Seignory of de Rais 70 kilometers southeast of Nantes and abutting La Mothe-Achard. It expands Gilles's prosperous seignories to the River Auzance.

Montaigu – The future King Louis XI, son of Charles VII, throws Jean de Siqueville, a captain of de Rais, into the prison in this chateau after his arrest at Tiffauges for pillaging. Located 15 kilometers from the latter stronghold, de Siqueville escapes and is never heard from again.

Montlucon – De Rais stays here at the Ecu de France after his debts mount in Orleans. He leaves two servants as collateral and a large, unpaid bill behind when he returns to his Chateaux.

Mortagne – Eustache Blanchet flees Tiffauges and resides at an inn here, 15 kilometers up-river on the Seine, after he suspects de Rais of murdering children. De Rais's henchmen kidnap him and keep him incommunicado in a dilapidated house in Machecoul so that he will not blab about Gilles's massacres.

Mothe-Achard (La) –* Exquisite Chateau and vasal seignory 65 kilometers south of Nantes. Gilles offers to give his family this property if they return Champtocé, Ingrandes and Machecoul to him. They readily accept his proposal.

Nantes – Capital of Brittany from 939 to 1532.
> **Biesse (meadow of)** – de Rais and his accomplices, Henriet and Poitou, are executed here on this island, situated to the south of the old center of the city. Today the same location is called boulevard des Martyrs Nantais de la Resistance.
> **Bouffay (Le)** - fortress at Nantes near its chateau where Gilles must deal with the secular court.
> **Chateau of the Dukes of Brittany** – after his arrest Gilles is lodged here in the new Tower and his ecclesiastical trial takes place in a large upper chamber. The accusations of families who lost children are heard in the lower chambers.
> **Notre-Dame-des-Carmes (or du Carmel)** – subsequent to Gilles's execution, his remains are taken to this Church for internment.
> **Suze (de La)** –* mansion on the rue Notre-Dame belonging to de Rais. He tries to conjure up the Devil here and also massacres numerous children in this exquisite house.

Orleans – A strategic city located on the Loire River occupied by the English. Joan of Arc with the assistance of Gilles de Rais, Dunois, La Hire and other French fighting legends recaptures it and rekindles the French spirit. De Rais stages his *Mystery of the*

Siege of Orleans here five years later which results in his financial downfall.

Paris – In September, 1429 Joan of Arc and twelve thousand Armagnac troops loyal to the newly anointed Charles VII attack Paris so as to liberate it from the Burgundians and their English allies. Joan of Arc is wounded. She requests de Rais remain with her for she presumes she is dying. She recovers, but Charles orders a retreat. Three years later the ten year old King of England, Henry VI, is crowned King of France at Notre Dame Cathedral by the above English and their sympathizers. Charles VII does not regain this city until 1436.

Parthenay – In 1428, High Constable de Richemont retires to this small estate which he owns, 50 kilometers west of Poitiers, after Gilles's scheming cousin, George de la Tremouille, ousts him from the Chinon Court.

Patay – This village, 20 kilometers northwest of Orleans, is reclaimed from the English by Joan and her troops in June, 1429. Gilles de Rais assists. The well-known English commander, John Talbot, is taken prisoner.

Poitiers – Gilles escorts Joan of Arc to this city after her meeting with Charles at Chinon so that she can be questioned by scholars and examined to ascertain whether she is a virgin.

Pornic –* Gilles owns the Chateau and its land.

Port-Launay – This village bordering Coueron, 15 kilometers from Nantes and on the right bank of the Loire estuary, is the location where an orphan, Jamie Bernard, was last seen as he and Perrine Martin (La Meffraye) headed off to Machecoul. She turns him over to de Rais so that he can be molested and murdered.

Port-Saint-Pere – 15 kilometers to the north of Machecoul. The Aise parents send their son to Machecoul to beg for alms. He never returns home.

Poitiers - In 1356 the second major French defeat during the Hundred Years War takes place in this village. Edward of England, the Black Prince, wins the battle.

Pouzages –* Located 30 kilometers southeast of Tiffauges. Catherine de Thouars separates from de Rais in 1434 and along with her daughter, Marie de Rais, lives in this enormous seignory and castle with its grand square keep.

Precigne –* More lands Gilles owns, 45 kilometers north of Angers.

Prigny -* Land and a chateau, 5 kilometers northwest of Bourgneuf, belonging de Rais.

Rais –* De Rais inherited this barony from his father and mother. It consists of 40 parishes located between the Loire and the Free Marshlands of Poitou and Brittany. The fortresses of Machecoul, Le Coustumier, Bourgneuf, Prince, Vue, Pornic, Touvois, Saint-Michel-Chef-Chef, Saint-Etienne-de-Mer-Morte, Prigny and half of the island of Bouin represent this confederation.

Reims – Ancient town. All French Kings have been anointed here since Clovis.

Riviere (La) –* Tiny property bordering Machecoul owned by de Rais. He gives it to one of his choirboys who he thinks sings like a nightingale.

Roche-Bernard (La) – Town where Peronne-Loessart gives up her child to Poitou for the promise of a new dress. The boy is murdered at Machecoul.

Rouen – Joan of Arc is held prisoner here and burned at the stake in this capital of Normandy on May 30, 1431.

Saint-Cyr-en-Rais – A boy from this village adjacent to Bourgneuf travels to Machecoul to beg for alms and never returns home.

Saint-Etienne-de-Mer-Morte –* 10 kilometers south of Machecoul. De Rais sells the chateau to the Treasurer of Brittany who acts as a front in this transaction for the Duke of Brittany. Furious that he has been duped and that he sold the property at a low price, Gilles marches 60 armed men to this village to retake it. He enters the church during Mass and threatens to kill the Treasurer's brother who is a tonsured priest. He demands the keys to the Castle from the brother and locks him up in the dungeon. These actions lead to Gilles's downfall. By violating the priest's immunity the Church can gather information about de Rais's behavior. Since Gilles entered Brittany without the Duke's permission, Jean V Of Brittany can also examine de Rais's conduct.

Saint-Etienne-de-Montluc – 20 kilometers northwest of Nantes. A tutor leaves his thirteen year old charge alone. When he returns to his house, the boy has vanished. Earlier an orphan also disappears from this hamlet.

Saint-Leger-des-Vignes – Jeannette Drouet sends two of her sons to Machecoul to ask for alms even though she lives near Nantes. Neither of them returns to the village.

Saint-Michel-Chef-Chef –* De Rais owns this chateau and surrounding lands, 40 kilometers west of Nantes.

Savenay –* Seignory belonging to de Rais, 35 kilometers northwest of Nantes.

Signon –* Gilles owns these lands located 5 kilometers northwest of Poitou.

Souche –* 15 kilometers northeast of Machecoul, de Rais owns this little seignory.

Sully-sur-Loire – Georges de La Tremouille owns the property 50 kilometers southeast of Orleans. In league with the English, La Tremouille's chateau is not besieged when the Goddamns attack Orleans, nor thereafter.

Suze (La) –* Significant property belonging to de Rais 20 kilometers southwest of Le Mans. Gilles cedes it to his brother in 1434 because of his deteriorating financial situation.

Tiffauges –* With its 18 towers, one of de Rais's most important fortresses (inherited from his wife). He performs his experiments in alchemy here and also tries to conjure up demons. Many children perish here. De Rais still possesses this great stronghold when he is executed.

Troyes – The debilited King VI signs a Treaty here granting the English rule over his kingdom and stripping his son, the future Charles VII, of his sovereign right to govern France. Jean V of Brittany in 1427 obtains his parliament's approval of this document and switches his allegiance once again to England. Joan of Arc escorted by Gilles de Rais retakes this town in July, 1429.

Vannes - Medieval capital of Brittany. Gilles's engagement to Beatrice de Rohan is announced here. In 1420 Jean V's wife pleads with his vassals to free him from a Penthievres prison where he has been made captive. 1437, Jean V makes Gilles his Lieutenant General. He issues this declaration from Vannes. He also signs an agreement with de Rais to purchase his Champtocé Castle. Gilles, in July, 1440 commits a brutal murder in this city. A month later the Duke and his brother, Arthur de Richemont, meet at Vannes and decide to seize Gilles'sTiffauges Fortress.

Verneuil – Charles VII, still Dauphin in 1424, is overcome by the English before this chateau, situated 30 kilometers west of Dreux. Verneuil remains in the English camp until 1449.

Voute (La) or Voulte (La) –* 20 kilometers east of Poitiers, this seignory of de Rais contains a chateau.

ACKNOWLEDGEMENTS

Many people encouraged me to write this story, but thank yous are due above all to Michael Denneny and Michael Putzel for their much welcomed criticisms and suggestions; Wendy Keller for her total belief in the project; my children, Serena Sterling and Graham Phillips as well as my daughter-in-law, Layla Phillips, for their wholehearted encouragement; my husband, Walter Phillips, Jr., for his endless patience, and his incredible grace and humor, who tolerated my obsession with this tale, always asking me the same pertinent question each night, "What's for dinner?"; the Bibliotheque de Nantes and the Free Library of Philadelphia whose staffs thoughtfully provided invaluable resources for this book; and finally to History Publishing Company, LLC, Publisher, Don Bracken, for his utmost support.

NOTES

Chapter One: BLUEBEARD'S CASTLE

1 Derison, Edward, ed. (1997) What Life was like in the Age of Chivalry: Medieval Europe, A.D. 800-1500. Alexandria, VA: Time Life Books, p.62.

2 Bataille, Georges. (1991) The Trial of Gilles de Rais. (Richard Robinson, Trans.) Los Angeles, California: Amok Books, (Original work published 1965), p. 272.

3 Bataille, p. 26.

4 Hyatte, Reginald. (1984) Laughter for the Devil. The Trials of Gilles de Rais. Companion-in-arms of Joan of Arc (1440). (Hyatte, Reginald, introduction & translation from Latin and French). Cranbury, New Jersey: Associated University Press, Inc. p.113.

5 Rouille, Joseph. (n.d.) Gilles de Rays, L'homme de la demesure. Cholet, France: Editions Pays & Terroirs, p. 31.

6 Battaille, p. 156.

7 Rouille, p. 31.

8 Bossard, Abbe Eugene. (1992) Gilles de Rais. Marechal de France, dit Barbe Blue. Grenoble, France: Jerome Millon (original work published in 1885), p.15.

9 http://www.crimelibrary.com/serial_killers/predators/rais/unbridled_4.html. The Childhood of Gilles, p. 3

10 http://fds.oup.com/www.oup.co.uk/pdf/0-19-811209

11 Jeary, Madeline. (1979) Sexuality and Family in Fifteenth Century France. Journal of Family History. Number 4. (Winter pp. 328-345).

12 Bossard, p. 22.

13 http://www.flowofhistory.com/units/west/10/FC73

14 http://wwwshus.edu/_his_hep/crecy

15 Bossard, p.23.

16 Bossard, p.16.

17 Bossard, p.15.

Chapter Two: A COUNTRY OF THIEVES / A BANQUET FOR KINGS

1 Lewis, D.B.Wyndham. (1952) The Soul of Marshall Gilles de RAIZ, with some account of his life and times, his abominable crimes, and

his expiation. London, England: Eyre & Spottiswoode, p.22.

2 http://xenophongroup.com/monjoie.htm

3 Gordon, Mary. (2000) Joan of Arc. New York, New York: Viking Penguines, a member of Penguin Putnam, pp.32-33.

4 http://xenophongroup.com/monjoie/yolande.htm

5 Vale, MGA. (1974) Charles VII. London, England: Eyre Methuen Ltd., p. 29.

6 Robb, David, M., Ph. D. and Garrison,J.J., M.A. (1953) ART in the Western World. New York, New York: Harper Brothers Publishers, p. 624.

7 Huysmans, J.K. (1972) LA-BAS (DOWN THERE). (Keen Wallace, trans.) New York, New York: Gramercy Books, p.45.

8 Aliki. (1983) A MEDIEVAL FEAST. New York, New York:Thomas Y. Crowell, pp. 5-6.

9 Aliki, pp.1-25.

10 Huysmans, p.44.

11 Vale, p .24.

12 Vale, p.27.

13 Vale, p.32.

14 Vale, pp..32.39.

15 Vale, p. 92.

16 Gordon, p.35

Chapter Three: BLUEBEARD BRAVE

1 Manchester, William Raymond. (1993) A World Lit only by Fire. The Medieval Mind and The Renaissance, Portrait of an Age. Boston, Massachusetts: Little Brown and Company, p.5.

2 Vincent, A. L.and Binns, Clare. (1926) Gilles de Rais:The original Bluebeard. London, England: A.M.
Philpot LTD., p.88.

3 Lewis, D.B.Wyndham. (1952) The Soul of Marshall Gilles De Raiz, with some account of his life and times, his abonimable crimes and his expiation. London, England:Eyre and Spottiswoode, p.30.

4 Bossard, Abbe Eugene. (1992) Gilles de Rais. Marechal de France, dit Barbe Blue. Grenoble, France : Jerome Millon (original work published in 1885), p. 31.

5 Paine, Albert Bigelow. (1927) The Girl In White Armor. New York, New York: The MacMillan Company, pp. 66-68.

6 Lewis, p.68
7 Paine, p.101.
8 Paine, p112.
9 Bossard, p.37.
10 Paine, p.109.

Chapter Four: THE INSPIRATION AND MARTYR OF
FRANCE

1 Morris, Charles. Historical Tales:French. Retrieved 07/07/2007 from http://www. main lesson.com/display,plp. author& morris& books =french & story=ampoule.com

2 http://encyclopedia2.the freedictionary.com/marshal

3 Lewis, D.B. Wyndham. (1952) The Soul of Marshal Gilles de Raiz, with some account of his life and times, his abominable crimes, and his expiation. London, England: Eyre & Spottiswoode, p.65.

4 Soisson, Janine et Pierre. (1981) Les Chateaux De La Loire. Geneva, Switzerland: Editions Minerva S.A., p.6.

5 Vincent, A.L.and Binns, Clare. (1926) Gilles de Rais: The original Bluebeard. London, England: A.M. Philpot LTD., pp 157-159.

6 Paine, Albert Bigelow. (1927) The Girl In White Armor. New York, New York:The MacMillan Company, p.200.

7 Paine, p. 250.

8 Paine, p. 185.

9 Gordon, Mary. (2000) Joan of Arc. New York, New York:Viking Penguins, a member of Penguin Putnam, Inc., pp. 32-33.

10 Paine, p.47.

11 Paine, p.199.

12 Sackeville-West, Vita. (1936) Saint Joan. New York, New York: Doubleday, pp.277-8.

13 Gordon, p.126.

14 Paine, p.253.

15 Paine, p.266.

16 http://www.crimelibrary.com/serial_killers/predators/rais_5html.," The Saint and Sinner" p.4.

17 Bataille, Geroges.(1965) Le Process de Gilles de Rais. Paris, France:Jacques Pauvent, p.33.

Chapter Five: THEATRICAL MAGNILOQUENCE /
STAGGERING RUIN

1 Vincent, A. L.and Binns, Clare. (1926) <u>Gilles de Rais:The Original Bluebeard.</u> London, England: A.M. Philpot, LTD, p. 97.
2 Vincent, pp.95-100.
3 Vincent, p.98.
4 Soisson, Janine et Pierre. (1981) <u>Les Chateaux De La Loire.</u> Geneva, Switzerland: Editions Minerva S.A.,
   p.. 80.
5 Rouille, Joseph. (n.d.) <u>Gilles de Rays. L'homme de la demesure.</u> Cholet, France: Editions Pays & Terroirs, p.67.
6 Lewis, D. B.Wyndham. (1952) <u>The Soul of Marshall Gilles de Raiz, with some account of his times, his abominable crimes, and his expiation.</u> London, England: Eyre & Spotiswoode, pp.95-96.
7 Lewis, p. 108.
8 Bossard, Abbe Eugene. (1992) <u>Gilles de Rais. Marechal de France, dit BarbeBlue.</u> Grenoble, France: Jerome Millon (original work published in 1885), p.92.
9 Manchester, William Raymond. (1993) <u>A World Lit only by Fire. The Medieval Mind and The Renaissance, Portrait of an Age.</u> Boston, Massachusetts: Little Brown and Company, p. 55.
10 Bataille, George. (1991) <u>The Trial of Gilles de Rais.</u> (Richard Robinson, Trans.) (original published 1965) Los Angeles, California: Amok Books, p.28.
11 Bossard, p.156.
12 Lewis, p.94.
13 Bossard, p.59.
14 Lewis,p.115.
15 Bataille, p.95.
16 http://www.freehoroscopesastrology.com/libra.asp
17 Bossard,p.15
18 Bossard, p.54.
19 Bossard, p.54.

Chapter Six: THE DARK SLOPE

1 Lewis, D. B. Wyndam. (1952) <u>The Soul of Marshall Gilles Re Raiz,with some account of his life and times, his abominable crimes, and his expiation.</u> London, England : Eyre and Spottiswoode, p.123.

2 Seligman, Kurt. (1997) <u>The History of Magic and The Occult.</u> New York, New York: Gramercy Books, p.118.

3 Bataille, Georges (1991). <u>The Trial of Gilles De Rais.</u> (Richard Robinson, Trans.) Los Angeles, CA: Amok Books (original work pubished1965), p.176.

4 Thoma, Richard. (2005) "Tragedy in Blue": <u>The Satanic Rites of Gilles De Rais.</u> (Candice Black, ed.). Washington, D.C.: Creation Books, p.73.

5 Bataille, p.196

6 Batallie,p. 196

7 Thoma, p.75.

8 Vincent, A.L.and Binns, Clare. (1926) <u>Gilles de Rais: the Original Bluebeard.</u> London, England: A.M.Philpot LTD., p.127.

9 Rouille, Joseph. (n.d.) <u>Gilles de Rays. l'homme de la demesure.</u> Cholet, France: Editions Pays & Terroire, p.74.

10 Bataille, p.111

11 Vincent, p.128

12 Bataille, p.195

13 Vincent, pp131-132.

14 Bataille, p.194.

15 Thoma, p.95

16 Bataliie, p.205

17 Hyatte, Reginald. (1984) <u>Laughter For The Devil,The Trials of Gilles de Rais, companion-in-arms of Joan of Arc (1440).</u> (Hyatte, Reginald, introduction & translation from the Latin and French). Cranbury, New Jersey: Associated University Press, Inc. p.89.

18 Vincent, p.134

19 Thoma, p.84

20 Bataille p.192, p.228-9

21 Bataille, p.120.

Chapter Seven: THERE BE MONSTERS HERE

1 http://www.bidstrup.com/phobianhistory.httm

2 http://www.fordham.edu/halsall/pwh/1979boswell.html

3 Huysman, J.K. (1972) <u>LA-BAS (DOWN THERE).</u> (Keene Wallace, trans.) New York, New York: Dover Publications Inc., p.154.

4 Bataille, Georges. (1991) <u>The Trial of Gilles De Rais.</u> (Richard Robinson, trans.) Los Angeles, California: Amok Books (original

work published 1965), pp. 272,275-6

5 Bataille, pp. 254-5.
6 Bossard, Abbe Eugene. (1992) Gilles De Rais, Marechal de France, dit Barbe Blue. Grenoble, France : Jerome Millon, (original work published 1885), p.160.
8 Thoma, Richard. (2005) "Tragedy in Blue" The Satanic Rites of Gilles De Rais. (Candice Black,ed.) Washington, D.C.:Creation Books,p.85.
9 Bossard, p. 163.
10 Hyatte, Reginald. (1984) Laughter For The Devil, The Trials of Gilles de Rais, companion-in-arms of Joan of Arc (1440). (Hyatte, Reginald, introduction & translation from the Latin and French). Cranbury, New Jersey: Associated University Press, Inc., p. 87.
12 Bataille, p 190.
15 Lewis, D. B. Wyndham. (1952) The Soul of Marshall Gilles De Raiz, with some account of his life and times, his abominable crimes, and his expiation. London, England: Eyre and Spottiswood, p.155.
16 Manchester, William Raymond. (1993) A World Lit only by Fire, The Medieval Mind and The Renaissance, Portrait of an Age. Boston, Massachusetts: Little Brown and Company, p.27
19 Bataille, p. 229.
22 http://www.geocities.com//kidhistory/ja/history2.htm
28 Mc Dermott, Terry. (2005) Perfect Soldiers. New York, New York: Harper Collins Publishers, Inc., p.xv.

30 Bataille, pp.225.
31 Bataille,p. 259.
32 Bataille, p.221.
33 Bataille, pp..22-23.
34 Vincent, A.L.and Binns, Clare. (1926) Gilles de Rais:The Original Bluebeard. London,England: A.M.Philpot, LTD., p. 34.
35 Lewis, p.151.
36 Bataille, p.231.

Chapter Eight: THE BRAZEN BLUNDER:ST. ETIENNE DE MER MORTE

1 Bossard, Abbe Eugene. (1992) Gilles De Rais, Marechal de France,dit Barbe Blue. Grenoble, France: Jerome Millon (original work published 1885), p.183.
2 Bataille, Georges. (1991) The Trial of Gilles De Rais. (Richard Robinson, trans.) Los Angeles, California: Amok Books (original work published 1965), p.155.
3 Bataille, p.243
4 Vincent, A.L.and Binns, Clare. (1926) Gilles de Rais, the Original Bluebeard. London, England: A.M. Philpot LTD., pp.160-161.

Chapter Nine: TRIAL:THE ADMINISTRATION OF MEDIEVAL JUSTICE

1 Hyatte, Reginald. (1984) Laughter For The Devil, The Trials of Gilles de Rais, companion-in-arms of Joan of Arc (1440). (Hyatte, Reginald, introduction & translation from Latin and French). Cranbury, New Jersey: Associated University Press, Inc., p.54.
2 Hyatte, p.57.
3 Reston, James, Jr. (2006) Dogs of God, Columbus, the Inquisition and the Defeat of the Moors. New York, New York: Anchor Books, p.200.
4 Bataille, George. (1991) TheTrial of Gilles De Rais. (Richard Robinson, trans.) Los Angeles, CA: Amok Books. (Original work published 1965), p.219.
5 Bataille, pp.228-229.
6 Bataille, pp.252-253.
7 Bataille, p.257.
8 Thoma, Richard (2005) "Tragedy in Blue" The Satanic Rites of

Gilles De Rais. (Candice Black, ed.) Washington, D.C: Creation Books, P.92.

9 Vincent, A.L and Binns, Clare. (1926) Gilles de Rais:The original Bluebeard. London, England: A. M. Philpot LTD., pp.165-166.

10 Bossard, Abbe, Eugene. (1992) Gilles de Rais. Marechal de France, dit Barbe Blue. Grenoble, France: Jerome Millon (Original work published 1885), p.221.

11 Hyatte, p.59.

12 Hyatte, p.58.

13 Hyatte, p.61.

14 Bossard, p.224.

15 Paul, the Apostle. Thessalonians, The Second Epistle, Chapter I, verse 8, The Holy Bible. (1852) New York, New York: American Bible Society, p.201.

16 Milton, John. (1941) The Complete Works of John Milton. (Harris Francis Fletcher, ed.) Cambridge, Massachusetts: The Riverside Press (original work circulated in the 16th century), pp. 177, 343.

17 Hyatte, p.58.

18 Lewis, D.B. Wyndham. (1952) The Soul of Marshall Gilles de Raiz, with some account of his life and times, his abominable crimes and his expiation. London, England: Eyre & Spottiswoode,p.178.

19 Bossard, p.236.

20 Hyatte, pp.20-21.

21 Bataille,p.277.

22 The American Heritage Illustrated Dictionary. (1987) . "dirge". (Pamela B. DeVinne, coordinating ed.) Boston, Massachusetts: Houghton Mifflin Company, p.483.

23 Bataille, p.278.

EPILOGUE

1 Bossard, Abbe Eugene. (1992) Gilles De Rais, Marechal de France, dit Barbe Blue. Grenoble, France : Jerome Millon (original work published 1885), p.236.

2 Bossard, p.313-15.

3 Rouille, Joseph. (n.d.) Gilles de Rays, l'homme de la demesure. Cholet, France: Editions Pays &Terroirs, pp.15, 149,150-3

4 Bossard, p.257.

5 Bataille, George (1991) The Trial of Gilles De Rais. (Richard

Robinson, trans) Los Angeles, CA : Amok Books (Original Work Published 1965), pp 61-62.

6 Hyatte, Reginald. (1984) Laughter ForThe Devil.The Trials of Gilles de Rais, Companion-in-arms of Joan of Arc (1440). (Hyatte, Reginald, introduction and translation from Latin and French). Cranbury, New Jersey: Associated University Press, Inc., p.156

7 Hyatte, pp.16-17, pp.22-23.

8 Davis, Don. (1991) The Milwaukee Murders Nightmare in Apartment 213 The True Story. New York, New York: St Martin's Paperbacks, New York: New York, p.183.

9 Miller, Alice. (1983) For Your Own Good:Hidden Cruelty in Child Rearing and the Roots of Violence. (Hildegarde Hannum, trans.) . New York, New York: Farrar Strause and Giroux, pp.170-197.

10 Eagleman, David. (2011). Incognito: The Secret Lives of the Brain. New York, New York: Pantheon Books, pp.151-154.

11 Styron, William. (1990) Darkness Visible, a Memoir of Madness. New York, New York: Vantage Books, pp.79-80.

12 Balzac, Honore de. (1960) "La Grande Breteche", Great French Stories. (Germaine Bree, ed.) New York, New York: Dell Publishing (original work published mid 19th century), p.115.

BIBLIOGRAPHY

Aliki. (1983). A MEDIEVAL FEAST. New York, New York: Thomas Y. Crowell

Balzac, Honore. (1960). "LA GRANDE BRETECHE", GREAT FRENCH STORIES (Germaine Bree, edited with introductions). New York, New York: Dell Publishing Company, pp. 113-136

Bataille, Georges. (1965) LE PROCES DE GILLES DE RAIS. (Jean-Jacques Pauvert, ed.). Paris, France: Societe Nouvelle des Editions Pauvert

Bataille, Georges. (1991) THE TRIAL OF GILLES DE RAIS. (Richard Robinson, trans.). Los Angeles, California: Amok Books (original published 1965)

Blanchard, Olivier, & Gerard, Alain. (N.D.) GILLES DE RAIS, Sur Les Empreintes. La Mothe-Achard, Vendee, France: Editions L'Etrave

Bossard, Abbe Eugene. (1992) GILLES DE RAIS, MARECHAL DE FRANCE, Dit BarbeBlue. Grenoble, France: Jerome Millon (original work published in 1885)

Crowley, Alester. (1930) GILLES DE RAIS, The Banned Lecture. New Orleans, Louisiana: Black Moon Publishing

Davis, Don. (1991) The MILWAUKEE MURDERS. Nightmare in Apartment 213: The True Story. New York, New York: St. Martin's Press

Derison, Edward, (ed.). (1997) WHAT LIFE WAS LIKE IN THE AGE OF CHIVALRY Medieval Europe,AD 800-1500. Alexandria, Virginia: Time-Life Books

Eagleman, David. (2011) INCOGNITO: The Secret Lives of the Brain. New York, New York: Pantheon Books

Erlanger, Phillippe, (1945) CHARLES VII ET SON MYSTERE. Paris, France: Gallimard

Fox, James Alan and Levin, Jack. (1996) OVERKILL. Mass Murder And Serial Killing Exposed. New York, New York: Dell Publishing

Garrison, J.J., MA & Robb, David M., Ph.D. (1953) ART IN THE WESTERN WORLD. New York, New York: Harper & Brothers Publishers

Gilcrest, Cherry. (1991) THE ELEMENTS OF ALCHEMY. Rockport, Massachussets: Element Books

Gordon, Mary. (2000) JOAN of ARC. New York, New York: Viking Penguin, a member of Penguin Putnam Inc.

Heers, Jacques. (N.D.) GILLES DE RAIS, Verites et Legends. Paris, France: Perrin

Huysmans, J.K. (1972) LA- BAS, Down There. (Keene Wallace, trans.). New
York, New York: Dover Publications, Inc.

Hyatte, Reginald. (1984). LAUGHTER FOR THE DEVIL, The Trials of Gilles de Rais, Companion-in-arms of Joan of Arc (1440). (Hyatte, Reginald, Introduction & translation from Latin and French). Cranbury, New Jersey: Associated University Press, Inc.

Lewis, Dominic Bevan Wyndham. (1952). THE SOUL OF MAR- SHALL GILLES DE RAIZ, With Some Account of His Life and Times, His Abominable Crimes, and His Expiation. London, England: Eyre and Spottiswoode.

Manchester, William, Raymond. (1993). A WORLD LIT ONLY BY FIRE, The Medieval Mind and The Renaissance, Portrait of an Age. Boston, Massachusetts: Element Books

McDermott, Terry. (2005) PERFECT SOLDIERS. New York, New York: The MacMillan Company
Miller, Alice (1983) FOR YOUR OWN GOOD. Hidden cruelty in child-rearing and the roots of violence. (Hildegard and Hunter Hannum trans), New York, New York: Farrar-Straus-Giroux

Milton, John (1941). THE COMPLETE WORKS OF JOHN MILTON. (Harris Francis Fletcher, ed.). Cambridge, Massachusetts: The Riverside Press (original work circulated in the 16th century)

Mondimore, Francis Mark, M.D. (2006) Depression,The Mood Disease. Baltimore, Maryland: The Johns Hopkins University Press

Paine, Albert Bigelow. (1927) THE GIRL IN WHITE ARMOR. New York, New York: The MacMillan Company

Prouteau, Gilbert. (1992). GILLES DE RAIS, ou La Gueule du Loup. Monaco: Edition du Rocher

Reston, James, Jr. (2006) DOGS OF GOD, Columbus, the Inquisition and the Defeat of the Moors. New York, New York: Anchor Books

Riviere, Daniel. (1986) HISTOIRE DE LA FRANCE. Paris, France: Hachette

Rouille, Joseph. (N.D.). GILLES DE RAYS, L'homme de la demesure. Cholet, France: Editions Pays & Terroirs

Seligman, Kurt. (1997) THE HISTORY OF MAGIC AND THE OCCULT. New York, New York: Gramercy Books

Senecal, Jacquemard. (1980) LE PRINTEMPS DU LOUP, Une Jeunesse de Gilles de Rais. Le Chateau L'Olonne, France: self published

Soisson, Janine et Pierre. (1981) LES CHATEAUX DE LA LOIRE. Geneva, Switzerland: Editions Minerva S.A.

Styron, William. (1990) DARKNESS VISIBLE, A Memoir of Madness. New York: New York: Vantage Books

The American Heritage Illustrated Encyclopedic Dictionary. (1987) (Pamela B. DeVinne, coordinating ed.) Boston, Massachusetts: Houghton Mifflin Company

The Holy Bible. (1852). New York, New York: American Bible Society

Thoma, Richard. (2005) "TRAGEDY IN BLUE", DARK STAR, The Satanic Rites of Gilles de Rais. (Candice Black, ed.). Washington, D.C.: Creations Books, pp. 51-102.

Tougeron, Herve, et.all. (1992-3) CAHIERS GILLES DE RAIS. No 1 - No 4. Nantes, France: Editions joca seria

Tuchman, Barabra W. (1978) A DISTANT MIRROR, The Calamitous 14th Century. New York, New York: Ballantine Books

Twain, Mark. (1989) JOAN of ARC. San Francisco, California: Ignatius Press (Original edition copyright 1896 &1899 by Harper & Brothers)

Vale, MGA. (1974) CHARLES VII. London, England: Eyre Methuen. Ltd

Vincent, A.L. and Binns, Clare. (1926) GILLES DE RAIS, the Original Bluebeard. London, England: A.M. Philpot

Vronsky, Peter. (2004) SERIAL KILLERS.The Method and Madness of Monsters. New York, New York:Berkley Books

West-Sackville, Vita. (1936) SAINT JOAN of ARC. New York, New York: Doubleday

Wolf, Leonard. (1980). BLUEBEARD, The Life and Crimes of Gilles de Rais. New York, New York: Clarkson N. Potter and Crown Publishers

INTERNET

http://www.bidstrup.com/phobianhistory.httm

http:www.mayoclinic.com/health/depression/DS00175/DSECTION= symptoms

http://www.emaxhealth.com/1357/vets-ptsd-suffer-more-medical-illnesses

http://www.emedicinehealth.com/bipolar-em htm

http://encyclopedia2.freedictionary.com/marshal
http://www.flowofhistory.com/units/west/10/FC73

http://www.fordham.edu/halsall/pwh/1979boswell.html

Gribben,Mark.Gilles de Rais.http://www.crimelibrary.com/serial.killers/predators/rais/unbridled 4.html

http://wwebsite,Lineone.net/farrago/killblair.htm.

Madeline,Jeary. (1979). Sexuality and Family in Fifteenth Century France. A MASK OR A MIRROR. Journal of Family History. Number 4. (Wint., pp. 328-345). Retrieved 7.07.2007 from http://www.the-orb.net/bibliographics/children.

http://www.medicinenet.com/posttraumatic-stress-disorder/p.2 htm

Medieval Incest Law-Theory & Practice. Retrieved 7,07,2007 from http://www.oup.co.uk/pfd/0-19-811209-2 www.oup.co.uk/pfd/0-19-811209-2

Morris, Charles. Historical Tales: French. Retrieved from http://www.mainlesson.com/display,php.author+morris+books=french+story=ampoule

http:/www.nami.org/bipolar/
http://www.nimh.nih.gov/health/publications/post-traumatic-stress-diso...
http://perso.orange.fr/jean-claude.colrat/2-sacre.htm,p.1.
http://perso.orange.fr/jean-claude.colorat/2rais.htm,p.1
http:/www.reuters.com/article/2011/05/02/us-soldiers-mental-illness-i
http://xenophongroup.com/montjoie.htm.

MUSIC RECORDINGS

Bob Dylan (1981) Heart of Mine. Loves Songs of Bob Dylan (Recorded by Maria Muldaur). (2006) Cleveland, Ohio: Telerac International

Simon & Garfunkle (1972). The Sound of Silence. Simon & Garfunkle's Greatest Hits. New York, New York: Columbia Records

INDEX